APPLAUSE FIRST FOLIO EDITIONS

The Tragedie of Anthonie and Cleopatra

BY

William Shakespeare

PREPARED & ANNOTATED BY

NEIL FREEMAN

APPLAUSE
NEW YORK • LONDON

The Applause Shakespeare Library

Folio Texts

AN APPLAUSE ORIGINAL

The Tragedie of Anthonie and Cleopatra

original concept devised by Neil Freeman

original research computer entry by Margaret McBride

original software programmes designed and developed by
James McBride and Terry Lim

Text layout designed and executed by Neil Freeman

Some elements of this text were privately published under the collective title of
The Freeman–Nichols Folio Scripts 1991–96

ISBN: 1-55783-377-X

Library of Congress Cataloging-in-Publication Data

Library of Congress Catalog Card Number: 99-65418

British Library Cataloging-in-Publication Data

A catalogue record of this book is available from the British Library

APPLAUSE BOOKS

1841 Broadway Suite 1100
New York, NY 10023
Phone (212) 765-7880
Fax: (212) 765-7875

Combined Book Services Ltd.
Units I/K Paddock Wood Dist. Ctr.
Paddock Wood,
Tonbridge Kent TN12 6UU
Phone 0189 283-7171
Fax 0189 283-7272

Printed in Canada

CONTENTS

ACKNOWLEDGEMENTS

My grateful thanks to all who have helped in the growth and development of this work. Special thanks to Norman Welsh who first introduced me to the Folio Text, and to Tina Packer who (with Kristin Linklater and all the members of Shakespeare & Co.) allowed me to explore the texts on the rehearsal floor. To Jane Nichols for her enormous generosity in providing the funding which allowed the material to be computerised. To James and Margaret McBride and Terry Lim for their expertise, good humour and hard work. To the National Endowment for the Arts for their award of a Major Artist Fellowship and to York University for their award of the Joseph G. Green Fellowship. To actors, directors and dramaturgs at the Stratford Festival, Ontario; Toronto Free Theatre (that was); the Skylight Theatre, Toronto and Tamanhouse Theatre of Vancouver. To colleagues, friends and students at The University of British Columbia, Vancouver; York University, Toronto; Concordia University, Montreal; The National Theatre School of Canada in Montreal; Equity Showcase Theatre, Toronto; The Centre for Actors Study and Training (C.A.S.T.), Toronto; The National Voice Intensive at Simon Fraser University, Vancouver; Studio 58 of Langara College, Vancouver; Professional Workshops in the Arts, Vancouver; U.C.L.A., Los Angeles; Loyola Marymount, Los Angeles; San Jose State College, California; Long Beach State College, California; Brigham Young University, Utah, and Hawaii; Holy Cross College, Massachussetts; Guilford College, North Carolina. To Chairman John Wright and Associate Dean Don Paterson for their incredible personal support and encouragement. To Rachel Ditor and Tom Scholte for their timely research assistance. To Alan and Chris Baker, and Stephanie McWilliams for typographical advice. To Jay L. Halio, Hugh Richmond, and G.B. Shand for their critical input. To the overworked and underpaid proofreading teams of Ron Oten and Yuuattee Tanipersaud, Patrick Galligan and Leslie Barton, Janet Van De Graaff and Angela Dorhman (with input from Todd Sandomirsky, Bruce Alexander Pitkin, Catelyn Thornton and Michael Roberts). And above all to my wife Julie, for her patient encouragement, courteous advice, critical eye and long sufferance!

SPECIAL ACKNOWLEDGEMENTS

Paul Sugarman and Glenn Young of Applause Books; Houghton Mifflin Company for permission to quote from the line numbering system developed for *The Riverside Shakespeare*: Evans, Gwynne Blakemore, Harry Levin, Anne Barton, Herschel Baker, Frank Kermode, Hallet D. Smith, and Marie Edel, editors, *The Riverside Shakespeare*. Copyright © 1974 by Houghton Mifflin Company.

DEFINITIONS OF AND GUIDE TO PHOTOGRAPHIC COPIES OF THE EARLY TEXTS

(see Appendix A for a brief history of the First Folio, the Quartos,
and their uneasy relationship with modern texts)

A QUARTO (Q)

A single text, so called because of the book size resulting from a particular method of printing. Eighteen of Shakespeare's plays were published in this format by different publishers at various dates between 1594–1622 prior to the appearance of the 1623 Folio. Of the eighteen quarto texts, scholars suggest that fourteen have value as source texts. An extremely useful collection of them is to be found in Michael J. B. Allen and Kenneth Muir, eds., *Shakespeare's Plays in Quarto* (Berkeley: University of California Press, 1981).

THE FIRST FOLIO (F1)[1]

Thirty-six of Shakespeare's plays (excluding *Pericles* and *Two Noble Kinsmen*, in which he had a hand) appeared in one volume published in 1623. All books of this size were termed Folios, again because of the sheet size and printing method, hence this volume is referred to as the First Folio; two recent photographic editions of the work are:

Charlton Hinman, ed., *The Norton Facsimile (The First Folio of Shakespeare)* (1968; republished New York: W. W. Norton & Company, Inc., 1996).

Helge Kökeritz, ed., *Mr. William Shakespeare's Comedies, Histories & Tragedies* (New Haven: Yale University Press, 1954).

THE SECOND FOLIO (F2)

Scholars suggest that the Second Folio, dated 1632 but perhaps not published until 1640, has little authority, especially since it created hundreds of new problematical readings of its own. Nevertheless, more than eight hundred modern text readings can be attributed to it. The most recent reproduction is D. S. Brewer, ed., *Mr.*

---

[1] For a full overview of the First Folio see the monumental two-volume work: Charlton Hinman, *The Printing and Proof Reading of the First Folio of Shakespeare* (2 volumes) (Oxford: Clarendon Press, 1963) and W. W. Greg, *The Editorial Problem in Shakespeare: a Survey of the Foundations of the Text*, 3rd. ed. (Oxford: Clarendon Press, 1954); for a brief summary, see the forty-six page publication from Peter W. M. Blayney, *The First Folio of Shakespeare* (Washington, DC: Folger Library Publications, 1991).

William Shakespeare's Comedies, Histories & Tragedies, the Second Folio Reproduced in Facsimile (Dover, NH: Boydell & Brewer Ltd., 1985).

The Third Folio (1664) and the Fourth Folio (1685) have even less authority, and are rarely consulted except in cases of extreme difficulty.

THE THIRD FOLIO (F3)

The Third Folio, carefully proofed (though apparently not against the previous edition) takes great pains to correct anomalies in punctuation ending speeches and in expanding abbreviations. It also introduced seven new plays supposedly written by Shakespeare, only one of which, *Pericles*, has been established as such. The most recent reproduction is D. S. Brewer, ed., *Mr. William Shakespeare's Comedies, Histories & Tragedies, the Third Folio Reproduced in Facsimile* (Dover, NH: Boydell & Brewer Ltd., 1985).

THE FOURTH FOLIO (F4)

Paradoxically, while the Fourth Folio was the most carefully edited of all, its concentration on grammatical clarity and ease of comprehension by its readers at the expense of faithful reproduction of F1 renders it the least useful for those interested in the setting down on paper of Elizabethan theatre texts. The most recent reproduction is D. S. Brewer, ed., *Mr. William Shakespeare's Comedies, Histories & Tragedies, the Fourth Folio Reproduced in Facsimile* (Dover, NH: Boydell & Brewer Ltd., 1985).

WELCOME TO THESE SCRIPTS

These scripts are designed to do three things:

1. show the reader what the First Folio (often referred to as F1) set down on paper, rather than what modern editions think ought to have been set down

2. provide both reader and theatre practitioner an easy journey through some of the information the original readers might have garnered from F1 and other contemporary scripts which is still relevant today

3. provide a simple way for readers to see not only where modern texts alter the First Folio, and how, but also allow readers to explore both First Folio and modern versions of the disputed passage without having to turn to an Appendix or a different text

all this, hopefully without interfering with the action of the play.

What the First Folio sets on paper will be the basis for what you see. In the body of the play-text that follows, the words (including spellings and capitalisations), the punctuation (no matter how ungrammatical), the structure of the lines (including those moments of peculiar verse or unusual prose), the stage directions, the act and scene divisions, and (for the most part) the prefixes used for each character will be as set in the First Folio.

In addition, new, on page, visual symbols specially devised for these texts will help point out both the major stepping stones in the Elizabethan debate/rhetorical process contained in the plays (a fundamental part of understanding both the inner nature of each character as well as the emotional clashes between them), and where and how (and sometimes why) modern texts have altered the First Folio information. And, unlike any other script, opposite each page of text will be a blank page where readers can make their own notes and commentary.

However, there will be the rare occasion when these texts do not exactly follow the First Folio.

Sometimes F1's **words or phrases** are meaningless; for example, the lovely misprinting of 'which' in *Twelfth Night* as 'wh?ch', or in *Romeo and Juliet* the type-setting corruptions of 'speeh' for 'speech' and the running of the two words 'not away' as 'notaway'. If there are no alternative contemporary texts (a Quarto version of the play) or if no modification was made by any of the later Folios (The Second Folio of 1632, The Third Folio of 1664, or The Fourth Folio of 1685, termed F2, F3, and F4 respectively) then the F1 printing will be set as is, no matter how peculiar, and the modern correction footnoted. However, if a more appropriate alternative is available in a Quarto (often referred to as Q) or F2, F3, or F4, that 'correction' will be set directly into the text, replacing the F1 reading, and footnoted accordingly, as in the case of 'wh?ch', 'speeh', and 'notaway'.

The only time F1's **punctuation** will be altered is when the original setting is so blurred that an accurate deciphering of what F1 set cannot be determined. In such cases, alternative punctuation from F2–4 or Q will be set and a footnote will explain why.

The only time F1's **line structure** will not be followed is when at the end of a very long line, the final word or part of the word cannot fit onto the single line, nor be set as a new line in F1 because of the text that follows and is therefore set above or below the original line at the right hand side of the column. In such rare cases these texts will complete the line as a single line, and mark it with a † to show the change from F1. In all other cases, even when in prose F1 is forced to split the final word of a speech in half, and set only a few letters of it on a new line—for example in *Henry the Fifth*, Pistoll's name is split as 'Pi' on one line and 'stoll' (as the last part of the speech) on the next—these texts will show F1 exactly as set.

Some liberties have to be taken with the **prefixes** (the names used at the beginning of speeches to show the reader which character is now speaking), for Ff (all the Folios) and Qq (all the Quartos) are not always consistent. Sometimes slightly different abbreviations are used for the same character—in *The Tempest*, King Alonso is variously referred to as 'Al.', 'Alo.', 'Alon.', and 'Alonso'. Sometimes the same abbreviation is used for two different characters—in *A Midsummer Nights Dream* the characters Quince, the 'director' and author of the Mechanicals play, and Titania, Queen of the fairies, are given the same abbreviation 'Qu.'. While in this play common sense can distinguish what is intended, the confusions in *Julius Caesar* between Lucius and Lucullus, each referred to sometimes as 'Luc.', and in *The Comedy of Errors*, where the twin brothers Antipholus are both abbreviated to 'Antiph.', cannot be so easily sorted out. Thus, whereas F1 will show a variety of abbreviated prefixes, these texts will usually choose just one complete name per character and stay with it throughout.

However, there are certain cases where one full name will not suffice. Sometimes F1 will change the prefix for a single character from scene to scene, the change usually reflecting the character's new function or status. Thus in *The Comedy of Errors*, as a drinking companion of the local Antipholus, the goldsmith Angelo is referred to by his given name 'Ang.', but once business matters go awry he very quickly becomes a businessman, referred to as 'Gold'. Similar changes affect most of the characters in *A Midsummer Nights Dream*, and a complex example can be found in *Romeo and Juliet*. While modern texts give Juliet's mother the single prefix Lady Capulet throughout (incorrectly since neither she nor Capulet are named as aristocrats anywhere in the play) both Ff and Qq refer to her in a wonderful character-revealing multiplicity of ways—Mother, Capulet Wife, Lady, and Old Lady—a splendid gift for actress, director, designer, and reader alike.

Surprisingly, no modern text ever sets any of these variations. Believing such changes integral to the development of the characters so affected, these texts will. In such cases, each time the character's prefix changes the new prefix will be set, and a small notation alongside the prefix (either by reference to the old name, or by adding the symbol •) will remind the reader to whom it refers.

Also, some alterations will be made to F1's **stage directions,** not to the words themselves or when they occur, but to the way they are going to be presented visually. Scholars agree F1 contains two different types of stage direction: those that came in the original manuscript from which the Playhouse copy of the play was made, and a second set that were added in for theatrical clarification by the Playhouse. The scholars conjecture that the literary or manuscript directions, presumably from Shakespeare, mainly dealing with entries and key actions such as battles, are those that F1 sets centred on a separate line, while the additional Playhouse directions, usually dealing with offstage sounds, music, and exits, are those F1 sets alongside the spoken dialogue, usually flush against the right hand side of the column. In performance terms there seems to be a useful distinction between the two, though this is only a rule of thumb. The centred manuscript (Shakespearean?) directions tend to stop or change the action of the play, that is, the scene is affected by the action the direction demands, whereas the Playhouse directions (to the side of the text) serve to underscore what is already taking place. (If a word is needed to distinguish the two, the centred directions can be called 'action' directions, because they are events in and of themselves, while the side-set directions could be called 'supportive' or 'continuous' since they tend not to distract from the current onstage action.)

Since F1 seems to visually distinguish between the two types (setting them on different parts of the page) and there seems to be a logical theatrical differentiation as to both the source and function of each, it seems only appropriate that these scripts also mark the difference between them. Both Ff and Qq's side-set directions are often difficult to decipher while reading the text: sometimes they are set so close to the spoken text they get muddled up with it, despite the different typeface, and oftentimes have to be abbreviated to fit in. These are drawbacks shared by most modern texts. Thus these texts will distinguish them in a slightly different way (see p. xxvi below).

Finally, there will be two occasional alterations to Ff's **fonts.** F1 used **italics** for a large number of different purposes, sometimes creating confusion on the page. What these texts will keep as italics are letters, poems, songs, and the use of foreign languages. What they will not set in italics are real names, prefixes, and stage directions. Also at the top of each play, and sometimes at the beginning of a letter or poem, F1 would set a large wonderfully **decorative opening letter,** with the second letter of the word being capitalised, the style tying in with the borders that surrounded the opening and closing of each play. Since these texts will not be reproducing the decorative borders, the decorative letters won't be set either.

MAKING FULL USE OF THESE TEXTS

WHAT MODERN CHANGES WILL BE SHOWN

WORDS AND PHRASES

Modern texts often tidy up F1's words and phrases. Real names, both of people and places, and foreign languages are often reworked for modern understanding; for example, the French town often set in F1 as 'Callice' is usually reset as 'Calais'. Modern texts 'correct' the occasional Elizabethan practice of setting a singular noun with plural verb (and vice versa), as well as the infrequent use of the past tense of a verb to describe a current situation. These texts will set the F1 reading, and footnote the modern corrections whenever they occur.

More problematical are the possibilities of choice, especially when a Q and F version of the same play show a different reading for the same line and either choice is valid—even more so when both versions are offered by different modern texts. Juliet's 'When I shall die,/Take him and cut him out in little starres' offered by Ff/Q1-3 being offset by Q4's 'When he shall die...' is a case in point. Again, these texts will set the F1 reading, and footnote the alternatives.

LINE STRUCTURE CHANGES RELATED TO PROBLEMS OF 'CASTING-OFF'

The First Folio was usually prepared in blocks of twelve pages at a time. Six pairs of pages would be prepared, working both forward and backward simultaneously. Thus from the centre of any twelve-page block, pages six and seven were set first, then five and eight, then four and nine, then three and ten, then two and eleven, and finally one and twelve. This meant each compositor had to work out very carefully how much copy would fit not only each sheet, but also how much would be needed overall to reach the outer edges of pages one and twelve to match it to the previously set text, (prior to page one) or about to be set text (after page twelve). Naturally the calculations weren't always accurate. Sometimes there was too little text left for too great a space: in such cases, if the manuscript were set as it should have been, a great deal of empty paper would be left free, a condition often described as 'white' space. Sometimes too much text remained for too small a space, and if the manuscript were to be set according to its normal layout, every available inch would be taken up with type (and even then the text might not fit), a condition that could be described as 'crammed space'.

Essentially, this created a huge design problem, and most commentators suggest when it arose the printing house policy was to sacrifice textual accuracy to neatness of design. Thus, so the argument goes, in the case of white space, extra lines of type would have to be created where (presumably) none originally existed. *Hamlet* provides an excellent example with the Polonius speech 'Indeed that's out of the air' starting at line 78 of what most modern texts term Act Two Scene 2. Q2 sets the four-line speech as prose, and most modern texts follow suit. However, F1, faced with a potentially huge white space problem at the bottom of the right hand column of p. 261 in the Tragedy section, resets the speech as eleven lines of very irregular verse! In the case of crammed space, five lines of verse might suddenly become three lines of prose, or in one very severe case of overcrowding in *Henry The Fourth Part Two*, words, phrases, and even half lines of text might be omitted to reduce the text sufficiently.

When such cases occur, this text will set F1 as shown, and the modern texts' suggested alternatives will be footnoted and discussed.

LINE STRUCTURE CHANGES NOT RELATED TO PROBLEMS OF 'CASTING-OFF'

In addition, modern texts regularly make changes to F1's line structure which are not related to 'white' or 'crammed' space, often to the detriment of both character and scene. Two major reasons are offered for the changes.

First, either (a few) prose lines suddenly appear in what essentially is a verse scene (or a few verse lines in a sea of prose) and the modern texts, feeling the scene should be standardised, restructure the offending lines accordingly. *The Tempest* is atrociously served this way[2], for where F1, the only source text, shows the conspirators Caliban, Stephano, and, very occasionally, Trinculo, speaking verse as well as prose even within the same speech (a sure sign of personal striving and inner disturbance) most modern texts readjust the lines to show only Caliban speaking verse (dignifying him more than he deserves) and Stephano and Trinculo only speaking prose (thus robbing them of their dangerous flights of fancy).

Second, some Ff verse lines appear so appallingly defective in terms of their rhythm and length that modern texts feel it necessary to make a few 'readjustments' of the lines around them to bring the offending lines back to a coherent, rhythmic whole. Many of the later plays are abominably served in this regard: in *Macbeth,* for example, over a hundred F1 passages involving more than 200 lines (90 percent of which were set by the usually reliable compositor A) have been altered by most modern texts. Most of these changes concentrate on regularising moments where a character is under tremendous upheaval and hardly likely to be speaking pure formal verse at that particular moment!

These changes come about through a mistaken application of modern grammat-

---

[2]   Commentators suggest the copy play used for setting F1, coming from Stratford as it did, and thus unsupervised by Shakespeare in the Playhouse preparation of the document, prepared by Ralph Crane, was at times defective, especially in distinguishing clearly between verse and prose: this is why most modern texts do not follow F1's choices in these dubious passages: readers are invited to explore *The Tempest* within this series, especially the footnotes, as a theatrical vindication of the original F1 setting

ical considerations to texts that were originally prepared not according to grammar but rhetoric. One of rhetoric's many strengths is that it can show not only when characters are in self-control but also when they are not. In a rhetorically set passage, the splutters of a person going through an emotional breakdown, as with Othello, can be shown almost verbatim, with peculiar punctuations, spellings, breaks, and all. If the same passage were to be set grammatically it would be very difficult to show the same degree of personal disintegration on the printed page.[3] F1's occasional weird shifts between verse and prose and back again, together with the moments of extreme linear breakdown, are the equivalents of human emotional breakdown, and once the anomalies of Elizabethan script preparation are accounted for,[4] the rhetorical breakdowns on F1's printed page are clear indications of a character's disintegration within the play. When modern texts tidy up such blemishes grammatically they unwittingly remove essential theatrical and/or character clues for reader and theatre person alike.

In these texts, F1's line structure will be set as is, and all such modern alterations (prose to verse, verse to prose, regularisation of originally unmetrical lines) will be shown. The small symbol ° will be added to show where modern texts suggest a line should end rather than where F1 shows it does. A thin vertical line will be set to the left alongside any text where the modern texts have converted F1's prose to verse, or vice versa. The more large-scale of these changes will be boxed for quicker reader recognition. Most of these changes will be footnoted in the text where they occur, and a comparison of the two different versions of the text and what each could signify theatrically will be offered. For examples of both, see p. xxiii below.

THE SPECIAL PROBLEMS AFFECTING WHAT ARE KNOWN AS 'SHARED' OR 'SPLIT' VERSE LINES

A definition, and their importance to the Shakespeare texts

Essentially, split lines are short lines of verse which, when placed together, form the equivalent of a full verse line. Most commentators suggest they are very useful in speeding the play along, for the second character (whose line attaches on to the end of the first short line) is expected to use the end of the first character's line as a

---

[3]   For a full discussion of this, readers are directed to Neil Freeman, *Shakespeare's First Texts* (Vancouver: Folio Scripts, 1994).

[4]   Readers are referred to an excellent chapter by Gary Taylor which analyses the whole background, conjectured and known, concerning the preparation of the first scripts. He points out the pitfalls of assuming the early texts as sole authority for all things Shakespearean: he examines the conjectured movement of the scripts from Shakespeare's pen to printed edition, and carefully examples the changes and alterations that could occur, (most notably at the hands of the manuscript copyists), as well as the interferences and revampings of the Playhouse, plus the effects of the first typesetters' personal habits and carelessness. Stanley Wells and Gary Taylor, *William Shakespeare: A Textual Companion* (Oxford: Clarendon Press, 1987), 1–68.

springboard and jump in with an immediate reply, enhancing the quickness of the debate. Thus in *Measure for Measure*, Act Two Scene 2, modern ll. 8–10, the Provost, trying to delay Claudio's execution, has asked Angelo whether Claudio has to die the following day: Angelo's questioning affirmation ends with a very pointed short line, followed immediately by a short line opening from the Provost.

Angelo	Did I not tell thee yea? hadst thou not order?
	Why do'st thou aske againe?
Provost	Lest I might be too rash:
	Under your good correction, I have seene
	When after execution . . .

If the Provost replies immediately after, or just as, Angelo finishes, an explosive dramatic tension is created. Allowing a minor delay before reply, as many actors do, will reduce the impact of the moment, and create a hesitation where one probably does not exist.

The occasional problem

So far so good. But the problems start when more than two short lines follow each other. If there are three short lines in succession, which should be joined, #1 and #2, or #2 and #3? Later in the same scene, Claudio's sister Isabella has, at the insistence of Claudio's friend Lucio, come to plead with Angelo for her brother's life. In Lucio's eyes she is giving up too easily, hence the following (modern ll. 45–49):

Lucio	You are too cold: if you should need a pin,
	You could not with more tame a tongue desire it:
	To him, I say.
Isabella	Must he needs die?
Angelo	Maiden, no remedie?

And here it seems fairly obvious Isabella and Angelo's lines should join together, thus allowing a wonderful dramatic pause following Lucio's urging before Isabella plucks up enough courage to try. Most modern texts set the lines accordingly, with Lucio's the short odd line out.

But what about the three lines contained in the exchange that follows almost straightaway?

Isabella	But you might doe't & do the world no wrong
	If so your heart were touch'd with that remorse, ·
	As mine is to him?
Angelo	Hee's sentenc'd, tis too late.
Lucio	You are too cold.
Isabella	Too late? why no: I that doe speak a word

> May call it againe: well, beleeve this
> (modern line numbering 53–56)

Does Angelo's 'Hee's sentenc'd...' spring off Isabella's line, leaving Isabella speechless and turning to go before Lucio urges her on again? Or does Angelo pause (to frame a reply?) before speaking, leaving Lucio to quickly jump in quietly giving Isabella no time to back off? Either choice is possible, and dramatically valid. And readers should be allowed to make their own choice, which automatically means each reader should able to see the possibility of such choices when they occur.

The problem magnified by the way modern texts set split/shared lines

However, because of a peculiarity faced by the modern texts not shared by Ff/Qq, modern texts rarely show such possibilities to their readers but make the choice for them. The peculiarity comes about from a change in text layout initiated in the eighteenth century.

Ff/Qq always set short lines directly under one another, as shown in the examples above. In 1778 George Steevens, a highly respected editor, started to show split lines a new way, by advancing the second split line to just beyond where the first split line finishes, viz.

Angelo	Did I not tell thee yea? hadst thou not order?
	Why do'st thou aske againe?
Provost	Lest I might be too rash:
	Under your good correction, I have seene
	When after execution...

Since that date all editions of Shakespeare have followed this practice, which is fine as long as there are only two short lines, but when three follow each other, a choice has to be made. Thus the second Isabella/Angelo/Lucio sequence could be set as either

Isabella	But you might doe't & do the world no wrong
	If so your heart were touch'd with that remorse,
	As mine is to him?
Angelo	Hee's sentenc'd, tis too late.
Lucio	You are too cold.
Isabella	Too late? why no: I that doe speak a word
	May call it againe: well, beleeve this...

(the usual modern choice), or

Isabella	But you might doe't & do the world no wrong
	If so your heart were touch'd with that remorse,
	As mine is to him?

Angelo	Hee's sentenc'd, tis too late.
Lucio	You are too cold.
Isabella	Too late? why no: I that doe speak a word
	May call it againe: well, beleeve this ...

This modern typesetting convention has robbed the reader of a very important moment of choice. Indeed, at the beginning of the twentieth century, Richard Flatter[5] suggested that what modern commentators consider to be split lines may not be split lines at all. He offers two other suggestions: pauses and hesitations could exist between each line, or the lines could in fact be spoken one on top of another, a very important consideration for the crowd responses to Anthony in the funeral scene of *Julius Caesar*. Either way, the universally adopted Steevens layout precludes the reader/theatre practitioner from even seeing such possibilities.

These texts will show the F1 layout as is, and will indicate via footnote when a choice is possible (in the case of three short lines, or more, in succession) and by the symbol } when the possibility of springboarding exists. Thus the Folio Texts would show the first Angelo/Provost example as:

Angelo	Did I not tell thee yea? hadst thou not order?
	Why do'st thou aske againe?
	}
Provost	Lest I might be too rash:
	Under your good correction, I have seene
	When after execution ...

In nearly all cases the } shows where most modern texts insist on setting a shared split line. However, readers are cautioned that in many of the later plays, the single line so created is much longer than pentameter, and often very a-rhythmic. In such cases the lines could have great value as originally set (two separate short lines), especially when a key debate is in process (for example, *Measure for Measure*, *The Tragedie of Cymbeline*, *Othello*, and *The Winters Tale*).

THE UNUSUAL SINGLE SPLIT LINE (PLEASE SEE 'A CAVEAT', P. XXXVIII)

So far the discussion has centred on short lines shared by two or more characters. Ff/Qq offer another complication rarely, if ever, accepted by most modern texts. Quite often, and not because of white space, a single character will be given two consecutive short lines within a single speech. *Romeo and Juliet* is chock full of this device: in the famous balcony scene (modern texts numbering 2.2.62–3) Juliet asks Romeo

How cam'st thou hither.

---

[5] Richard Flatter, *Shakespeare's Producing Hand* (London: Heinemann, 1948, reprint).

> Tell me, and wherefore?
> The Orchard walls are high, and hard to climbe

The first two lines (five syllables each) suggest a minute pause between them as Juliet hesitates before asking the all important second line (with its key second part 'and wherefore'). Since Qq rarely set such 'single split lines' most modern texts refuse to set any of them, but combine them:

> How cams't thou hither. Tell me and wherefore?

This basically F1 device is set by all the compositors and followed by all other Folios. This text will follow suit, highlighting them with the symbol → for quick recognition, viz.:

> How cam'st thou hither. →
> Tell me, and wherefore?
> The Orchard walls are high, and hard to climbe

SENTENCE AND PUNCTUATION STRUCTURES

A CHARACTER'S THOUGHTFUL & EMOTIONAL JOURNEY

A quick comparison between these texts and both the Ff/Qq's and the modern texts will reveal two key differences in the layout of the dialogue on the printed page—the bolding of major punctuation, and the single line dropping of text whenever a new sentence begins.

The underlying principle behind these texts is that since the handwritten documents from which they stem were originally intended for the actor and Playhouse, in addition to their poetical values, the Ff/Qq scripts represent a theatrical process. Even if the scripts are being read just for pleasure, at the back of the reader's mind should be the notion of characters on a stage and actors acting (and the word 'process' rather than 'practice' is deliberate, with process suggesting a progression, development, or journey).

The late Jean-Louis Barrault gave a wonderful definition of acting, and of this journey, suggesting an actor's job was to strive to remain in 'the ever-changing present'. If something happens onstage (an entry, an exit, a verbal acceptance or denial of what the actor's character has suggested), the 'present' has changed, and the character must readjust accordingly. Just as onstage, the actor should be prepared for the character to re-adjust, and in rehearsal should be examining how and why it does, so should the reader in the library, armchair, or classroom.

In many ways, the key to Shakespeare is discovering how each character's mind works; perceiving the emotions and intellects as they act and react helps the reader understand from where the poetical imagination and utterance stem.

Certain elements of each character's emotional and intellectual journey, and where it changes, are encoded into the sentence structure of Ff/Qq.

Elizabethan education prepared any schooled individual (via the 'petty school' and the private tutor) for the all important and essential daily rough and tumble of argument and debate. Children were trained not only how to frame an argument so as to win it hands down, but also how to make it entertaining so as to enthrall the neutral listener.

The overall training, known as 'rhetoric', essentially allowed intellect and emotion to exist side by side, encouraging the intellect to keep the emotion in check. The idea was not to deny the emotions, but ensure they didn't swamp the 'divinity' of reason, the only thing separating man from beast. While the initial training was mainly vocal, any written matter of the period automatically reflected the ebb and flow of debate. What was set on the printed page was not grammar, but a representation of the rhetorical process.

DROPPING A LINE TO ILLUSTRATE F1'S SENTENCE STRUCTURE

Put at its simplest, in any document of the period, each sentence would represent a new intellectual and emotional stage of a rhetorical argument. When this stage of the argument was completed, a period would be set (occasionally a question mark or, much more rarely, an exclamation mark—both followed by a capital letter) signifying the end of that stage of the argument, and the beginning of the next.

Thus in the First Folio, the identification of each new sentence is an automatic (and for us, four hundred years later, a wonderful) aid to understanding how a character is reacting to and dealing with Barrault's ever-changing present.

To help the reader quickly spot the new steppingstone in an argument, and thus the point of transition, these texts highlight where one sentence ends and the new one begins by simply dropping a line whenever a new sentence starts. Thus the reader has a visual reminder that the character is making a transition to deal with a change in the current circumstances of the scene (or in the process of self-discovery in the case of soliloquies).

This device has several advantages. The reader can instantly see where the next step in the argument begins. The patterns so created on the page can quickly illuminate whenever a contrast between characters' thought patterns occurs. (Sometimes the sentences are short and precise, suggesting the character is moving quickly from one idea to the next. Sometimes the sentences are very long, suggesting the character is undergoing a very convoluted process. Sometimes the sentences contain nothing but facts, suggesting the character has no time to entertain; sometimes they are filled with high-flown imagery, perhaps suggesting the character is trying to mask a very weak argument with verbal flummery.) The patterns can also show when a character's style changes within itself, say from long and convoluted to short and precise, or vice versa. It can also immediately pinpoint when a character is in trouble and not arguing coherently or logically, something modern texts often alter out of grammatical necessity.

With patience, all this could be gleaned from the modern texts (in as far as they set the Ff sentence structure, which they often don't) and from a photostat of the First Folio, by paying special attention to where the periods are set. But there is one extra very special advantage to this new device of dropping a line: this has to do once more with the Elizabethan method of setting down spoken argument on paper, especially when the character speaking is not in the best of all possible worlds.

If an Elizabethan person/character is arguing well, neatly, cleanly, tidily, then a printed representation of that argument would also be clean, neat, and tidy—to modern eyes it would be grammatically acceptable. If the same character is emotionally upset, or incapable of making a clear and tidy argument, then the on-paper representation would be muddy and untidy—to modern eyes totally ungrammatical and often not acceptable. By slightly isolating each sentence these texts very quickly allow the reader to spot when a sentence's construction is not all that it should be, say in the middle of Viola's so-called ring speech in *Twelfth Night* (Act Two Scene 2), or Helena's declaration of love for Bertram in *All's Well That Ends Well* (Act One Scene 3), or the amazing opening to *As You Like It*, where Orlando's opening litany of complaint against his brother starts with a single sentence twenty lines long.

This is especially relevant when a surprising modern editorial practice is accounted for. Very often the Ff sentence structures are markedly altered by modern texts, especially when the Ff sentences do not seem 'grammatical'—thus Orlando's twenty-line monster is split into six separate, grammatically correct sentences by all modern texts. And then there is the case of Shylock in *The Merchant of Venice*, a Jewish man being goaded and tormented beyond belief by the very Christians who helped his daughter elope with a Christian, taking a large part of Shylock's fortune with her. A sentence comparison of the famous Act Three Scene 1 speech culminating in 'Hath not a Jew eyes?' is very instructive. All modern texts set the speech as between fifteen and seventeen sentences in length: whatever the pain, anger, and personal passion, the modern texts encourage dignity and self-control, a rational Shylock. But this is a Shylock completely foreign to both Q1 and Ff. Q1 show the same speech as only four sentences long, Ff five—a veritable onflow of intellect and passion all mixed together, all unstoppable for the longest period of time—a totally different being from that shown by the modern texts. What is more, this is a totally different Shylock from the one seen earlier in the Ff/Q1 version of the play, where, even in the extremes of discomfort with the old enemy Anthonio, his sentence structures are rhetorically balanced and still grammatical to modern eyes.

Here, with Shylock, there are at least three benefits to dropping the sentence: the unusualness of the speech is immediately spotted; the change in style between this and any of his previous speeches can be quickly seen; and, above all, the moment where the speech moves from a long unchecked outpouring to a quick series of brief, dangerously rational sentences can be quickly identified. And these advantages will be seen in such changed sentence circumstances in any play in any of these texts.

THE HIGHLIGHTING OF THE MAJOR PUNCTUATION IN THESE TEXTS

A second key element of rhetoric encoded into the Ff/Qq texts clearly shows the characters' mind in action. The encoding lies in the remaining punctuation which, unlike much modern punctuation, serves a double function, one dealing with the formation of the thought, the other with the speaking of it.

Apart from the period, dealt with already, essentially there are two sets of punctuation to consider, minor and major, each with their own very specific functions.

Shakespearean characters reflect the mode of thinking of their time. Elizabethans were trained to constantly add to or modify thoughts. They added a thought to expand the one already made. They denied the first thought so as to set up alternatives. They elaborated a thought so as to clarify what has already been said. They suddenly moved into splendid puns or non-sequiturs (emotional, logical, or both) because they had been immediately stimulated by what they or others had just said. The **minor punctuation** (essentially the comma [,] the parenthesis or bracket [( )], and the dash) reflects all this.

In establishing thought processes for each character, minor punctuation shows every new nuance of thought: every tiny punctuation in this category helps establish the deftness and dance of each character's mind. In *As You Like It* (Act Three Scene 2, modern line numbering 400–402) the Ff setting of Rosalind's playing with her beloved Orlando has a wonderful coltish exuberance as she runs rings round his protestations of love:

> Love is meerely a madnesse, and I tel you,
> deserves as well a darke house,* and a whip,* as madmen do:

Her mind is adding extra thoughts as she goes: the Ff commas are as much part of her spirit and character as the words are—though most modern texts create a much more direct essayist, preaching what she already knows, by removing the two Ff commas marked *.[6]

A similar situation exists with Macbeth, facing Duncan whom he must kill if he is

---

[6] Unfortunately, many modern texts eradicate the F and Q minor punctuation arguing the need for light (or infrequent) punctuation to preserve the speed of speech. This is not necessarily helpful, since what it removes is just a new thought marker, not an automatic indication to pause: too often the result is that what the first texts offer a character as a series of closely-worked out dancing thought-patterns (building one quick thought—as marked by a comma—on top of another) is turned into a series of much longer phrases: often, involved and reactive busy minds are artificially turned into (at best) eloquent ones, suddenly capable of perfect and lengthy rationality where the situation does not warrant such a reaction, or (at worst) vapid ones, speaking an almost preconceived essay of commentary or artificial sentimentality.

to become king (Act One Scene 4, modern line numbering 22–27). Ff show a Macbeth almost swamped with extra thoughts as he assures Duncan

> The service,* and the loyaltie I owe,
> In doing it,* payes it selfe.
> Your highnesse part,* is to receive our Duties,
> And our Duties are to your Throne,* and State,
> Children,* and Servants; which doe but what they should,*
> By doing every thing safe toward your Love
> And Honour.

The heavy use of minor punctuation—especially when compared with most modern texts which remove the commas marked *, leaving Macbeth with just six thoughts compared to Ff's twelve—clearly shows a man ill at ease and/or working too hard to say the right thing. Again the punctuation helps create an understanding of the character.

However, while the minor punctuation is extremely important in the discovery process of reading and/or rehearsal, paradoxically, it mustn't become too dominant. From the performance/speaking viewpoint, to pause at each comma would be tantamount to disaster. There would be an enormous dampening effect if reader/actor were to pause at every single piece of punctuation: the poetry would be destroyed and the event would become interminable.

In many ways, minor punctuation is the Victorian child of Shakespearean texts, it must be seen but not heard. (In speaking the text, the new thought the minor punctuation represents can be added without pausing: a change in timbre, rhythm, or pitch—in acting terms, occurring naturally with changes in intention—will do the trick.)

But once thoughts have been discovered, they have to be organised into some form of coherent whole. If the period shows the end of one world and the start of the new, and if the comma marks a series of small, ever-changing, ever-evolving thoughts within each world, occasionally there must be pause for reflection somewhere in the helter-skelter of tumbling new ideas. This is the **major punctuation's** strength; major punctuation consisting of the semicolon [;], and the colon [:].

Major punctuation marks the gathering together of a series of small thoughts within an overall idea before moving onto something new. If a room full of Rodin sculptures were analogous to an Elizabethan scene or act, each individual piece of sculpture would be a speech, the torso or back or each major limb a separate sentence. Each collective body part (a hand, the wrist, the forearm, the upper arm) would be a series of small thoughts bounded by major punctuation, each smaller item within that part (a finger, a fingernail, a knuckle) a single small thought separated by commas. In describing the sculpture to a friend one might move from the smaller details (the knuckle) to the larger (the hand) to another larger (the wrist) then another (the forearm) and so on to the whole limb. Unless the speaker is emotionally moved by the recollection, some pauses would be essential, certainly after finishing the whole description of the arm (the sentence), and probably after each major collective of the hand, the wrist, etc. (as marked by the major punctuation), but not after every small bit.

As a rule of thumb, and simply stated, the colon and semicolon mark both a thinking and a speaking pause. The vital difference between major and minor punctuation, whether in the silent reading of the text or the performing of it aloud, is you need not pause at the comma, bracket, or dash; you probably should at the colon, semicolon, and period.

Why the Major Punctuation is Bolded in These Texts.

In speaking the text or reading it, the minor punctuation indicates the need to key onto the new thought without necessarily requiring a pause. In so doing, the inherent rhythms of speech, scene, and play can clip along at the rate suggested by the Prologue in *Romeo and Juliet,* 'the two hours traffic of the stage', until a pause is absolutely necessary. Leave the commas alone, and the necessary pauses will make themselves known.

The 'major' punctuation then comes into its own, demanding double attention as both a thinking and speaking device. This is why it is bolded, to highlight it for the reader's easier access. The reader can still use all the punctuation when desired, working through the speech thought by thought, taking into account both major and minor punctuation as normal. Then, when needed, the bolding of the major punctuation will allow the reader easy access for marking where the speech, scene, or play needs to be broken down into its larger thinking/speaking (and even breathing) units without affecting its overall flow.

The Blank Pages Within the Text

In each text within this series, once readers reach the play itself they will find that with each pair of pages the dialogue is printed on the right-hand page only. The left-hand page has been deliberately left blank so that readers, actors, directors, stage managers, teachers, etc. have ample space for whatever notes and text emendations they may wish to add.

PRACTICAL ON-PAGE HELP FOR THE READER

THE VISUAL SYMBOLS HIGHLIGHTING MODERN ALTERATIONS

THE BOX

This surrounds a passage where the modern texts have made whole-scale alterations to the Ff text. Each boxed section will be footnoted, and the changes analysed at the bottom of the page.

THE FOOTNOTES

With many modern texts the footnotes are not easily accessible. Often no indication is given within the text itself where the problem/choice/correction exists. Readers are forced into a rather cumbersome four-step process. First, they have to search through the bottom of the page where the footnotes are crammed together, often in very small print, to find a line number where an alteration has been made. Then they must read the note to find out what has been altered. Then they must go back to the text and search the side of the page to find the corresponding line number. Having done all this, finally they can search the line to find the word or phrase that has been changed (sometimes complicated by the fact the word in question is set twice in different parts of the line).

These texts will provide a reference marker within the text itself, directly alongside the word or phrase that is in question. This guides the reader directly to the corresponding number in the footnote section of the bottom of each page, to the alteration under discussion — hopefully a much quicker and more immediate process.

In addition, since there are anywhere between 300 and 1,100 footnotes in any one of these texts, a tool is offered to help the reader find only those notes they require, when they require them. In the footnote section, prior to the number that matches the footnote marker in the text, a letter or combination of letters will be set as a code. The letter 'W', for example, shows that the accompanying footnote refers to word substitutions offered by modern texts; the letters 'SD' refer to an added or altered stage direction; the letters 'LS' show the footnote deals with a passage where the modern texts have completely altered the line-structure that F1 set. This enables readers to be selective when they want to examine only certain changes, for they can quickly skim through the body of footnotes until they find the code they want, perhaps those dealing with changes in prefixes (the code 'P') or when modern alterations have been swapping lines from verse to prose or vice versa (the code 'VP'). For full details of the codes, see pp. xxxiii–xxxv below.

Readers are urged to make full use of the footnotes in any of the Recommended Texts listed just before the start of the play. They are excellent in their areas of expertise. To attempt to rival or paraphrase them would be redundant. Thus the footnotes in these scripts will hardly ever deal with word meanings and derivations; social or political history; literary derivations and comparisons; or lengthy quotations from scholars or commentators. Such information is readily available in the *Oxford English Dictionary* and from the recommended modern texts.

Generally, the footnotes in these scripts will deal with matters theatrical and textual and will be confined to three major areas: noting where and how the modern texts alter F1's line structure; showing popular alternative word readings often selected by the modern texts (these scripts will keep the F1 reading unless otherwise noted); and showing the rare occasions where and how these scripts deviate from their source texts. When the modern texts offer alternative words and/or phrases to F2-4/Qq, the original spelling and punctuation will be used. Where appropriate, the footnotes will briefly refer to the excellent research of the scholars of the last three centuries, and to possible theatrical reasons for maintaining F1's structural 'irregularities'.

THE SYMBOL °

This will be used to show where modern texts have altered F1's line structure, and will allow the reader to explore both the F1 setting and the modern alternative while examining the speech where it is set, in its proper context and rightful position within the play. For example, though F1 is usually the source text for *Henry the Fifth* and sets the dialogue for Pistoll in prose, most modern texts use the memorial Q version and change his lines to (at times extraordinarily peculiar) verse. These texts will set the speech as shown in F1, but add the ° to show the modern texts alterations, thus:

Pistoll	Fortune is Bardolphs foe, and frownes on him:° for he hath stolne a Pax, and hanged must a be:° a damned death:° let Gallowes gape for Dogge, let Man goe free,° and let not Hempe his Wind-pipe suffocate:° but Exeter hath given the doome of death,° for Pax of little price.°
	Therefore goe speake,° the Duke will heare thy voyce;° and let not Bardolphs vitall thred bee cut° with edge of Penny-Cord, and vile reproach.°
	Speake Captaine for his Life, and I will thee requite.°

(Henry V, These Scripts, 2.1.450–459)

Read the speech utilising the ° to mark the end of a line, and the reader is exploring what the modern texts suggest should be the structure. Read the lines ignoring the ° and the reader is exploring what the F1 text really is. Thus both F1 and modern/Q versions can be read within the body of the text.

THE VERTICAL LINE TO THE LEFT OF THE TEXT

This will be used to mark a passage where modern editors have altered F1's verse to prose or vice versa. Here is a passage in a predominantly prose scene from *Henry V.* Modern texts and F1 agree that Williams and Fluellen should be set in prose. However, the F1 setting for Henry could be in verse, though most modern texts set it in prose too. The thin vertical line to the left of the text is a quick reminder to the reader of disagreement between Ff and modern texts (the F1 setting will always be shown, and the disputed section will be footnoted accordingly).

King Henry	Twas I indeed thou promised'st to strike,	
	And thou hast given me most bitter termes.	
Fluellen	And please your Majestie, let his Neck answere	
	for it, if there is any Marshall Law in the World.	
King Henry	How canst thou make me satisfaction?	
Williams	All offences, my Lord, come from the heart: ne-	
	ver came any from mine, that might offend your Ma-	
	jestie.	*(Henry V,* These Scripts, 4.1.240–247)

THE SYMBOL } SET TO THE RIGHT OF TEXT, CONNECTING TWO SPEECHES

This will be used to remind readers of the presence of what most modern texts consider to be split or shared lines, and that therefore the second speech could springboard quickly off the first, thus increasing the speed of the dialogue and debate; for example:

Angelo	Did I not tell thee yea? hadst thou not order?
	Why do'st thou aske againe?
Provost	Lest I might be too rash: }
	Under your good correction, I have seene
	When after execution . . .

Since there is no definitive way of determining whether Shakespeare wished the two short lines to be used as a shared or split line, or used as two separate short lines, the reader would do well to explore the moment twice. The first time the second speech could be 'springboarded' off the first as if it were a definite shared line; the second time round a tiny break could be inserted before speaking the second speech, as if a hesitation were deliberately intended. This way both possibilities of the text can be examined.

THE SYMBOL → TO THE RIGHT OF THE TEXT, JOINING TWO SHORT LINES SPOKEN BY A SINGLE CHARACTER

This indicates that though Ff has set two short lines for a single character, perhaps hinting at a minute break between the two thoughts, most modern texts have set the two short lines as one longer one. Thus the first two lines of Juliet's

How cam'st thou hither. →

> Tell me, and wherefore?
> The Orchard walls are high, and hard to climbe

can be explored as one complete line (the interpretation of most modern texts), or, as F1 suggests, as two separate thoughts with a tiny hesitation between them. In most cases these lines will be footnoted, and possible reasons for the F1 interpretation explored.

THE OCCASIONAL USE OF THE †

This marks where F1 has been forced, in a crowded line, to set the end of the line immediately above or below the first line, flush to the right hand column. These texts will set the original as one complete line—the only instance where these scripts do not faithfully reproduce F1's line structure.

THE OCCASIONAL USE OF THE † TOGETHER WITH A FOOTNOTE (ALSO SEE P. XXXVII)

This marks where a presumed F1 compositorial mistake has led to a meaningless word being set (for example 'speeh' instead of 'speech') and, since there is a 'correct' form of the word offered by either F2–4 or Qq, the correct form of the word rather than the F1 error has been set. The footnote directs the reader to the original F1 setting reproduced at the bottom of the page.

PATTERNED BRACKETS { } SURROUNDING A PREFIX OR PART OF A STAGE DIRECTION

These will be used on the infrequent occasions where a minor alteration or addition has been made to the original F1 setting.

THE VARIED USE OF THE * AND ∞

This will change from text to text. Sometimes (as in *Hamlet*) an * will be used to show where, because of the 1606 Acte To Restraine The Abuses of Players, F1 had to alter Qq's 'God' to 'Heaven'. In other plays it may be used to show the substitution of the archaic 'a' for 'he' while in others the * and /or the ∞ may be used to denote a line from Qq or F2–4 which F1 omits.

THE SYMBOL •

This is a reminder that a character with several prefixes has returned to one previously used in the play.

THE VISUAL SYMBOLS HIGHLIGHTING KEY ITEMS WITHIN THE FIRST FOLIO

THE DROPPING OF THE TEXT A SINGLE LINE

This indicates where one sentence ends, and a new one begins (see pp. xvii–xviii).

THE BOLDING OF PUNCTUATION

This indicates the presence of the major punctuation (see pp. xviii–xxi).

UNBRACKETED STAGE DIRECTIONS

These are the ones presumed to come from the manuscript copy closest to Shakespeare's own hand (F1 sets them centred, on a separate line). They usually have a direct effect on the scene, altering what has been taking place immediately prior to its setting (see p. ix).

BRACKETED STAGE DIRECTIONS

These are the ones presumed to have been added by the Playhouse. (F1 sets them alongside the dialogue, flush to the right of the column.) They usually support, rather than alter, the onstage action (see p. ix).

(The visual difference in the two sets of directions can quickly point the reader to an unexpected aspect of an entry or exit. Occasionally an entry is set alongside the text, rather than on a separate line. This might suggest the character enters not wishing to draw attention to itself, for example, towards the end of *Macbeth*, the servant entering with the dreadful news of the moving Byrnane Wood. Again, F1 occasionally sets an exit on a separate line, perhaps stopping the onstage action altogether, as with the triumphal exit to a 'Gossips feast' at the end of *The Comedy of Errors* made by most of the reunited and/or business pacified characters, leaving the servant Dromio twins onstage to finish off the play. A footnote will be added when these unusual variations in F1's directions occur.)

As with all current texts, the final period of any bracketed or unbracketed stage direction will not be set.

ACT, SCENE, AND LINE NUMBERING SPECIFIC TO THIS TEXT

Each of these scripts will show the act and scene division from F1. They will also indicate modern act and scene division, which often differs from Ff/Qq. Modern texts suggest that in many plays full scene division was not attempted until the eighteenth century, and act division in the early texts was sometimes haphazard at best. Thus many modern texts place the act division at a point other than that set in Ff/Qq, and nearly always break Ff/Qq text up into extra scenes. When modern texts add an act or scene division which is not shared by F1, the addition will be shown in brackets within the body of each individual play as it occurs. When Ff set a new Act or scene, for clarity these texts will start a fresh page, even though this is not Ff/Qq practice

ON THE LEFT HAND SIDE OF EACH PAGE

Down the left of each page, line numbers are shown in increments of five. These refer to the lines in this text only. Where F1 prints a line containing two sentences, since these scripts set two separate lines, each line will be numbered independently.

ON THE TOP RIGHT OF EACH PAGE

These numbers represent the first and last lines set on the page, and so summarise the information set down the left hand side of the text.

AT THE BOTTOM RIGHT OF EACH PAGE: USING THESE SCRIPTS WITH OTHER TEXTS

At times a reader may want to compare these texts with either the original First Folio, or a reputable modern text, or both. Specially devised line numbers will make this a fairly easy proposition. These new reference numbers will be found at the bottom right of the page, just above the footnote section.

The information before the colon allows the reader to compare these texts against any photographic reproduction of the First Folio. The information after the colon allows the reader to compare these texts with a modern text, specifically the excellent *Riverside Shakespeare.*[7]

Before the colon: any photostat of the First Folio

A capital letter plus a set of numbers will be shown followed by a lowercase letter. The numbers refer the reader to a particular page within the First Folio; the capital letter before the numbers specifies whether the reader should be looking at the right hand column (R) or left hand column (L) on that particular page; the lower case letter after the numbers indicates which compositor (mainly 'a' through 'e') set that particular column. An occasional asterisk alongside the reference tells the reader that though this is the page number as set in F1, it is in fact numbered out of sequence, and care is needed to ensure, say in *Cymbeline,* the appropriate one of two 'p. 389s' is being consulted.

Since the First Folio was printed in three separate sections (the first containing the Comedies, the second the Histories, and the third the Tragedies),[8] the pages and section in which each of these scripts is to be found will be mentioned in the introduction accompanying each play. The page number refers to that printed at the top of the reproduced Folio page, and not to the number that appears at the bottom of the page of the book which contains the reproduction.

Thus, from this series of texts, page one of *Measure for Measure* shows the ref-

---

[7]   Gwynne Blakemore Evans, Harry Levin, Anne Barton, Herschel Baker, Frank Kermode, Hallet D. Smith, and Marie Edel, eds., *The Riverside Shakespeare* (Copyright © 1974 by Houghton Mifflin Company). This work is chosen for its exemplary scholarship, editing principles, and footnotes.

[8]   The plays known as Romances were not printed as a separate section: *Cymbeline* was set with the Tragedies, *The Winter's Tale* and *The Tempest* were set within the Comedies, and though *Pericles* had been set in Q it did not appear in the compendium until F3. *Troilus and Cressida* was not assigned to any section, but was inserted between the Histories and the Tragedies with only 2 of its 28 pages numbered.

erence 'L61–c'. This tells the reader that the text was set by compositor 'c' and can be checked against the left hand column of p. 61 of the First Folio (*Measure For Measure* being set in the Comedy Section of F1).

Occasionally the first part of the reference seen at the bottom of the page will also be seen within the text, somewhere on the right hand side of the page. This shows the reader exactly where this column has ended and the new one begins.

(As any photostat of the First Folio clearly shows, there are often sixty-five lines or more per column, sometimes crowded very close together. The late Professor Charlton Hinman employed a brilliantly simple line-numbering system (known as TLN, short for Through Line Numbering System) whereby readers could quickly be directed to any particular line within any column on any page.

The current holders of the rights to the TLN withheld permission for the system to be used in conjunction with this series of Folio Texts.)

After the colon: *The Riverside Shakespeare*

Numbers will be printed indicating the act, scene, and line numbers in *The Riverside Shakespeare,* which contain the information set on the particular page of this script. Again, using the first page of *Measure For Measure*, the reference 1.1.1–21 on page one of these scripts directs the reader to Act One Scene 1 of *The Riverside Shakespeare*; line one in *The Riverside Shakespeare* matches the first line in this text, while the last line of dialogue on page one of this text is to be found in line twenty-one of the *Riverside* version of the play.

COMMON TYPESETTING PECULIARITIES OF THE FOLIO AND QUARTO TEXTS
(And How These Texts Present Them)

There are a few (to modern eyes) unusual contemporary Elizabethan and early Jacobean printing practices which will be retained in these scripts.

THE ABBREVIATIONS, 'S.', 'L.', 'D.', 'M.'

Ff and Qq use standard printing abbreviations when there is not enough space on a single line to fit in all the words. The most recognisable to modern eyes includes 'S.' for Saint; 'L.' for Lord; 'M.' for Mister (though this can also be short for 'Master', 'Monsieur', and on occasions even 'Mistress'); and 'D.' for Duke. These scripts will set F1 and footnote accordingly.

'Ÿ', 'W', AND ACCENTED FINAL VOWELS

Ff/Qq's two most commonly used abbreviations are not current today, viz.:

ÿ, which is usually shorthand for either 'you'; 'thee'; 'thou'; 'thy'; 'thine'; or 'yours'

w, usually with a ¨ above, shorthand for either 'which'; 'what'; 'when'; or 'where'. Also, in other cases of line overcrowding, the last letter of a relatively unimportant word is omitted, and an accent placed over the preceding vowel as a marker, e.g. 'thä' for 'than'. For all such abbreviations these scripts will set F1 and footnote accordingly.

THE SPECIAL CASE OF THE QUESTION AND EXCLAMATION MARKS ('?' AND '!')

USAGE

Elizabethan use of these marks differs somewhat from modern practice. Ff/Qq rarely set an exclamation mark: instead the question mark was used either both as a question mark and as an exclamation point. Thus occasionally the question mark suggests some minor emphasis in the reading.

SENTENCE COUNT

When either mark occurs in the middle of a speech, it can be followed by a capitalised or a lowercase word. When the word is lowercase (not capitalised) the sentence continues on without a break. The opposite is not always true: just because the following word is capitalised does not automatically signify the start of a new sentence, though more often than not it does.

Elizabethan rhetorical writing style allowed for words to be capitalised within a sentence, a practice continued by the F1 compositors. Several times in *The Winters Tale,* highly emotional speeches are set full of question marks followed by capitalised words. Each speech could be either one long sentence of ongoing passionate rush, or up to seven shorter sentences attempting to establish self-control.

The final choice belongs to the individual reader, and in cases where such alternatives arise, the passages will be boxed, footnoted, and the various possibilities discussed.

THE ENDING OF SPEECHES WITH NO PUNCTUATION, OR PUNCTUATION OTHER THAN A PERIOD

Quite often F1–2 will not show punctuation at the end of a speech, or sometimes set a colon (:) or a comma (,) instead. Some commentators suggest the setting of anything other than a period was due to compositor carelessness, and that omission occurred either for the same reason, or because the text was so full it came flush to the right hand side of the column and there was no room left for the final punctuation to be set. Thus modern texts nearly always end a speech with the standard period (.), question mark (?), or exclamation mark (!), no matter what F1–2 have set.

However, omission doesn't always occur when a line is full, and F2, though making over sixteen hundred unauthorised typographical corrections of F1 (more than eight hundred of which are accepted by most modern texts), rarely replaces an offending comma or colon with a period, or adds missing periods — F3 is the first to make such alterations on a large scale basis. A few commentators, while acknowledging some of the omissions/mistakes are likely to be due to compositor or scribal error, suggest that ending the speech with anything other than a period (or not ending the speech at all) might indicate that the character with the speech immediately following is in fact interrupting this first speaker.

These texts will set F1, footnote accordingly, and sometimes discuss the possible effect of the missing or 'incorrect' punctuation.

THE SUBSTITUTIONS OF 'i/I' FOR 'j/J' AND 'u' FOR 'v'

In both Ff/Qq words now spelled as 'Jove' or 'Joan' are often set as 'Iove' or 'Ioan'. To avoid confusion, these texts will set the modern version of the word. Similarly, words with 'v' in the middle are often set by Ff/Qq with a 'u'; thus the modern word 'avoid' becomes 'auoid'. Again, these texts will set the modern version of the word, without footnote acknowledgement.

ALTERNATIVE SETTINGS OF A WORD WHERE DIFFERENT SPELLINGS MAINTAIN THE SAME MEANING

Ff/Qq occasionally set, what appears to modern eyes, an archaic spelling of a word for which there is a more common modern alternative, for example 'murther' for murder, 'burthen' for burden, 'moe' for more, 'vilde' for vile. Some modern texts set the Ff/Qq spelling, some modernise. These texts will set the F1 spelling throughout.

ALTERNATIVE SETTINGS OF A WORD WHERE DIFFERENT SPELLINGS SUGGEST DIFFERENT MEANINGS

Far more complicated is the situation where, while an Elizabethan could substitute one word formation for another and still imply the same thing, to modern eyes the substituted word has a entirely different meaning to the one it has replaced. The following is by no means an exclusive list of the more common dual-spelling, dual-meaning words:

anticke–antique	mad–made	sprite–spirit
born–borne	metal–mettle	sun–sonne
hart–heart	mote–moth	travel–travaill
human–humane	pour–(powre)–power	through–thorough
lest–least	reverent–reverend	troth–truth
lose–loose	right–rite	whether–whither

Some of these doubles offer a metrical problem too; for example 'sprite', a one syllable word, versus 'spirit'. A potential problem occurs in *A Midsummer Nights Dream*, where provided the modern texts set Q1's 'thorough', the scansion pattern of elegant magic can be established, whereas F1's more plebeian 'through' sets up a much more awkward and clumsy moment.

These texts will set the F1 reading, and footnote where the modern texts' substitution of a different word formation has the potential to alter the meaning (and sometimes scansion) of the line.

'THEN' AND 'THAN'

These two words, though their neutral vowels sound different to modern ears, were almost identical to Elizabethan speakers and readers, despite their different meanings. Ff and Qq make little distinction between them, setting them interchangeably. In these scripts the original printings will be used, and the modern reader should soon get used to substituting one for the other as necessary.

'I', AND 'AY'

Ff/Qq often print the personal pronoun 'I' and the word of agreement 'aye' simply as 'I'. Again, the modern reader should quickly get used to this and make the substitution whenever necessary. The reader should also be aware that very occasionally either word could be used and the phrase make perfect sense, even though different meanings would be implied.

'MY SELFE/HIM SELFE/HER SELFE' VERSUS 'MYSELF/HIMSELF/ HERSELF'

Generally Ff/Qq separate the two parts of the word, 'my selfe' while most modern texts set the single word 'myself'. The difference is vital, based on Elizabethan philosophy. Elizabethans regarded themselves as composed of two parts, the corporeal 'I', and the more spiritual part, the 'selfe'. Thus when an Elizabethan character refers to 'my selfe', he or she is often referring to what is to all intents and purposes a separate being, even if that being is a particular part of him- or herself. Thus soliloquies can be thought of as a debate between the 'I' and 'my selfe', and in such speeches, even though there may be only one character onstage, it's as if there were two distinct entities present.

These texts will show F1 as set.

FOOTNOTE CODE
(shown in two forms, the first alphabetical,
the second grouping the codes by topic)

To help the reader focus on a particular topic or research aspect, a special code has been developed for these texts. Each footnote within the footnote section at the bottom of each page of text has a single letter or series of letters placed in front of it guiding readers to one specific topic; thus 'SPD' will direct readers to footnotes just dealing with songs, poems, and doggerel.

ALPHABETICAL FOOTNOTE CODING

A	asides
AB	abbreviation
ADD	a passage modern texts have added to their texts from F2–4/Qq
ALT	a passage (including act and scene division) that has been altered by modern texts without any Ff/Qq authority
COMP	a setting probably influenced by compositor interference
F	concerning disputed facts within the play
FL	foreign language
L	letter or letters
LS	alterations in line structure
M	Shakespeare's use of the scansion of magic (trochaic and seven syllables)
N	a name modern texts have changed or corrected for easier recognition
O	F1 words or phrases substituted for a Qq oath or blasphemy
OM	passage, line, or word modern texts omit or suggest omitting
P	change in prefix assigned to a character
PCT	alterations to F1's punctuation by modern and/or contemporary texts
Q	material rejected or markedly altered by Qq not usually set by modern texts
QO	oaths or blasphemies set in Qq not usually set by modern texts
SD	stage directions added or altered by modern texts
SP	a solo split line for a single character (see pp. xv–xvi above)

SPD	matters concerning songs, poems, or doggerel
?ST	where, because of question marks within the passage, the final choice as to the number of sentences is left to the reader's discretion
STRUCT	a deliberate change from the F1 setting by these texts
UE	an unusual entrance (set to the side of the text) or exit (set on a separate line)
VP	F1's verse altered to prose or vice versa, or lines indistinguishable as either
W	F1's word or phrase altered by modern texts
WHO	(in a convoluted passage) who is speaking to whom
WS	F1 line structure altered because of casting off problems (see pp. x–xi above)

FOOTNOTE CODING BY TOPIC

STAGE DIRECTIONS, ETC.

A	asides
P	change in prefix assigned to a character
SD	stage directions added or altered by modern texts
UE	an unusual entrance (set to the side of the text) or exit (set on a separate line)
WHO	(in a convoluted passage) who is speaking to whom

LINE STRUCTURE AND PUNCTUATION, ETC.

L	letter or letters
LS	alterations in line structure
M	Shakespeare's use of the scansion of magic (trochaic and seven syllables)
PCT	alterations to F1's punctuation by modern and/or contemporary texts
SPD	matters concerning songs, poems, or doggerel
?ST	where, because of question marks within the passage, the final choice as to the number of sentences is left to the reader's discretion
SP	a solo split line for a single character (see pp. xv–xvi above)
VP	F1's verse altered to prose or vice versa, or lines indistinguishable as either

WS   F1 line structure altered because of casting off problems (see pp. x–xi above)

CHANGES TO WORDS AND PHRASES

AB   abbreviation

F   concerning disputed facts within the play

FL   foreign language

N   a name modern texts have changed or corrected for easier recognition

O   F1 words or phrases substituted for a Qq oath or blasphemy

QO   oaths or blasphemies set in Qq not usually set by modern texts

W   F1's word or phrase altered by modern texts

CHANGES ON A LARGER SCALE AND OTHER UNAUTHORISED CHANGES

ADD   a passage modern texts have added to their texts from F2–4/Qq

ALT   a passage (including act and scene division) that has been altered by modern texts without any Ff/Qq authority

COMP   a setting probably influenced by compositor interference

OM   passage, line, or word modern texts omit or suggest omitting

Q   material rejected or markedly altered by Qq not usually set by modern texts

STRUCT   a deliberate change from the F1 setting by these texts

ONE MODERN CHANGE FREQUENTLY NOTED IN THESE TEXTS

'MINUTE' CHANGES TO THE SYLLABLE LENGTH OF FF LINES

As noted above on pages xi–xii, modern texts frequently correct what commentators consider to be large scale metric deficiencies, often to the detriment of character and scene. There are many smaller changes made too, especially when lines are either longer or shorter than the norm of pentameter by 'only' one or two syllables. These changes are equally troublesome, for there is a highly practical theatrical rule of thumb guideline to such irregularities, viz.:

if lines are slightly **longer** than pentameter, then the characters so involved have too much information coursing through them to be contained within the 'norms' of proper verse, occasionally even to the point of losing self-control

if lines are slightly **shorter** than ten syllables, then either the information therein contained or the surrounding action is creating a momentary (almost need to breath) hesitation, sometimes suggesting a struggle to maintain self-control

These texts will note all such alterations, usually offering the different syllable counts per line as set both by F1 and by the altered modern texts, often with a brief suggestion as to how the original structural 'irregularity' might reflect onstage action.

FINALLY, A BRIEF WORD ABOUT THE COMPOSITORS [9]

Concentrated research into the number of the compositors and their habits began in the 1950s and, for a while, it was thought five men set the First Folio, each assigned a letter, 'A' through 'E'.

'E' was known to be a seventeen-year-old apprentice whose occasional mishaps both in copying text and securing the type to the frame have led to more than a few dreadful lapses, notably in *Romeo and Juliet*, low in the left column on p. 76 of the Tragedies, where in sixteen F1 lines he commits seven purely typographical mistakes. Compositor 'B' set approximately half of F1, and has been accused of being cavalier both with copying text and not setting line ending punctuation when the line is flush to the column edge. He has also been accused of setting most of the so called 'solo' split lines, though a comparison of other compositors' habits suggests they did so too, especially the conglomerate once considered to be the work of a single compositor known as 'A'. It is now acknowledged that the work set by 'A' is probably the work of at least two and more likely five different men, bringing the total number of compositors having worked on F1 to nine ('A' times five, and 'B' through 'E').

It's important to recognise that the work of these men was sometimes flawed. Thus the footnotes in these texts will point the reader to as many examples as possible which current scholarship and research suggest are in error. These errors fall into two basic categories. The first is indisputable, that of pure typographical mistakes ('wh?ch' for 'which'): the second, frequently open to challenge, is failure to copy exactly the text (Qq or manuscript) which F1 has used as its source material.

As for the first, these texts place the symbol † before a footnote marker within the text (not in the footnote section), a combination used only to point to a purely typographical mistake. Thus in the error-riddled section of *Romeo and Juliet* quoted above, p. 109 of this script shows fourteen footnote markers, seven of them coupled with the symbol †. Singling out these typographical-only markers alerts the reader to compositor error, and that (usually) the 'correct' word or phrase has been set within the text. Thus the reader doesn't have to bother with the footnote below unless they have a morbid curiosity to find out what the error actually is. Also, by definition, the more † appearing in a passage, the worse set that passage is.

As to the second series of (sometimes challengeable) errors labelled poor copy work, the footnotes will alert the reader to the alternative Qq word or phrase usage preferred by most modern texts, often discussing the alternatives in detail, especially when there seems to be validity to the F1 setting.

---

[9]   Readers are directed to the ground breaking work of Alice Walker, and also to the ongoing researches of Paul Werstine and Peter W. M. Blayney.

Given the fluid state of current research, more discoveries are bound to be published as to which compositor set which F1 column long after these texts go to print. Thus the current assignation of compositors at the bottom of each of these scripts' pages represents what is known at this moment, and will be open to reassessment as time goes by.

A CAVEAT: THE COMPOSITORS AND 'SINGLE SPLIT LINES' (SEE PP. XV–XVI)

Many commentators suggest single split lines are not Shakespearean dramatic necessity, but compositorial invention to get out of a typesetting dilemma. Their argument is threefold:

first, as mentioned on pp. x–xi, because of 'white space' a small amount of text would have to be artificially expanded to fill a large volume of what would otherwise be empty space: therefore, even though the column width could easily accommodate regular verse lines, the line or lines would be split in two to fill an otherwise embarrassing gap

second, even though the source documents the compositors were using to set F1 showed material as a single line of verse, occasionally there was too much text for the F1 column to contain it as that one single line: hence the line had to be split in two

third, the device was essentially used by compositor B.

There is no doubt that sometimes single split lines did occur for typesetting reasons, but it should be noted that:

single split lines are frequently set well away from white space problems

often the 'too-much-text-for-the-F1-column-width' problem is solved by setting the last one or two words of the overly lengthy line either as a new line, or as an overflow or underflow just above the end of the existing line without resorting to the single split line

all compositors seem to employ the device, especially the conglomerate known as 'A' and compositor E.

As regards the following text, while at times readers will be alerted to the fact that typographical problems could have had an influence on the F1 setting, when single split lines occur their dramatic potential will be discussed, and readers are invited to explore and accept or reject the setting accordingly.

INTRODUCTION TO THE TEXT OF
THE TRAGEDIE OF ANTHONIE, AND CLEOPATRA [1]
pages 340 - 368 of the Tragedy Section [2]
All Act, Scene, and line numbers will refer to the
Applause text below unless otherwise stated.

Current research places the play as number thirty or thirty-one in the canon. It was set in tandem with *The Tragedie of Cymbeline.*

The play was entered in the Stationer's Register May 20 1608 [3], and because Samuel Daniel's revisions of his *The Tragedie of Cleopatra*, (originally written 1594) published in 1607, seem so dependent on *The Tragedie of Anthonie and Cleopatra*, scholars point to a 1606 composition date for Shakespeare's play.

SCHOLARS' ASSESSMENT

F1 is the sole authority. Because of its length; irregular stage directions; occasional characters who though named seem to play no part in the scene (for example, see footnote #3, page 4, with the rest annotated throughout); the mess of the Messengers (footnote #3, page 10); and the prefix confusion of Alexas or Charmian (where most modern texts reassign the speech from the former to the latter, see footnote #1, page 7); the text could not come from a prompt-book. [4] Yet its finished condition, far finer than most plays emanating from foul papers, suggests a fair transcript from Shakespeare. *The New Cambridge Shakespeare Antony and Cleopatra* (see Recommended Texts below) coins the ingenious term 'producer's' rather than 'prompter's' copy.

Campbell [5] offers the paradoxical

> The Folio text is an unusually good one except for many misprints, most of which were corrected in the Second Folio . . .

---

[1] The Catalogue, headers and most of the dialogue (129 references) set 'Anthony'; 'Anthonie' is set on the Title page and five times in the dialogue; 'Antony' is set three times in the dialogue. For a detailed examination, see Wells, Stanley and Taylor, Gary (eds.). *William Shakespeare: A Textual Companion.* Oxford: Clarendon Press. 1987. pages 549 - 555: for a detailed analysis of the play's contents, see any of the Recommended Modern Texts.

[2] *Mr. William Shakespeare's Comedies, Histories, & Tragedies, 1623.*

[3] The log of The Stationer's Company through which ownership of a text was established, and via which all texts were regulated and licensed.

[4] A manuscript prepared by the Playhouse (copied from either fair or foul papers) with detailed information added necessary for staging a theatrical performance. The term 'foul papers' refers to Shakespeare's first draft, with all the original crossings out and blots intact.

[5] Campbell, Oscar James and Edward G. Quinn (eds.). *The Reader's Encyclopedia Of Shakespeare.* New York: Thomas Y. Crowell. 1966. page 24

and there are sufficient claims of 'errors' in punctuation and mislineation and ambiguous lineation for many editors to go after the F1 text with a hatchet. *A Textual Companion* lists more than 180 passages involving over three hundred and forty lines that needed to be altered for *The Oxford Shakespeares.* [6]

Thankfully M. R. Ridley, editor of *The Arden Shakespeare Antony and Cleopatra* (see Recommended Texts below) offers a clear-cut rebuttal of serious punctuation alteration, 'I think therefore that in the punctuation of the early texts we have, pretty certainly, at least "playhouse punctuation", and very possibly a great deal of Shakespeare's own' (page xviii).

Would that he were so tolerant of so-called mislineation for there are many short starting lines and crammed pages which mark much of this 'Stratford' play. [7] Mercifully the editor of one of the latest editions, is:

> Shakespeare's verse, especially in his late plays, constantly warns us not to
> impose preconceived notions of metrical conventionality (page 267

Apart from not trying to restructure passages of three successive short lines,[8] he also goes against what he calls 'a virtually unanimous editorial tradition' of combining two or more half-lines, especially when they 'do not produce very plausible pentameter verse'. He then succinctly adds, especially as regards this play,

> Shakespeare did occasionally write hexameter lines, to be sure, [9] but to add such
> hypothetically constructed hexameters by the hundreds to the meagre store of
> undoubted hexameters occurring elsewhere is to increase the percentage out of
> all recognisable proportion.

Would all editors share David Bevington's common-sense and seemingly theatrical approach in his *New Cambridge Shakespeare* (1990 edition).[10]

---

[6] Wells, Stanley and Taylor, Gary (eds.). *The Oxford Shakespeare, William Shakespeare, The Complete Works, Original Spelling Edition* and *Modern Spelling Edition*. Oxford: The Clarendon Press. 1986

[7] As they do one other Stratford pxlay, *The Tragedy of Coriolanus.* The term 'Stratford plays' refers to those final plays sent in from Stratford after Shakespeare left London: since he was not on hand to decipher problems in his foul papers, scholars claim in these plays problems of ambiguous lines and irregular verse are far greater than normal. The plays involved include *Coriolanus, Cymbeline, The Winters Tale, The Tempest,* and *Henry VIII.*

[8] See the General Introduction, pages xiii.

[9] Iambic lines of six strong stresses, usually twelve syllables long.

[10] Yet his generosity does not extend to what most editors consider verse-prose mislineation. As most editors, he alters Agrippa's F1 tentative prose first murmurings of how Cæsar's sister Octavia and Anthony might marry, back to the traditional formal verse, thus supporting Ridley's rather wry comment 'an oasis of prose cannot have been intended in the middle of a straight run of regular verse.' (*The Arden Shakespeare Antony and Cleopatra,* page 238)

THE TEXT

was set by compositors B (44 columns) and E (14).

F1'S STAGE MANAGEMENT OF THE PLAY

PREFIXES

There are several minor problems, most of which would have been cleared up by a book-holder.

• **VARIABLE SPELLINGS OFFERED FOR SOME NAMES**

There is both 'Camidius' (four times in the dialogue and twice in stage directions) and 'Camidias' (the first stage direction). There is 'Ventigius' (twice in the dialogue and one stage direction) and 'Ventidius' (twice in stage directions and three times in dialogue). Then there is the character known either as 'Dercetius' (prefix page 114) or 'Decretas' (stage direction and as the character names himself, both page 120).

Also, it seems whoever added or set the stage directions was neither familiar with, nor had worked on, the rest of the text, for here more than in any other play, there are some very weird mis-spellings of names: 'Cleopater' for 'Cleopatra' (page 41) though this is also set twice in earlier dialogue; 'Menes' for 'Menas' (page 53); 'Cæsur' for 'Cæsar' (page 106); and 'Dollabello' and 'Dollabella" (twice) for 'Dolabella' (page 83) - who is also referred to by Cæsar as 'Dollabella' (page 120).

• **THE PROBLEM OF THE ABBREVIATED PREFIXES FOR MENACRATES OR MENAS**

Some modern texts correct the single F1 - 3 setting of Menacrates to the historically correct Menecretes. Even so, the prefix 'Mene.' would normally apply just to Mene{a}crates, but a problem arises on page 27 (line 720). Here, although the prefix 'Mene' is used, at the end of the sequence Pompey immediately refers to the character as Menas. As a result, though both men are among the few friends and supporters aligned with Pompey, some commentators suggest wiping out Mene{a}crates completely.

Yet there may be a virtue in maintaining the two as separate characters (apart from the fact both are referred to as distinct individuals, rather dismissively as 'Pyrates' by a Messenger to Cæsar, line 517 page 20). From the text, Menas seems to be more a practical soldier, while, if most of the earlier 'Mene' dialogue does stand apart, Menc{a}crates seems to be more the strategist.

F1'S USUAL LACK OF NUMBERING FOR GENERIC CHARACTERS

This badly skews the scene with the 'Company of Soldiers' (from the dialogue apparently finishing their watch) who meet 'other Soldiers' (page 96). The speaking members of the Company, numbered #1 and #2, greet the others and in turn are greeted by another number #1, and it's evident from the dialogue this is not the number #1 who has just been speaking. Most modern texts renumber the second #1 as #3. This number #1/#3 finishes with the words 'goodnight, goodnight.' but no exit is set, so it is not clear if anyone does leave. A generalised direction follows 'They place themselves in every corner of the Stage', and in the ensuing conversation the prefixes are numbers #1 through #4. So it's not clear whether #1 and #2 refer to members of the first or second group.

- **THE OCCASIONALLY TOTALLY INCORRECT PREFIX**

Prefixes are occasionally set for characters who are not part of the scene or who have just left it. Thus 'Anthony' is set instead of 'Agrippa' (page 61, footnote #2, line 1661), even though Anthony was never part of the scene - simply mentioned two lines earlier. 'Ventidius' is set instead of 'Camidius', though Ventidius was neither part of the scene nor even mentioned (page 77, footnote #2, line 2090). And page 121, footnote #7, line 3378, 'Dolabella' is set instead of 'Agrippa', even though Dolabella left the scene some thirty lines earlier to carry out Cæsar's order.

STAGE DIRECTIONS

Since the manuscripts upon which F1 is based were originally prepared for the theatre, it would be second nature for the actors and prompt book holder to fill in many of the smaller details in performance without extra annotation. Thus these minor details would not make their way to F1's publisher (the house of Jaggard) and in the printing it was never considered a necessity to add such missing details, since, as often as not, they weren't really missing if the text in question was closely followed. In this play, some details can be so seen, some not.

- **DETAILS THAT CAN BE GLEANED BY FOLLOWING THE ACTION OF THE PLAY**

As usual, F1 leaves the inner movement of one or two characters within large scale scenes (such as Pompey and Menas' withdrawal and return, pages 55 - 7) to the reader's imagination. Some musical cues are omitted, especially if referred to within the text, as with Enobarbus' 'This is to horse' (page 62, line 1676), probably referring to an offstage trumpet, which most modern texts add just before his line.

. And, as usual, the dialogue often renders directions unnecessary, as with Cleopatra and Charmian placing the asps on their bodies (pages 136 - 7), and with Cleopatra handing to Cæsar a list of all her possessions where the words

> This is the breef: of Money, Plate & Jewels
> I am posses't of, 'tis exactly valewed,
>
> (page 129, lines 3613 - 4)

are all that the first actors and F1 require.

Sometimes minor characters are left out of large-scale entries, as with the Banquet entry (page 53), which modern texts suggest should include both the Boy who sings more than a hundred lines later, and the Servants to pass around all the drink; with Towrus who should accompany Cæsar's army (page 77); and Thidias with Cæsar, Agrippa and Dollabella (page 83).

Also, some **exits**, especially for supernumeraries, are taken for granted if they arise out of the dialogue, as with someone going to get the 'man from Scicion' and the withdrawal of the Messengers once Anthony is told of the death of his first wife, Fulvia (page 10, line 219). And, as usual, even if not mentioned, dead bodies are expected to be removed at the end of a scene, as Enobarbus' (page 106), and Eros' (page 116).

* WHEN THE DIALOGUE SIMPLY ISN'T DETAILED ENOUGH

In the sequence when Cleopatra is supposedly handing to Cæsar an inventory of all she possesses, she calls upon her treasurer Seleucus to back her up. He promptly betrays her by revealing the list only contains half her assets. Which command does he then obey, Cleopatra's threatening command 'Prythee go hence/Or I shall shew the Cynders of my spirits', or Cæsar's 'Forbeare Seleucus.' , for no further direction is set for him.

The situation is even more marked with the death of Anthony, which could occur anywhere between his last line 'I can no more' (line 3293 page 118) and Cleopatra's next five lines.

Also there is no clear indication as to how the Clowne sneaks the asps past the guards (page 134, line 3747) save for the reference to 'figs'. Thus most modern texts sensibly suggest the supposed 'figs' and thus the asps are in a basket which the Clowne then leaves behind.

* THE LACK OF ANY DETAILS IN THE CAPTURE OF CLEOPATRA

Sometimes it has to be inspired guesswork that deciphers the action from the dialogue, as in the following where, as the Roman Proculeius is lulling Cleopatra with a false assessment of Cæsar's empathy for her, something unexplained through dialogue alone occurs at the bracketed letters A through D

Proculeius	This Ile report (deere Lady)	
	Have comfort, for I know your plight is pittied	
	Of him that caus'd it.	(A)
Proculeius	You see how easily she may be surpriz'd:	
	Guard her till Cæsar come.	
Iras	Royall Queene.	
Charmian	Oh Cleopatra, thou art taken Queene.	
Cleopatra	Quicke, quicke, good hands.	(B)
Proculeius	Hold worthy Lady, hold:	(C)
	Doe not your selfe such wrong, who are in this	
	Releev'd, but not betraid.	
Cleopatra	What of death too that rids our dogs of languish	
Proculeius	Cleopatra, do not abuse my Masters bounty, by	
	Th'undoing of your selfe:	(D)

(page 125, lines 3480 - 93)

At A, most modern texts have the Roman general Gallus plus Soldiers enter and quickly capture Cleopatra and her Court. This is only surmised from an innocuous order from Cæsar some fifty lines earlier 'Gallus, go you along' (page 123, line 3430) and even then there is no mention of Soldiers or capture. Since at D Proculeius asks Cleopatra not to abuse Cæsar's 'bounty' by 'Th'undoing of your selfe', editors suggest at B, Cleopatra pulls a knife on herself and at C Proculeius disarms her.

- **QUESTIONABLE ALTERING OF THE TIMING OF SOME DIRECTIONS**

Undoubtedly some stage directions seem to be set too early. Probably this is because they were added by the Playhouse as a form of warning cue for the original actors, musicians or stage-hands, as with the side-set 'far off', presumably referring to a music cue, four lines before Anthony comments that the sound refers to their forces having caused the enemy to 'retyre' (page 102, footnote #6).

In such cases, alterations by modern texts are welcome. But not all alterations are. First, there are those **unfortunate alterations made because the modern texts think the direction is set too late.** But in what seems to be late, F1 has probably set an important clue that it is the on-stage person who is driving the action surrounding the entry. By reversing direction and dialogue, modern texts often stop the play with the entry, thus reducing both the drive of usually the more important character as well as the speed of the play.

This is especially so with the centre set direction 'Enter a Servant with Thidias' (page 90). F1 shows Anthony calling 'Is he whipt' before the direction is set. Most modern texts set the direction first then the line. This is theatrical foolishness, for Anthony is often impatient, and the original F1 setting may be yet a further illustration of this, with him yelling off-stage (probably goaded to it by his ongoing quarrel with Cleopatra).

Second, **the passion for altering timing in the name of tidiness sometimes causes modern texts to completely eradicate a silent stage moment**, as with the deliberate snub of Anthony by Cleopatra early in the play. F1 sets

{Alexas}	My Lord approaches.
	Enter Anthony with a Messenger
Cleopatra	We will not looke upon him:
	Go with us.
	[Exeunt]

(page 8, lines 175 - 7)

Most modern texts reset this as

{Alexas}	My Lord approaches.
Cleopatra	We will not looke upon him:
	Go with us.
	[Exeunt]
	Enter Anthony with a Messenger

which totally ruins Cleopatra's calculated effect (via her highly visible F1 public snub, exiting only after he enters) of letting Anthony know her displeasure that he has ignored her to receive word of his wife.

There is also, at least as set in F1, the wonderful kindness from Cleopatra to the eunuch Mardian in sparing him the sight of her death: by judicious tidying most modern texts remove this possibility, see footnote #1 page 124 for details.

* **MOMENTS IN THE STAGE ACTION THAT NEED RESOLVING**

Nevertheless, certain decisions are required of the reader

- how many Servitors does Anthony bid farewell to, four (as F1 suggests), five or six: see footnote #2 to page 94
- commentators suggest that, in addition to Eros, one other should enter with Anthony in what modern texts term Act Four Scene 5 (page 99), see footnote #3
- modern texts restructure the sequence of Cleopatra's helping Anthony don his armour: see footnote #4 to page 97

And finally, a stage direction for Alexas incorrectly suggests he is returning from Cæsar, when in fact he is coming from Anthony (page 22).

ASIDES & WHO-TO'S.

These present little problem, save for the occasional breaking off by Pompey of his private conversation with Menas to join in the general drunken banter (e.g. line 1501, page 55), and the working out whether some of Enobarbus' more pointed comments are intended to be heard by all those around him or not.

In these and similar cases, the modern texts offer additional stage directions. In many such cases this text will not, but it will footnote the more difficult and obscure references, with annotations as to extra stage directions (coded SD), or asides (coded A), or as to who is speaking to whom (coded WHO).

MODERN INTERVENTIONS

VARIATIONS IN VERSE AND PROSE

These are legion, with much of F1's prose being reset as verse to the detriment of many of the characters. The distinction is not one of mere pedantry. Verse implies some harmony and grace in self-expression; prose a more prosaic, everyday quality to the dialogue,. And it can be very useful to note when such changes occur, for the transition between them usually shows a change in attitude within, or between, the speakers involved.

* **F1's PROSE AS A CLUE TO CHANGES IN CHARACTER BEHAVIOUR**

With Enobarbus, it might be that he is truly at ease in prose, as in his private straightforward man-to-man exchange with Menas (pages 51 - 3). Thus it shouldn't be surprising that his more sardonic passive-aggressive commentaries also slip into prose. And it would seem that when he goes too far he succeeds in dragging others out of verse down to his prose level.

This happens with Anthony after Enobarbus' suggestion that for all the fine protestations of 'Love' for each other between Cæsar and Anthony, once the Pompey situation has been dealt with they will have time to wrangle again ('Or if you borrow . . .', pages 32, lines 866 and on); and with Cleopatra during the quarrel over his recommendation to Anthony that she should not be present during the 'warres' against Cæsar ('I will be even with thee.' pages 73 - 4, lines 1994 - 2004). Most modern texts set Enobarbus in verse, the overall pattern of the scenes.

A mixture of verse and prose also seems to be a characteristic of Cleopatra at her most skittish, as with her determination to write to Anthony yet again ('Who's borne that day . . .' page 24, lines 646 - 53) and dangerous, as with her second meeting with the unfortunate Messenger who brought her news of Anthony's marriage to Octavia (pages 64 - 7). Most modern texts set both sequences as verse.

- **THE SUDDEN APPEARANCE OF PROSE AS MOMENTS OF RELAXATION**

What was suggested above for Enobarbus and Menas, can be equally applied to Charmian and the Soothsayer (pages 4 - 7). F1 sets both Charmian's opening wheedling of Alexas to produce the Soothsayer, and her sensual responses to the Soothsayer's (accurately gloomy but unrecognised) forecast in prose. Most modern texts set verse, suggesting a formality which was most definitely not part of the original scene.

METRIC (LINE STRUCTURE) ALTERATIONS

These are at a premium too. Because of the metrical freedoms Shakespeare explores in this play, many verse lines are longer or shorter than the norm of ten syllables [11]. Most modern texts readjust both them and the lines around them to establish metric regularity. Thus normalcy is created where original F1 irregularities show the character(s) so affected undergoing great strain. Often a totally different state of mind, of thought process, and of speech pattern, is created

---

[11] Now well into the mature stages of his writing, (*The Tragedie of Anthonie and Cleopatra* coming after about 80% of his work has been completed), Shakespeare has already shown in *The Tragedie of Macbeth*, and *The Tragedie of King Lear* and will continue to show in *The Tragedie of Coriolanus* and *The Tempest*, a much freer metric convention than in his early plays - unconsciously created by the dramatic situation, not poetic necessity.

As the passions or actions of the characters swell beyond the bounds of normal experience and expression, he creates lines longer than the iambic norm. And, in contrast, he creates lines shorter than the norm when action is required to fill the gap, or the speaker or listener is so moved or stunned by the words just uttered that they cannot complete a line of normal length.

Couple all this to a play which deals with political manipulations and conflict at the highest levels, treason, and passionate love, and it is hardly surprising that at times speech and breath patterns show enormous varieties from the iambic pentameter's norm of good behaviour and even tempered utterance.

from the one(s) originally set, doing enormous disservice to character and scene. Many of these alterations are footnoted under the coding 'LS', and the following can serve as example.

● **HIGHLIGHTING THE SMALLEST OF MOMENTS**

Minor linear variations can add wonderful personal delicacies, as with Anthony's enticing Cleopatra - angered by his spending time with Messengers from Rome - by embellishing her original suggestion that they should wander through the city

No Messenger but thine, and all alone, to night	(12)
Wee'l wander through the streets, and note	(8)
The qualities of the people. Come my Queene	
(page 3, lines 66 - 8)	

F1's two off-balanced lines can suggest all sorts of seductive verbal excitements and delays, nuzzling and physical attentions. Most modern texts reset the lines as normal pentameter.

No Messenger but thine, and all alone,	(10)
To night wee'l wander through the streets, and note	(10)
The qualities of the people. Come my Queene	

Metric irregularities also underscore the deep personal reactions beneath what seems a calm stoic acceptance, as with the Messenger delivering news to Anthony of his wife Fulvia's death

Messenger	Fulvia thy wife is dead.	(6 - 7)
Anthony	Where dyed she.	(3)
Messenger	In Scicion, her length of sicknesse,	(9)
	With what else more serious,	(6 - 7)
	Importeth thee to know, this beares.	(8)
Anthony	Forbeare me	(3)
	There's a great Spirit gone, thus did I desire it:	
	(page 10, lines 219 - 25)	

F1's hesitations allow for self-control by both men. Modern texts create instead one long pause and two overlylong lines.

Messenger	Fulvia thy wife is dead.	
Anthony	Where dyed she.	(9 - 10)
Messenger	In Scicion,	(4)
	Her length of sicknesse, with what else more serious,	(11 - 12)
	Importeth thee to know, this beares.	
Anthony	Forbeare me	(11)
	There's a great Spirit gone, thus did I desire it:	

The variations can establish undercurrents of alarm, as with Enobarbus' concern that Cleopatra really may be considering betraying Anthony as he watches her toying with the pomposity of Cæsar's envoy, Thidias. In suggesting that Cæsar realises Cleopatra accepted Anthony through fear rather than love, Thidias continues

Thidias	The scarre's upon your Honor, therefore he	
	Does pitty, as constrained blemishes	
	Not as deserved.	(4 - 5)*
Cleopatra	He is a God,	(4)*
	And knowes what is most right. Mine Honour,	(9)*
	Was not yeelded, but conquer'd meerely.	(9)*
Enobarbus	To be sure of that, I will aske Anthony.	(11)
	Sir, sir, thou art so leakie	(7)*
	That we must leave thee to thy sinking, for	
	Thy deerest quit thee.	

(page 87, lines 2379 - 2389)

F1's first four fleeting asterisked hesitations allow for Cleopatra's wondrous sarcasm to be gently aired for the amusement of all who truly know her. The fifth allows a moment for Enobarbus' concern. By restructuring, mainly through shared lines, most modern texts wipe out all the teasing delicacies and nuances offered by F1's short lines, setting an onrush instead.

Thidias	The scarre's upon your Honor, therefore he	
	Does pitty, as constrained blemishes	
	Not as deserved.	
Cleopatra	He is a God, and knowes	(10 - 11)
	What is most right. Mine Honour, was not yeelded,	(11)
	But conquer'd meerely.	
Enobarbus	To be sure of that,	(10)
	I will aske Anthony. Sir, sir, thou art so leakie	(13)
	That we must leave thee too thy sinking, for	
	Thy deerest quit thee.	

Similar restructuring affects a myriad of moments, including the death of Eros (page 113, lines 3148 - 50); Anthony's failure to commit quick suicide (page 114, lines 3166 - 71); and Cleopatra's first questioning the Clowne as to whether he has brought the asps (page 134, lines 3748 - 50).

• F1's METRIC VARIATIONS AND OCTAVIUS CÆSAR

Above all, the restructuring totally destroys the manic nature of Cæsar. Time and time again, in his moments of anger and thwarted ambition, F1 sets him totally erratic long opening lines, as in his first face to face meeting with Anthony. He responds to Anthony's blunt telling him he has no business being concerned at Anthony's involvement with Cleopatra (page 29, line 780) thus

I must be laught at, if or for nothing, or a little, I   (15)

And his double displeasure at being ignored while Anthony was revelling (page 31, line 828) is expressed as

> I wrote to you when rioting in Alexandria you   (13 - 15)

which all modern texts try (unsuccessfully) to reduce to normal pentameter here and throughout the rest of the play by readjusting the opening of each of his speeches to form split lines with the previous speaker , viz

> {Anthony)   or being, concerne you not.
>
> Cæsar   I must be laught at,   (11 - 12)
>   If or for nothing, or a little, I (10)

and

> {Anthony)   But say I could not helpe it.
>
> Cæsar   I wrote to you   (11)
>   When rioting in Alexandria you   (9 - 11)

Cæsar's F1 pattern of momentary irregularity never changes, even at the end when, having already won the war, wanting Anthony's surrender he orders with wondrous drawling pauses

> Cæsar   Go to him Dollabella, bid him yeeld,
>   Being so frustrate, tell him,   (6 - 7)
>   He mockes the pawses that he makes.   (8)
>
> Dolabella   Cæsar, I shall.
>   (4)
>   (page 120, lines 3341 - 44)

Unfortunately the seemingly languid basking in triumph offered by the F1 short lines is quickly transformed into a speedier sense of determination by the modern texts' unsuccessful attempt at regularisation.

> Cæsar   Go to him Dollabella, bid him yeeld,
>   Being so frustrate, tell him, he mockes   (8 - 9)
>   The pawses that he makes.
>
> Dolabella   Cæsar, I shall.   (10)

BREAKS IN PERSONAL DECORUM

Single split lines abound [12], as with Anthony, who has already moved to verse, suddenly losing patience with Enobarbus' pointed still-in-prose comments tying together how thankful Anthony should be about the death of his first wife with distasteful remarks about Anthony's 'business' with Cleopatra. He shuts Enobarbus up with

---

[12]   These are two or more short verse lines, set for a single character, which if placed together (as poets, scholars and commentators suggest), would form a single full line of verse. These lines are rarely reproduced as set by any modern text : see the General Introduction, pages xv - xvi for further discussion.

> No more light Answeres: (5)
> Let our Officers (5)
> Have notice what we purpose. I shall breake
>
> (page 12, lines 285 - 8)

And at times such splits can underscore debating points, as with Cleopatra's double rebuke of Anthony's seeking her agreement for his return (temporarily) to Rome. The pauses inherent in F1's setting of her response

> Why should I think you can be mine, & true
> (Though you in swearing shake the Throaned Gods)
> Who have been false to Fulvia? (7 - 8)
> Riotous madnesse, (4 - 5)
> To be entangled with those mouth-made vowes
>
> (page 15, lines 352 - 6)

followed closely by lines 359 - 62

> Nay pray you seeke no colour for your going,
> But bid farewell, and goe: (6)
> When you sued staying (5)
> Then was the time for words: No going then

are as potent as a physical slap across the face. Most modern texts reset each pair of short lines as one.

PUNCTUATION

To requote M.R. Ridley from page xl, 'I think therefore that in the punctuation of the early texts we have, pretty certainly, at least "playhouse punctuation", and very possibly a great deal of Shakespeare's own'. Nevertheless, modern texts alter F1's punctuation in the usual ways [13], often making bland 'corrections' where F1's ungrammatical settings offer much more emotion, as with Cleopatra's questioning of Alexas about her beloved Anthony from whom he has just returned. The comma of F1's

> What was he sad,* or merry?

(page 23, lines 629), suggests she expects Anthony should have been sad, the 'merry' coming as an almost treacherous after-thought. Modern texts' retinkering to

> What was he,* sad or merry?   or,   What,* was he sad or merry?

reduces her wonderful self-centredness to nothing more than urgent questioning. Other similarly diminishing repunctuations include Anthony's F1 page 16, line 421

> You'l heat my blood no more?

The question mark, in its contemporary function as exclamation point, suggests the line might simply be a statement or even a threat that there will be no more sex between him and Cleopatra. Either is a far cry from the usual modern resetting of

---

[13] For further details see Freeman, Neil H.M. *Shakespeare's First Texts.* Vancouver. 1994

l

You'l heat my blood! No more!

One of the most damaging repunctuations affects the nervousness of the unnamed Egyptian whom Cleopatra has forced to be her ambassador to Cæsar. The F1 setting with all its peculiar (asterisk marked) punctuation expresses his discomfort superbly

Ægyptian	A poore Egyptian yet,* the Queen my mistris
	Confin'd in all,* she has her Monument *
	Of thy intents, desires,* instruction,
	That she preparedly may frame her selfe
	To'th'way shee's forc'd too.

(pages 122, lines 3408 - 12)

which most modern texts reset as the much more self-controlled (the punctuation alterations again marked *)

Ægyptian	A poore Egyptian yet; * the Queen my mistris,*
	Confin'd in all * she has, * her Monument,*
	Of thy intents, desires* instruction,
	That she preparedly may frame her selfe
	To'th'way shee's forc'd too.

And sometimes even what appears the most stupid F1 punctuation mistake may have value, see footnote #3 to page 138 as example.

COMBINATIONS OF UNBALANCED DEVICES (when all irregularities blend together)

These are superb indicators of extreme awkwardness as with Pompey's first meetings with Cæsar and Anthony and all the Roman might. The irregularities as a whole suggest a man somewhat out of his depth (pages 47 - 50). Most modern texts regularise the sequence throughout.

DEBATE

Though Spevack [14] finds 499 shared split lines [15], this is the one play where his calculations must be readjusted for the enormous alterations made to F1 by his research text *The Riverside Shakespeare* [16]. Nevertheless many still remain, and serve to speed on a very long play, especially when characters are cross-examining one another as with Cleopatra and Enobarbus (page 7), or one character intercedes during heated discussions as with Anthony's jumping on Lepidus'

---

[14] Spevack, M. *A Complete And Systematic Concordance To The Works Of Shakespeare.* (9 vols.) Hildesheim. Georg Holms. 1968 - 1980

[15] Two or more short verse lines, set for two or more characters, which if placed together (as poets, scholars and commentators suggest), would form a single full line of verse: see the General Introduction, pages xii - xv for further discussion.

[16] Gwynne Blakemore Evans, Harry Levin, Anne Barton, Herschel Baker, Frank Kermode, Hallet D. Smith, and Marie Edel, eds., *The Riverside Shakespeare* (Copyright © 1974 by Houghton Mifflin Company).

attempt to control the angry Cæsar (page 31) who has just dropped the grace of verse for more direct angry prose.

However, great care must be taken not to push every successive short line together to create a full verse line. The prime example comes at the opening of this first negotiating scene where most modern texts combine five short speeches totalling eleven syllables into one line, thus

Cæsar	Welcome to Rome.			
Anthony		Thanke you.		
Cæsar			Sit.	
Anthony				Sit sir.
Cæsar				Nay then.

(page 29, lines 773 - 77)

setting up a speedy exchange. However F1 allows the actor/reader to choose whether the lines should all be jammed together or no

Cæsar	Welcome to Rome.	(4)
Anthony	Thanke you.	(2)
Cæsar	Sit.	(1)
Anthony	Sit sir.	(2)
Cæsar	Nay then.	(2)

F1 sets up a tighter and unforgiving opening, at one and the same time both stiffly formal and silly in Cæsar's insistence on the observing of protocol.

FACTS

T.J. King suggests there are 3,484 spoken lines and that twelve actors can play nineteen principal roles. Four boys each play a principal female role. Thirteen men can play thirty-seven smaller speaking roles and forty-six mutes: three boys can play twelve mutes. [17]

The 'CATALOGUE' lists the play as *Anthony and Cleopater.* There are two headers, the left is *The Tragedie of,* the right *Anthony and Cleopatra.* The title above the text is *THE TRAGEDIE OF Anthonie, and Cleopatra.* What should be page 360 is incorrectly set as 380 with the same number then repeated in its correct order as part of *The Tragedy of Cymbeline.* There are three catch word variations.

F1 sets no Act or Scene Division.

Neil Freeman,
Vancouver, B.C.
Canada, 1998

---

[17] This assumes a certain number of attendants in the 'traines' of Cleopatra and Octavia: King, T.J. *Casting Shakespeare's Plays.* Cambridge. Cambridge University Press. 1992

RECOMMENDED MODERN TEXTS WITH EXCELLENT SCHOLARLY FOOTNOTES AND RESEARCH

The footnotes in this text are concise, and concentrate either on matters theatrical or choices in word or line structure which distinguish most modern editions and this Folio based text. Items of literary, historical, and linguistic concern have been well researched and are readily available elsewhere. One of the best **research** works in recent years is

Wells, Stanley, and Gary Taylor, eds. *William Shakespeare: A Textual Companion.* Oxford: Clarendon Press, 1987.

For the re-editing of the 'Messenger mess', page 10, readers are guided to

Wells, Stanley. *Re-editing Shakespeare For The Modern Reader.* Clarendon Press. 1984

In terms of modern **texts,** readers are urged to consult at least one of the following:

Evans, Gwynne Blakemore, Harry Levin, Anne Barton, Herschel Baker, Frank Kermode, Hallet D. Smith, and Marie Edel, eds. *The Riverside Shakespeare.* Copyright © 1974 by Houghton Mifflin Company.

Ridley, M. R. (ed.). *Antony and Cleopatra.* The Arden Shakespeare. 1954

Bevington, D. (ed.). *Antony and Cleopatra.* The New Cambridge Shakespeare. 1990

THE TRAGEDIE OF ANTHONIE, AND CLEOPATRA
Dramatis Personæ

THE ROMANS

THE THREE TRIUMVIRS OF ROME
Mark ANTHONY
LEPIDUS
Octavius CÆSAR
OCTAVIA, Cæsar's sister, later wife to Mark Anthony

A RIVAL TO THE THREE TRIUMVIRS
Sextus POMPEY
His Supporters

MENAS   MENECRATES   VARRIUS

SUPPORTERS OF OCTAVIUS CÆSAR

MECENAS   THIDIAS
AGRIPPA   GALLUS
TOWRUS   DOLABELLA
            PROCULEIUS

SUPPORTERS OF MARK ANTHONY
Domitius ENOBARBUS

DEMETRIUS   EROS
PHILO   CAMIDIUS
VENTIDIUS   SCARRUS
SILLIUS   DECRETAS

MESSENGERS
a CENTERIE, and the soldiers of his WATCH
members of Mark Anthony's GUARD
a SOLDIER
Anthony's Schoolmaster, acting as an AMBASSADOR
a GUARD
a singing BOY

THE EGYPTIANS
Queene CLEOPATRA

HER ATTENDANTS

CHARMIAN   IRAS
ALEXAS   DIOMED
MARDIAN, an Eunuch   SELEUCAS, her Treasurer

a MESSENGER
an EGYPTIAN, acting as an Ambassador for Cleopatra
a CLOWNE
a SOOTHSAYER

Souldiers   Attendants   Captaines   Servants

This Cast List has been specially prepared for this edition, and will not be found in the Facsimile

THE
TRAGEDIE OF
Anthonie, and Cleopatra

Actus Primus. Scœna Prima

ENTER DEMETRIUS AND PHILO

Philo †

Nay†, but this dotage of our Generals
Ore-flowes the measure :   those his goodly eyes
That o're the Files and Musters of the Warre,
Have glow'd like plated Mars : → ¹
5 Now bend, now turne
The Office and Devotion of their view
Upon a Tawny Front.
　　　　　　His Captaines heart,
Which in the scuffles of great Fights hath burst
10 The Buckles on his brest, reneages all temper,
And is become the Bellowes and the Fan
To coole a Gypsies Lust.

FLOURISH. ENTER ANTHONY, CLEOPATRA HER LADIES, THE
TRAINE, WITH EUNUCHS FANNING HER

Looke where they come :
Take but good note, and you shall see in ² him
15 (The triple Pillar of the world) transform'd
Into a Strumpets Foole.
　　　　　　　　　Behold and see.

Cleopatra

If it be Love indeed, tell me how much.

L 340 - b : 1. 1. 1 - 14

SP 1　this is the first of many cases when two short Ff lines have been joined as one in most modern texts: in this case
the Ff setting could have come about because the enlarged decorative 'N' that opens the play, extending downward
four lines, allowed insufficient space for a full line to be set: if the Ff setting is to be maintained the break is at a
highly auspicious moment, with Philo pausing as he contrasts the gaze of the once warlike-Anthony with the
current Anthony-the-lover

W 2　Ff = 'in', one modern gloss = 'e'en'

	Anthony	There's beggery in the love that can be reckon'd [1]
20	Cleopatra	Ile set a bourne how farre to be belov'd.
	Anthony	Then must thou needes finde out new Heaven, new Earth.

ENTER A MESSENGER [2]

	Messenger	Newes (my good Lord) from Rome.
	Anthony	Grates me, the summe.
25	Cleopatra	Nay heare them Anthony.

Fulvia perchance is angry: Or who knowes,
If the scarse-bearded Cæsar have not sent
His powrefull Mandate to you.
                    Do this, or this;
30 Take in that Kingdome, and Infranchise that:

Perform't, or else we damne thee.

Anthony	How, my Love?
Cleopatra	Perchance?
	Nay, and most like: [3]

35 You must not stay heere longer, your dismission
Is come from Cæsar, therefore heare it Anthony. [4]

Where's Fulvias Processe? (Cæsars I would say) both?

Call in the Messengers: As I am Egypts Queene,
Thou blushest Anthony, and that blood of thine
40 Is Cæsars homager: else so thy cheeke payes shame,
When shrill-tongu'd Fulvia scolds.
                    The Messengers.

Anthony	Let Rome in Tyber melt, and the wide Arch
	Of the raing'd Empire fall: Heere is my space,
45| Kingdomes are clay: Our dungie earth alike	L 340-b
	Feeds Beast as Man; the Noblenesse of life
	Is to do thus: [5] when such a mutuall paire,

[PCT 1] F1-2 = no punctuation (possibly as if Cleopatra interrupts him), F3-4 and most modern texts set a period

[P 2] arguing that the Messenger would be waiting outside, some modern texts give the entry and lines to a Servant, who then exits later as part of the 'Traine', post line 70

[LS 3] the actor has choice as to which two of these three short lines may be joined as one line of split verse

[PCT 4] F1 sets a faint mark which may be punctuation: F2/most modern texts set a period

[SD 5] most modern texts suggest that Anthony illustrates 'to do thus' by embracing Cleopatra

And such a twaine can doo't, in which I binde
One paine of punishement, the world to weete
50   We stand up Peerelesse.
                                                }

Cleopatra   Excellent falshood:
Why did he marry Fulvia, and not love her?

Ile seeme the Foole I am not.
                              Anthony ° will be himselfe. ¹
55 **Anthony**   But stirr'd by Cleopatra.°

Now for the love of Love, and her soft houres,
Let's not confound the time with Conference harsh;
There's not a minute of our lives should stretch
Without some pleasure now. ²
60   What sport to night?

Cleopatra   Heare the Ambassadors.
                                                }
Anthony   Fye wrangling Queene:
Whom every thing becomes, to chide, to laugh,
To weepe: who ³ every passion fully strives
65   To make it selfe (in Thee) faire, and admir'd.

⁴ No Messenger but thine, and all alone,° to night
Wee'l wander through the streets, and note °
The qualities of people.
                              Come my Queene,
70   Last night you did desire it.
                                    Speake not to us.

[Exeunt with the Traine]

Demetrius   Is Cæsar with Anthonius priz'd so slight?

Philo   Sir sometimes when he is not Anthony,
He comes too short of that great Property

LS ₁ this is one of the many occasions when most modern texts reduce the overlylong Ff line at the end of a speech (here 14 syllables) by combining the latter half with the subsequent short line from the next speaker: while this may be more correct metrically, in this case the restructuring to two almost regular pentameter lines reduces both the impact of Cleopatra's (passionate) challenging definition of their actions, and the need for Anthony's highly intimate (short line) reply

W ₂ though most modern texts agree with Ff and set this as 'now', one gloss = 'new'

W ₃ some modern texts follow F2 and set 'whose', others the more recent gloss 'how': F1 = 'who'

LS ₄ this is the first example of a metrically unbalanced pair of lines (here 12/8 syllables) which modern texts reset as two regular lines (10/10): (see the Introduction to this play for further details:) yet the Ff setting sets up Anthony's inner turbulence as he initiates a most unusual love adventure for the pair of them: the modern setting removes any indication of excitement

75

Demetrius

Which still should go with Anthony.

[1] I am full sorry,° that hee approves the common
Lyar,° who thus speakes of him at Rome; but I will hope °
of better deeds to morrow.

Rest you happy.°

[Exeunt]

ENTER ENOBARBUS, LAMPRIUS, A SOUTHSAYER,[2] RANNIUS, LUCILLI-
US, CHARMIAN, IRAS, MARDIAN THE EUNUCH,
AND ALEXAS [3]

[Most modern texts create a new scene here, Act One Scene 2]

80 **Charmian**

L.[4] Alexas, sweet Alexas, most anything Alexas,
almost most absolute Alexas, where's the Soothsayer
that you prais'd so to'th'Queene?

[5] Oh that I knewe this
Husband, which you say,° must change [6] his Hornes with
85 Garlands.°

Alexas Soothsayer.

Soothsayer Your will?

Charmian Is this the Man?

Is't you sir that know things?

VP [1]

R 340 - b : 1. 1. 58 - 1. 2. 9

as the °'s show, most modern texts set this speech as verse, thus maintaining the standards of the scene so far: perhaps they do so because they adjudge the original compositor, erring on the side of caution, set prose simply because he might have thought there was too little space left in the column to set it as verse: however, the Ff setting, with its drop from the grace of verse to the more immediacy of prose, suggests a wonderful change for Demetrius, who at the top of the scene was told how Anthony had changed, now voices surprise himself

W [2]

F1-3 = 'Southsayer', F4/most modern texts = 'Soothsayer'

SD/P [3]

many modern texts exclude the Romans Lamprius, Rannius and Lucillius, and the Egyptian Mardian the Eunuch from the entry since they do not speak in the scene: in addition the Soothsayer is sometimes brought on after Alexas' first calling for him, and Enobarbus is sometimes brought in with his first line, giving orders for the setting up of the food and drink: however, in the footnote to the opening of scene II, page 8-9, *The Arden Shakespeare Anthony And Cleopatra*, op. cit., the excellent editor M.R.Ridley points out the importance of both the order of the entry, as is always the case with Shakespeare, and the fact that the silent figures, staying with their own kind, set up the two opposing cultures (Roman and Egyptian), thus providing a neat visual illustration of the tensions underlying the play

AB [4]

most modern texts expand Ff's 'L.' to 'Lord'

VP [5]

Ff unequivocally set the scene up to the entry of Cleopatra in prose (with the possible exception of Enobarbus' first two lines and Charmian's two line attempt to find out how many children she will have), which seems to emphasise the informality of the occasion: most modern texts make various attempts to set some of the characters' words as verse, noticeably the Soothsayer and (less frequently) Charmian: such changes will be marked ° accordingly, but not always footnoted

W [6]

most modern texts = 'charge', Ff = 'change'

90	Soothsayer	[1] In Natures infinite booke of Secrecie,° a little I can read.°
	Alexas	Shew him your hand.
	Enobarbus	Bring in the Banket quickly:° Wine enough, R 340 - b Cleopatra's health to drinke.° [2]
95	Charmian	Good sir, give me good Fortune.
	Soothsayer	I make not, but foresee.
	Charmian	Pray then, foresee me one.
	Soothsayer	You shall be yet ° farre fairer then you are.
	Charmian	He meanes in flesh.°
100	Iras	No, you shall paint when you are old.
	Charmian	Wrinkles forbid.°
	Alexas	Vex not his prescience,[3] be attentive.
	Charmian	Hush.°
	Soothsayer	You shall be more beloving, then beloved.°
105	Charmian	I had rather heate my Liver with drinking.°
	Alexas	Nay, heare him.
	Charmian	Good now some excellent Fortune: Let mee be married to three Kings in a forenoone, and Widdow them all: Let me have a Childe at fifty, to whom Herode
110		of Jewry may do Homage. Finde me to marrie me with Octavius Cæsar, and companion me with my Mistris.
	Soothsayer	You shall out-live the Lady whom you serve.°
	Charmian	Oh excellent, I love long life better then Figs.°
115	Soothsayer	You have seene and proved a fairer former fortune,° then that which is to approach.°

VP [1] if, as Ff suggest, these are the only verse lines for Enobarbus in the scene, that could offer great contrast to the other, less formal conversation in the scene - especially since he says no more until addressed directly by Cleopatra after her entry

SD [2] most modern texts add a stage direction for various Servants to quickly bring in food and drink, then exit

W [3] F1-2/most modern texts = 'prescience', F3 = 'patience'

Charmian Then belike my Children shall have no names:°
Prythee how many Boyes and Wenches must I have.°[1]

Soothsayer If every of your wishes had a wombe,° & foretell[2] every wish, a Million.°

Charmian Out Foole, I forgive thee for a Witch.°

Alexas You thinke none but your sheets are privie to
your wishes.

Charmian Nay come, tell Iras hers.

Alexas Wee'l know all our Fortunes.

Enobarbus Mine, and most of our Fortunes to night, shall
be drunke to bed.

Iras There's a Palme presages Chastity, if nothing els.

Charmian E'ne as the o're-flowing Nylus presageth Famine.

Iras Go you wilde Bedfellow, you cannot Soothsay.

Charmian Nay, if an oyly Palme bee not a fruitfull Prog-
nostication, I cannot scratch mine eare.
Prythee tel her
but a worky day Fortune.

Soothsayer Your Fortunes are alike.

Iras But how, but how, give me particulars.

Soothsayer I have said.

Iras Am I not an inch of Fortune better then she?

Charmian Well, if you were but an inch of fortune better
then I: where would you choose it.

Iras Not in my Husbands nose.

Charmian Our worser thoughts Heavens mend.

L 341 - b : 1. 2. 35 - 62

VP 1 if indeed, as Ff suggest, these are the only verse lines for Charmian in the scene, they allow a wonderful momentary mood swing into the more graceful, passionate verse, as she discusses her fecundity, before reverting to the more everyday prose

W 2 most modern texts = 'fertile', Ff = 'foretell'

Alexas	[1] Come, his Fortune, his Fortune.	

Oh let him
mary a woman that cannot go, sweet Isis, I beseech thee,
and let her dye too, and give him a worse, and let worse
follow worse, till the worst of all follow him laughing to
his grave, fifty-fold a Cuckold.

Good Isis heare me this
Prayer, though thou denie me a matter of more waight:
good Isis I beseech thee.

Iras Amen, deere Goddesse, heare that prayer of the
people.

For, as it is a heart-breaking to see a handsome
man loose-Wiv'd, so it is a deadly sorrow, to beholde a
foule Knave uncuckolded: Therefore deere Isis keep decorum, and Fortune him accordingly.

Charmian Amen.

Alexas Lo now, if it lay in their hands to make mee a
Cuckold, they would make themselves Whores, but
they'ld doo't.

ENTER CLEOPATRA [2]

Enobarbus	Hush, heere comes Anthony.	L 341-b
Charmian	Not he, the Queene.	
Cleopatra	Save you, my Lord. [3]	
Enobarbus	No Lady.	
Cleopatra	Was he not heere?	
Charmian	No Madam. [4]	

L 341 - b / R 341 - b : 1. 2. 62 - 81

[P1] most modern texts assign this speech to Charmian: they suggest that the original compositor mistook the italicised name 'Alexas' within Charmian's speech and set it as a separate prefix: they argue the speech should continue from her previous ' . . . Heavens mend. Alexas. Come his Fortune, his Fortune . . . ': Ff assign the speech to Alexas, and if this is maintained the 'him' referred to would have to be either the neutered Egyptian Mardian, or one of the Romans, possibly Enobarbus - either choice would make for fascinating playing, the former presumably creating laughter, the latter (teasing) tension

[SD 2] to allow for Enobarbus' 'mistake' in the following line, most modern texts delay the entry one line: however, given the dimensions of the Elizabethan stage it is possible that she would have to begin her entry here to arrive at the group in time for her line: there is also the possibility that Enobarbus is being sarcastic, suggesting that wherever Cleopatra may be, Anthony is not far behind

[W 3] F2 and most modern texts = 'Saw you my Lord.', F1 = 'Save you, my Lord.'

[LS 4] the actor has choice as to how these six short lines may be joined as lines of split verse

Cleopatra	He was dispos'd to mirth, but on the sodaine
170	A Romane thought hath strooke him. $\rightarrow$ [1]
	Enobarbus?
Enobarbus	Madam.
Cleopatra	Seeke him, and bring him hither : wher's Alexias? [2]
Alexas	Heere at your service. $\rightarrow$ [3]
175	My Lord approaches.

ENTER ANTHONY, WITH A MESSENGER [4]

Cleopatra	We will not looke upon him : $\rightarrow$ [5]
	Go with us.

[Exeunt]

Messenger	Fulvia thy Wife, $\rightarrow$ [6]
	First came into the Field.

180	Anthony	Against my Brother Lucius?
	Messenger	I : ° but soone that Warre had end,
		And the times state ° [7]

Made friends of them, joynting their force 'gainst Cæsar,
Whose better issue in the warre from Italy, [8]
185 Upon the first encounter drave them.

}

R 341 - b : 1. 2. 82 - 94

[SP 1] this splendidly theatrical Ff split line (7/4 syllables) allows Cleopatra to express publicly her displeasure with one Roman, Anthony, before switching attention to his closest countryman, Enobarbus

[N 2] F2 and most modern texts = 'Alexas', F1 = 'Alexias'

[SP 3] theatrically this Ff split line (5/5 syllables) allows Alexas time to decorously greet Cleopatra and/or recognise the fact that Anthony's imminent appearance may disturb even more the already upset-with-Anthony mood of Cleopatra: most modern texts set the two lines as one

[SD 4] most modern texts delay Anthony's entry until after Cleopatra's exit, thus totally denying her the effect she presumably intends her exit to have upon him

[SP 5] the Ff split line (7/3 syllables) allows both groups, Roman and Egyptian, a moment of amazement at Cleopatra's decision: this could create a moment of inaction on the part of her entourage, thus necessitating the (short) command of the second line: most modern texts set the two lines as one

[SP 6] Ff mark both this Messenger speech and the opening of his next two longer ones with short lines, (4 or 5/6 syllables) as if he is taking great care in delivering the bad news, and this might explain why Anthony takes steps to reassure him how the news will be received, lines 189 - 192 below: In each instance most modern texts combine the two short lines

[SP 7] see the previous footnote

[PCT 8] Ff set the comma at the end of the line, most modern texts advance the comma to ', from Italy'

Anthony	Well, what worst. [1]
Messenger	The Nature of bad newes infects the Teller.
Anthony	When it concernes the Foole or Coward: On.
	Things that are past, are done [2] with me.

190

'Tis thus,
Who tels me true, though in his Tale lye death,
I heare him as he flatter'd.

Messenger	Labienus ° (this is stiffe-newes)
	Hath with his Parthian Force ° [3]

195

Extended Asia: from Euphrates ° his conquering
Banner shooke, from Syria ° to Lydia,
And to Ionia,° whil'st ——

Anthony	Anthony thou would'st say.
Messenger	Oh my Lord.° [4]

200

Anthony	Speake to me home,
	Mince not the generall tongue,° name
	Cleopatra as she is call'd in Rome: ° [5]

Raile thou in Fulvia's phrase, and taunt my faults
With such full License, as both Truth and Malice

205

Have power to utter.
                                    Oh then we bring forth weeds,
When our quicke windes [6] lye still, and our illes told us
Is as our earing: fare thee well awhile. †[7]

Messenger	At your Noble pleasure.

[Exit Messenger]
ENTER ANOTHER MESSENGER

R 341 - b : 1. 2. 94 - 112

W [1] Ff = 'worst', which seems a firm demand from Anthony to be told everything: some modern texts set 'worse'

PCT [2] to emphasis the above at least one modern text ends the sentence here, starting a new one as 'With me tis thus,/Who . . .'

SP [3] see footnote #6, previous page

LS [4] with the mixture of long and short lines, (7/7 or 8/6 or 7/13/10-12/7/6/3 syllables) Ff show both the Messenger's passion momentarily getting the better of him , and then a form of recovery, and Anthony's encouraging him to continue: most modern texts regularise the passage as shown (10 or 11/10 or 11/9/10 or 11/10 or 11/10)

LS [5] with two short lines followed by a third more normal, (4/7 or 8/10 syllables), Anthony's efforts at self control are clearly delineated with the minor hesitations Ff offer: once again most modern texts regularise the passage to two lines of almost normal pentameter as shown (10 or 11/10)

W [6] most modern texts = 'minds', Ff = 'windes'

W [7] F2 and most modern texts = 'awhile', F1 = 'awhlle'

210	Anthony	From Scicion [1] how the newes? [2]
		Speake there.

1st. Messenger	The man from Scicion,
	Is there such an one?
2nd. Messenger	He stayes upon your will. [3]

215	Anthony	Let him appeare: [4]
		These strong Egyptian Fetters I must breake,
		Or loose my selfe in dotage.

ENTER ANOTHER MESSENGER WITH A LETTER

What are you?

3rd. Messenger	Fulvia thy wife is dead.
220	Anthony	Where dyed she.° [5] }

{3rd.} Messenger [6]	In Scicion,° her length of sicknesse,
	With what else more serious,°
	Importeth thee to know, this beares.
Anthony	Forbeare me ° [7] [8]

225		There's a great Spirit gone, thus did I desire it:
		What our contempts doth [9] often hurle from us,	R 341-b
		We wish it ours againe.
		The present pleasure,

R 341-b / L 342-b : 1. 2. 113 - 124

N 1 most modern texts set Ffs 'Scicion' as the more historically correct 'Sicyon'

W 2 though most modern texts agree with Ff and set 'how the news', some use the gloss 'ho, the news'

P/LS 3 in *Re-editing Shakespeare For The Modern* (see Recommended Texts), the problem of playing these three lines is explored in detail pages, 37-41, and a highly practical reassignment of speeches is proposed, viz.

(1st Messenger becomes)	2nd. Messenger	The man from Scicion.
(this line reassigned to)	Anthony	Is there such an one?
(this line stays with Ff prefix)	2nd. Messenger	He stayes upon your will.

SD 4 most modern texts add a stage direction for the [2nd.] Messenger to withdraw

LS 5 while most modern texts' setting of one full verse line may be metrically correct, the Ff setting of two short lines (6 or 7/3 syllables) allows Anthony greater silence for the news to sink home

LS 6 Ffs four irregular lines allow for the Messenger's careful passing the details on via the letter he bears, and for Anthony's still being unable to respond in full verse voice, (9/7/8/3 syllables): the modern text resetting, with just one short first line leaves a single pause and then creates a totally different mood, of onrush (4/12/11)

PCT 7 F1-3 set no punctuation, allowing Anthony to flow two separate thoughts together: F4 sets a comma, and most modern texts stop the flow completely by setting a period

SD 8 most modern texts, following up on Anthony's request to be left alone ('Forbeare me'), here direct the Messenger to withdraw, thus leaving Anthony alone on stage

W 9 F1 = 'contempts doth', F2 = 'contempts do', one modern gloss = 'contempt doth'

230   By revolution lowring, does become
The opposite of it selfe: she's good being gon,
The hand could plucke her backe, that shov'd her on.

I must from this enchanting Queene breake off,
Ten thousand harmes, more then the illes I know
My idlenesse doth hatch.

ENTER ENOBARBUS [1]

235   How now Enobarbus.

Enobarbus   What's your pleasure, Sir?

Anthony   I must with haste from hence.

Enobarbus   Why then we kill all our Women.
                          We see how
240   mortall an unkindnesse is to them, if they suffer our de-
parture death's the word.

Anthony   I must be gone.

Enobarbus   Under a compelling an [2] occasion, let women die.
It were pitty to cast them away for nothing, though be-
245   tweene them and a great cause, they should be esteemed
nothing. Cleopatra catching but the least noyse of this,
dies instantly: I have seene her dye twenty times uppon
farre poorer moment: I do think there is mettle in death,
which commits some loving acte upon her, she hath such
250   a celerity in dying.

Anthony   She is cunning past mans thought.

Enobarbus   Alacke Sir no, her passions are made of nothing
but the finest part of pure Love.
                       We cannot cal her winds
255   and waters, sighes and teares: They are greater stormes
and Tempests then Almanackes can report.
                            This cannot
be cunning in her;   if it be, she makes a showre of Raine
as well as Jove.

260   **Anthony**   Would I had never seene her.

L 342 - b : 1. 2. 125 - 152

[SD][1] most modern texts delay the entry until after Anthony's next line, thus making Enobarbus' entry dependent upon being summoned: the Ff setting suggests Enobarbus might enter unbidden and then Anthony catches sight of him

[W][2] modern texts argue Ff's 'Under a compelling an occasion' is unclear, and most leave out 'an': glosses have included 'Under as compelling an occasion' and 'Under so compelling an occasion'

Enobarbus	Oh sir, you had then left unseene a wonderfull peece of worke, which not to have beene blest withall, would have discredited your Travaile.
Anthony	Fulvia is dead.
265 Enobarbus	Sir.
Anthony	Fulvia is dead.
Enobarbus	Fulvia?
Anthony	Dead.
Enobarbus	Why sir, give the Gods a thankefull Sacrifice:
270	when it pleaseth their Deities to take the wife of a man from him, it shewes to man the Tailors of the earth: com- forting therein, that when olde Robes are worne out, there are members to make new.
	If there were no more
275	Women but Fulvia, then had you indeede a cut, and the case to be lamented: This greefe is crown'd with Conso- lation, your old Smocke brings foorth a new Petticoate, and†¹ indeed the teares live in an Onion, that should water this sorrow.
280 Anthony	The businesse she hath broached in the State, Cannot endure my absence.
Enobarbus	And the businesse you have broach'd heere can- not be without you, especially that of Cleopatra's, which wholly depends on your abode.
285 Anthony	No more light² Answeres: →³ Let our Officers Have notice what we purpose.
	I shall breake The cause of our Expedience to the Queene,
290	And get her love⁴ to part.
	For not alone The death of Fulvia, with more urgent touches Do strongly speake to us: but the Letters too

---

L 342 - b : 1. 2. 153 - 181

^W¹ F2 and most modern texts = 'and', F1 = 'aud'

^W² F1 and most modern texts = 'light', F2 = 'like'

^{SP}³ the two short Ff lines (5/5 syllables) allow Anthony a moment to shift from reflection and discussion to matters
of immediate practicality: most modern texts join both lines together

^W⁴ the Ff setting of 'love' suggests Anthony as well as Cleopatra will have very strong personal stakes in the proposed
parting: most modern texts make the statement much more prosaic by substituting 'leave'

Of many our contriving Friends in Rome,
295   Petition us at home.
                        Sextus Pompeius
Have [1] given the dare to Cæsar, and commands
The Empire of the Sea.
                    Our slippery people,   L 342 - b
300   Whose Love is never link'd to the deserver,
Till his deserts are past, begin to throw
Pompey the great, and all his Dignities
Upon his Sonne, who high in Name and Power,
Higher then both in Blood and Life, stands up
305   For the maine Souldier.
                     Whose quality going on,
The sides o'th'world may danger.
                       Much is breeding,
Which like the Coursers heire,[2] hath yet but life,
310   And not a Serpents poyson.
                      Say our pleasure,
To such whose places under us, require [3]
Our quicke remove from hence.

Enobarbus   I shall doo't. [4]

ENTER CLEOPATRA, CHARMIAN, ALEXAS, AND IRAS
[Most modern texts create a new scene here, Act One Scene 3]

315 **Cleopatra**   Where is he?

    Charmian   I did not see him since.

    Cleopatra   See where he is, → [5]
                    Whose with him, what he does:
                    I did not send you.
320   If you finde him sad,
                    Say I am dauncing : if in Myrth, report
                    That I am sodaine sicke.
                          Quicke, and returne. [6]

W [1] F1 = 'Have', F2 and most modern texts = 'Hath'

W [2] several modern texts alter the F1-2 setting (and possible pun) by substituting the modern 'hair' for the original 'heire': F3-4 offer a different pun with 'hare'

W [3] F1 = 'To such whose places under us, require': F2 and some modern texts = 'To such whose place is under us, requires': other modern texts keep the F1 setting, but move the comma from 'us' to after 'require'

SD [4] most modern texts have the men exit here, and set a new scene with Cleopatra's entry: however, the Ff setting would allow them just to retire to a safe distance

SP [5] the Ff two short lines (4/6 syllables) allow Cleopatra a moment's hesitation while deciding what action to take: most modern texts join the two lines together

SD [6] most modern texts indicate that someone (usually Alexas) exits to carry out Cleopatra's order

	Charmian	Madam, me thinkes if you did love him deerly,
325		You do not hold the method, to enforce
		The like[†1] from him.
	Cleopatra	What should I do, I do not?
	Charmian	In each thing give him way, crosse him in nothing.
	Cleopatra	Thou teachest like a foole : the way to lose him.
330	Charmian	Tempt him not so too farre.

                              I wish [2] forbeare,
In time we hate that which we often feare.

ENTER ANTHONY

            But heere comes Anthony.

	Cleopatra	I am sicke, and sullen.
335	Anthony	I am sorry to give breathing to my purpose.
	Cleopatra	Helpe me away deere Charmian, I shall fall,
		It cannot be thus long, the sides of Nature
		Will not sustaine it.
	Anthony	Now my deerest Queene.
340	Cleopatra	Pray you stand farther from mee.
	Anthony	What's the matter?
	Cleopatra	I know by that same eye ther's some good news.
		What sayes the married woman you may goe? [3]
		Would she had never given you leave to come.
345		Let her not say 'tis I that keepe you heere,
		I have no power upon you : Hers you are.
	Anthony	The Gods best know.
	Cleopatra	Oh never was there Queene
350		So mightily betrayed : yet at the first [†4]
		I saw the Treasons planted.

W 1 the *Norton* reproduction shows F1 as setting what looks like either 'lrke' or 'ltke'; the *Yale* reproduction looks more like 'like': F2/most modern texts = 'like'

W 2 though most modern texts agree with Ff and set 'I wish', one gloss = 'Iwis'

PCT 3 Ff = 'What sayes the married woman you may goe?': for clarity modern texts put a comma either after 'What' (or even follow F4 and set 'What!'), or after 'woman' (with perhaps a question or exclamation mark)

W 4 F2 and most modern texts = 'first', F1 = 'fitst'

Anthony	Cleopatra. ⟩	

Cleopatra	Why should I think you can be mine, & true,
	(Though you in swearing shake the Throaned Gods)
	Who have been false to Fulvia? → [1]
355	Riotous madnesse,
	To be entangled with those mouth-made vowes,
	Which breake themselves in swearing. ⟩

Anthony	Most sweet Queene.

Cleopatra	Nay pray you seeke no colour for your going,
360	But bid farewell, and goe : → [2]
	When you sued staying,
	Then was the time for words : No going then,
	Eternity was in our Lippes, and Eyes,
	Blisse in our browes bent : none our parts so poore,
365	But was a race of Heaven.
	They are so still,
	Or thou the greatest Souldier of the world,
	Art turn'd the greatest Lyar. ⟩

Anthony	How now Lady?	R 342 - b

370 **Cleopatra**	I would I had thy inches, thou should'st know
	There were a heart in Egypt. ⟩

Anthony	Heare me Queene :
	The strong necessity of Time, commands
	Our Services[†3] a-while : but my full heart
375	Remaines in use with you.
	Our Italy,
	Shines o're with civill Swords ; Sextus Pompeius
	Makes his approaches to the Port of Rome,
	Equality of two Domesticke powers,
380	Breed scrupulous faction : The hated growne to strength
	Are newly growne to Love : The condemn'd Pompey,
	Rich in his Fathers Honor, creepes apace
	Into the hearts of such, as have not thrived
	Upon the present state, whose Numbers threaten,
385	And quietnesse growne sicke of rest, would purge
	By any desperate change : My more particular,

R 342 - b / L 343 - b : 1. 3. 26 - 54

[SP 1] the Ff two short lines (7 or 8/4 or 5 syllables) allow the impact of Cleopatra's very public taunt to strike home: most modern texts join the two lines as one

[SP 2] see the previous footnote, (6/5 syllables)

[▼ 3] F2 and most modern texts = 'Services', F1 = 'Servicles'

And that which most with you should safe my going,
Is Fulvias death.

Cleopatra Though age from folly could not give me freedom
390   It does from chilishnesse.
                           Can Fulvia dye?

Anthony She's dead my Queene.

Looke heere, and at thy Soveraigne leysure read
The Garboyles she awak'd: at the last, best,
395   See when, and where shee died.

Cleopatra O most false Love!

Where be the Sacred Violles thou should'st fill
With sorrowfull water?
                    Now I see, I see,
400   In Fulvias death, how mine receiv'd shall be.

Anthony Quarrell no more, but bee prepar'd to know
The purposes I beare: which are, or cease,
As you shall give th'advice.
                    By the fire
405   That quickens Nylus slime, I go from hence
Thy Souldier, Servant, making Peace or Warre,
As thou affects. [1]

Cleopatra Cut my Lace, Charmian come,
But let it be, I am quickly ill, and well,
410   So Anthony loves.

Anthony My precious Queene forbeare,
And give true evidence to his Love, which stands
An honourable Triall.

Cleopatra So Fulvia told me.

415 I prythee turne aside, and weepe for her,
Then bid adiew to me, and say the teares
Belong to Egypt.
                    Good now, play one Scene
Of excellent dissembling, and let it looke
420   Like perfect Honor.

Anthony You'l heat my blood [2] no more?

[1] F1 and some modern texts = 'affects', F2 and most modern texts = 'affectst'

[2] F1's 'You'l heat my blood no more?' makes theatrical sense, especially if the question mark is seen in its Elizabethan context as an exclamation point: most modern texts alter the meaning by setting 'You'll heat my blood: no more!'

Cleopatra	You can do better yet : but this is meetly.	
Anthony	Now by [1] Sword.	
Cleopatra	And Target.	}
425	Still he mends.	
	But this is not the best.	
	Looke prythee Charmian,	
	How this Herculean Roman do's become	
	The carriage of this chase.	
430	**Anthony** Ile leave you Lady.	
	Cleopatra Courteous Lord, one word : [2]	
	Sir, you and I must part, but that's not it :	
	Sir, you and I have lov'd, but there's not it :	
	That you know well, something it is I would :	
435	Oh, my Oblivion is a very Anthony,	
	And I am all forgotten.	
	}	
	Anthony But that your Royalty	
	Holds Idlenesse your subject, I should take you	
	For Idlenesse it selfe.	
	}	
440	**Cleopatra** 'Tis sweating Labour,	
	To beare such Idlenesse so neere the heart	
	As Cleopatra this.	
	But Sir, forgive me,	L 343 - b
	Since my becommings kill me, when they do not	
445	Eye well to you.	
	Your Honor calles you hence,	
	Therefore be deafe to my unpittied Folly,	
	And all the Gods go with you.	
	Upon your Sword	
450	Sit Lawrell [3] victory, and smooth successe	
	Be strew'd before your feete.	
	Anthony Let us go.	
	Come :° Our separation so abides and flies,° [4]	
	That thou reciding heere, goes yet with mee ;	
455	And I hence fleeting, heere remaine with thee.	
	Away.	

W [1] F2 and most modern texts = 'my', F1 does not set the word

LS [2] the actor has choice as to which two of these three short lines may be joined as one line of split verse

W [3] F1 and some modern texts = 'Lawrell', i.e. 'laurel': F2 and other modern texts = 'Lawrell'd'

LS [4] the Ff setting (6 + 3/11 syllables) allows for Anthony to register Cleopatra's speech of reconciliation, and pause
before replying in kind: most modern texts set two regular lines as shown (10/10)

[Exeunt]

ENTER OCTAVIUS READING A LETTER, LEPIDUS, AND THEIR TRAINE

[Most modern texts create a new scene here, Act One Scene 4]

Cæsar	You may see Lepidus, and henceforth know,
	It is not Cæsars Naturall vice, to hate
	One ¹ great Competitor.
460	From Alexandria
	This is the newes : He fishes, drinkes, and wastes
	The Lampes of night in revell : Is not more manlike
	Then Cleopatra : nor the Queene of Ptolomy
	More Womanly then he.
465	Hardly gave audience

> ² Or vouchsafe ³ to thinke he had Partners.
> You
> Shall ° finde there a man, who is th'abstracts ⁴ of all faults,°
> That all men follow.
>
> 470 Lepidus   I must not thinke
> There are,° evils enow to darken all his goodnesse :°

His faults in him, seeme as the Spots of Heaven,
More fierie by nights Blacknesse ; Hereditarie,
Rather then purchaste : what he cannot change,
475 Then what he chooses.

Cæsar   You are too indulgent.
Let's ⁵ graunt it is not
Amisse to tumble on the bed of Ptolomy,
To give a Kingdome for a Mirth, to sit
480 And keep the turne of Tipling with a Slave,
To reele the streets at noone, and stand the Buffet
With knaves that smels ⁶ of sweate : Say this becoms him
(As his composure must be rare indeed,
Whom these things cannot blemish) yet must Anthony
485 No way excuse his foyles,⁷ when we do beare

ᵂ ₁ most modern texts = 'Our': Ff's = 'One' (which to this editor seems more supercilious)

ᴸˢ ₂ the Ff irregular setting allows both the virulently anti-Anthony Cæsar a characteristic moment of long line verbal explosion before re-establishing control, and the more cautious Lepidus a moment of hesitation before he openly disagrees with Cæsar (10/12/5 + 4/13 syllables): most modern texts readjust the passage (11/11/10/11), creating a slightly overheated passage as shown

ᵂ ₃ F1 = 'Vouchsafe', most modern texts = 'Vouchsaf'd', F2-4 = 'did vouchsafe'

ᵂ ₄ F1 = 'th'abstracts', F2 and most modern texts = 'the abstract', F3 = 'th'abstract'

ᵂ ₅ Ff = 'Let's', some modern texts = 'Let us'

ᵂ ₆ F1 and some modern texts = 'smels', F2 and most modern texts = 'smell'

ᵂ ₇ Ff = 'foyles', some modern texts = 'soils'

18

So great waight in his lightnesse.
                              If he fill'd
His vacancie with his Voluptuousnesse,
Full surfets, and the drinesse of his bones,
490   Call on him for't.
                         But to confound such time,
That drummes him from his sport, and speakes as lowd
As his owne State, and ours, 'tis to be chid: [1]
As we rate Boyes, who being mature in knowledge,
495   Pawne their experience to their present pleasure,
And so rebell to judgement.

ENTER A MESSENGER

Lepidus   Heere's more newes.

Messenger   Thy biddings have beene done, & everie houre
                     Most Noble Cæsar, shalt thou have report
500   How 'tis abroad.
                                     Pompey is strong at Sea,
                     And it appeares, he is belov'd of those
                     That only have feard Cæsar: to the Ports
                     The discontents repaire, and mens reports
505   Give him much wrong'd. [2]
                                                        }
Cæsar   I should have knowne no lesse,
                     It hath bin taught us from the primall state
                     That he which is was wisht, untill he were:
                     And the ebb'd man, → [3]
510   Ne're lov'd, till ne're worth love,
                     Comes fear'd, [4] by being lack'd.
                                        This common bodie,
                     Like to a Vagabond Flagge upon the Streame,
                     Goes too, and backe, lacking [5] the varrying tyde   R 343 - b
515   To rot it selfe with motion.
                                                    }
Messenger [6]   Cæsar I bring thee word,

[PCT 1] for supposed clarity some modern texts set "tis to be chid/As we rate Boyes', thus removing Ff's emphatic colon

[SD 2] most modern texts set an exit for the Messenger here, even though Cæsar gives no verbal indication to leave: ee also footnote #6 below

[SP 3] the Ff setting (4/6 syllables) allows Cæsar a hesitation as he formulates his maxim: most modern texts join the lines

[W 4] Ff = 'fear'd', most modern texts set either 'dear'd' or 'lov'd'

[W 5] Ff = 'lacking', most modern texts = 'lackeying'

[P/SD 6] since Ff offer no entry for any other character, they seem to suggest this is the same Messenger who, having waited for Cæsar to finish his ruminations, now offers further bad news: most modern texts set an entry for, and give the lines to, a Second Messenger

19

Menacrates [1] and Menas famous Pyrates
Makes the Sea serve them, which they eare and wound
With keeles of every kinde.
520   Many hot inrodes
They make in Italy, the Borders Maritime
Lacke blood to thinke on't, and flush youth revolt,
No Vessell can peepe forth : but 'tis as soone
Taken as seene : for Pompeyes name strikes more
525   Then could his Warre resisted. [2]
                                  }

Cæsar   Anthony,
Leave thy lascivious Vassailes. [3]
                         When thou once
Was [4] beaten from Medena, where thou slew'st
530   Hirsius, and Pausa [5] Consuls, at thy heele
Did Famine follow, whom thou fought'st against,
(Though daintily brought up) with patience more
Then Savages could suffer.
                        Thou did'st drinke
535   The stale of Horses, and the gilded Puddle
Which Beasts would cough at.
                     Thy pallat thê [†6] did daine
The roughest Berry, on the rudest Hedge.

Yea, like the Stagge, when Snow the Pasture sheets,
540   The barkes of Trees thou brows'd.
                      On the Alpes,
It is reported thou did'st eate strange flesh,
Which some did dye to looke on : And all this
(It wounds thine Honor that I speake it now)
545   Was borne so like a Soldiour, that the cheeke
So much as lank'd not.

Lepidus   'Tis pitty of him.

Cæsar   Let his shames quickely [7]
Drive him to Rome, 'tis time we twaine

[N 1] F4 and most modern texts set the historically correct 'Menecrates', F1-3 = 'Menacrates'

[SD 2] most modern texts here add a stage direction for the Messenger's exit

[W 3] F1-2 = 'Vassailes', F3 = 'Vassails', F4 = 'Vassals': most modern texts change the emphasis from people to drink by setting 'wassails'

[W 4] F1 = 'Was', F2 = 'Wert', some modern texts = 'Wast'

[N/F 5] F4/most modern texts = historically correct 'Modena', 'Hirtius' and 'Pansa': F1-3 = 'Medena', 'Hirsius' and 'Pausa'

[AB 6] F1 = 'thê', (printed as such because of lack of column width): F2/most modern texts = 'then'

[LS 7] the actor has choice as to which two of these three short lines may be joined as one line of split verse

550		Did shew our selves i'th'Field, and to that end
		Assemble me [1] immediate counsell, Pompey
		Thrives in our Idlenesse.
	Lepidus	To morrow Cæsar,
		I shall be furnisht to informe you rightly
555		Both what by Sea and Land I can be able
		To front this present time.
	Cæsar	Til which encounter,° it is my busines too.
		Farwell.°[2]
	Lepidus	Farwell my Lord, what you shal know mean time
560		Of stirres abroad, I shall beseech you Sir
		To let me be partaker.
	Cæsar	Doubt not sir, I knew[3] it for my Bond.

[Exeunt]
ENTER CLEOPATRA, CHARMIAN, IRAS, & MARDIAN
[Most modern texts create a new scene here, Act One Scene 5]

	Cleopatra	Charmian.
	Charmian	Madam.
565	**Cleopatra**	Ha, ha,° give me to drinke Mandragoru.[4]
	Charmian	Why Madam? °
	Cleopatra	That I might sleepe out this great gap of time:[5]
		My Anthony is away.
	Charmian	You thinke of him too much.
570	**Cleopatra**	O 'tis Treason.
	Charmian	Madam, I trust not so.
	Cleopatra	Thou, Eunuch Mardian?
	Mardian	What's your Highnesse pleasure?[6]

[W][1] F1 = 'me', F2 and most modern texts = 'we'

[LS][2] Ff's two irregular lines (6/13 or 14 syllables) allow a hesitation before a blurt (often seen when things are not quite going the way Cæsar would like): most modern texts reverse and reduce both moments by restructuring to 11/8 or 9 syllables

[W][3] Ff = 'knew', most modern texts = 'know'

[W][4] most modern texts = 'Mandragora', F1 = 'Mandragoru', F2-4 = 'Mandragoras'

[PCT][5] with the colon Ff set two phrases for Cleopatra, the second explaining the (attempted) explanation of the first: most modern texts remove the colon

[LS][6] the actor has choice as to how these six short lines may be joined as one line of split verse: also some modern texts attempt (not particularly successfully) to regularise the opening of the scene as the symbols ° show

Cleopatra	Not now to heare thee sing.

575

                                I take no pleasure
In ought an Eunuch ha's : Tis well for thee,
That being unseminar'd, thy freer thoughts
May not flye forth of Egypt.
                              Hast thou Affections?

580   **Mardian**   Yes gracious Madam.

         Cleopatra   Indeed?

         Mardian   Not in deed Madam, for I can do nothing
But what in deede is honest to be done :
Yet have I fierce Affections, and thinke

585   What Venus did with Mars.
                                  }

         Cleopatra   Oh Charmion :
Where think'st thou he is now?
                        Stands he, or sits he?   L 344 · b
Or does he walke?

590   Or is he on his Horse?
Oh happy horse to beare the weight of Anthony!

Do bravely Horse, for wot'st thou whom thou moov'st,
The demy Atlas of this Earth, the Arme [1]
And Burganet of men.

595   Hee's speaking now,
Or murmuring, where's my Serpent of old Nyle,
(For so cals me :) Now I feede my selfe
With most delicate poyson.
                         Thinke on me

600   That am with Phœbus amorous pinches blacke,
And wrinkled deepe in time.
                        Broad-fronted Cæsar,
When thou was't heere above the ground, I was
A morsell for a Monarke : and great Pompey

605   Would stand and make his eyes grow in my brow,
There would be anchor this Aspect, and dye
With looking on his life.

               ENTER ALEXAS FROM {ANTHONY} [†2]

         Alexas   Soveraigne of Egypt, haile.

L 344 - b / R 344 - b : 1. 5. 9 - 34

[W1] most modern texts agree with Ff and set the sensual 'Arme': one modern gloss suggests the more intellectual 'Acme'

[F/SD2] all modern texts correctly show Alexas as coming from 'Anthony': Ff all suggest (incorrectly) he comes from 'Caesar'

Cleopatra		How much unlike art thou Marke Anthony?
610		Yet comming from him, that great Med'cine hath

> With his Tinct gilded thee.
>
> How goes it ° with my brave Mark Anthonie? ° ¹

Alexas		Last thing he did (deere Queene†²)
		He kist the last of many doubled kisses ³
615		This Orient Pearl.
		His speech stickes in my heart.

Cleopatra   Mine eare must plucke it thence.
)

Alexas   Good Friend, quoth he :

620
Say the firme Roman to great Egypt sends
This treasure of an Oyster :   at whose foote
To mend the petty present, I will peece
Her opulent Throne, with Kingdomes.
                                                All the East,
(Say thou) shall call her Mistris.
625   So he nodded,
And soberly did mount an Arme-gaunt ⁴ Steede,
Who neigh'd so hye, that what I would have spoke,
Was beastly dumbe ⁵ by him.

Cleopatra   What was he sad, or merry? ⁶
)

630 **Alexas**   Likc to the time o'th'yeare, between ÿ ⁷ extremes.

Of hot and cold, he was nor sad nor merrie.

Cleopatra   Oh well divided disposition :   Note him,
Note him good Charmian, 'tis the man ;   but note him.

R 344 - b : 1. 5. 35 - 54

ᴸˢ ₁ Ffs irregularity (6/10 syllables) sets up a fully theatrical pause, allowing Cleopatra to pause awaiting some form of reply from Alexas and, when none is forthcoming, to ask the obvious question: some modern texts set a different irregularity (9/7) which diminishes the Ff subtext, and over-emphasises the already highlighted short six syllable line that follows

ᵂ ₂ F2 and most modern texts = 'Queene': F1 = 'Qu ene'

ᴾᶜᵀ ₃ Ff = 'He kist the last of many doubled kisses', most modern texts = 'He kist - the last of many doubled kisses -'

ᵂ ₄ the Ff phrase 'Arme-gaunt' has caused much discussion and created many glosses, see Appendix 1, *The Arden Shakespeare, Anthony and Cleopatra*, op. cit., and *William Shakespeare: A Textual Companion*, op. cit., page 550, footnote 1.5.47/492: the more plausible glosses include 'termagaunt', 'war-gaunt', and 'arrogant'

ᵂ ₅ most modern texts = 'dumb'd', Ff = 'dumbe'

ᴾᵀ ₆ though most modern texts agree with Ff and set 'What was he sad, or merry?' (usually with a comma after 'What'), one gloss = 'What was he, sad or merry?'

ᵂ ₇ F1 = 'ÿ', (set as such because of lack of column width): F2/most modern texts = 'the'

23

He was not sad, for he would shine on those
635   That make their lookes by his.
                          He was not merrie,
Which seem'd to tell them, his remembrance lay
In Egypt with his joy, but betweene both.
Oh heavenly mingle!
640   Bee'st thou sad, or merrie,
The violence of either thee becomes,
So do's it no mans [1] else.
                           Met'st thou my Posts?

Alexas	I Madam, twenty severall Messengers.

645   Why do you send so thicke?

Cleopatra   [2] Who's borne that day,° when I forget to send
to Anthonie,° shall dye a Begger.
                       Inke and paper Char-
650   mian.°
             Welcome my good Alexas.
                    Did I Charmian,° e-
ver love Cæsar so?

Charmian   Oh that brave Cæsar! °

Cleopatra	Be choak'd with such another Emphasis,
655		Say the brave Anthony.
Charmian	The valiant Cæsar.
Cleopatra	By Isis, I will give thee bloody teeth,
	If thou with Cæsar Paragon againe : [3]
	My man of men.
660	**Charmian**	By your most gracious pardon,
	I sing but after you.
Cleopatra	My Sallad dayes,
	When I was greene in judgement, cold in blood,
	To say, as I saide then.

[W] [1] F2 and most modern texts = 'man', F1 = 'mans'

[VP] [2] Ff set Cleopatra's speech in prose, perhaps suggesting a shift in inner mood as she considers all the love
letters she has and will send to Anthony: most modern texts reset it as verse and adjust Charmian's wounding
comments accordingly: they presumably did so assuming the First Folio compositor was overcautious as he
reached the bottom of page 344, and set prose simply because he was afraid he had too much text for the remaining
column space

[W] [3] F2 and most modern texts = 'paragon againe', F1 = 'parago nagaine'

665   But come, away,
    Get me Inke and Paper,   R 344 - b

he shall have every day a severall greeting,° or Ile unpeo-
ple Egypt.° [1]

[Exeunt]
ENTER POMPEY, MENECRATES, AND MENAS,[2] IN
WARLIKE MANNER
[Most modern texts create a new scene here, Act Two Scene 1]

Pompey   If the great Gods be just, they shall assist
670   The deeds of justest men.

Menecrates   [3] Know worthy Pompey,° that what they do delay, they not deny.°

Pompey   Whiles we are sutors to their Throne, decayes °
the thing we sue for.

675 Menecrates We ignorant of our selves,°

Begge often our owne harmes, which the wise Powres
Deny us for our good : so finde we profit
By loosing of our Prayers.
               }

Pompey   I shall do well :
680   The people love me, and the Sea is mine ;
My powers are Cressent, and my Auguring hope
Sayes it will come to'th'full.
                    Marke Anthony
In Egypt sits at dinner, and will make
685   No warres without doores.
                     Cæsar gets money where
He looses hearts : Lepidus flatters both,

R 344 - b / L 345 - b : 1. 5. 75 - 2. 1. 14

[VP 1] F1 sets the last two lines of the scene in the top of the left column on page 345, one of the most textually
crowded pages of the play: though the speech started in verse these final lines are shown as prose, perhaps a
result of the overcrowding (though the images deal with love-letters, exactly the same as her previous Ff prose
speech, lines 646 - 652, footnote #2, page 24: F2-4 set the lines the same way, even though F4 does not follow the
same page layout: most modern texts reset these two lines as verse as shown

[P 2] Ff give just one prefix throughout the scene, 'Mene.', which would suggest that all the speeches so assigned
belong to 'Menecrates': however, Pompey's speech, line 713, addresses a character he refers to as 'Menas', suggesting
the subsequent reply, lines 720 - 4, should be assigned to 'Menas': modern texts redistribute the speeches between
Menas and Menecrates in various ways (see the Introduction to this text, and *William Shakespeare, A Textual
Companion*, op. cit., page 550, footnote to 2.1.2 et al), and one commentator suggests ignoring Menecrates
completely: this text will follow Ff and assign all the 'Mene.' speeches to 'Menecrates' except for lines 720 - 4
mentioned above

[VP 3] Ff show the two speeches from Menecrates and Pompey as prose, perhaps because of the overcrowded page
referred to in footnote #1 above: most modern texts reset them as verse and adjust the surrounding lines
accordingly

		Of both is flatter'd : but he neither loves,
		Nor either cares for him.
690	**Menecrates**	Cæsar and Lepidus ° are in the field,
		A mighty strength they carry.° [1]

	Pompey	Where have you this?
		'Tis false.

Menecrates From Silvius, Sir.

695 **Pompey** He dreames : I know they are in Rome together
Looking for Anthony : but all the charmes of Love,
Salt Cleopatra soften thy wand [2] lip,
Let Witchcraft joyne with Beauty, Lust with both,
Tye up the Libertine in a field of Feasts, [3]
700 Keepe his Braine fuming.
                              Epicurean Cookes,
Sharpen with cloylesse sawce his Appetite,
That sleepe and feeding may prorogue his Honour,
Even till a Lethied dulnesse ——

ENTER VARRIUS

705 How now Varrius?

Varrius This is most certaine, that I shall deliver :
Marke Anthony is every houre in Rome
Expected.
                    Since he went from Egypt, 'tis
710 A space for farther Travaile.

Pompey I could have given lesse matter
A better eare.
                    Menas, I did not thinke
This amorous Surfetter would have donn'd his Helme
715 For such a petty Warre : His Souldiership
Is twice the other twaine : But let us reare
The higher our Opinion, that our stirring
Can from the lap of Egypts Widdow, plucke
The neere [4] Lust-wearied Anthony.

LS 1 in this case the modern restructuring to two long lines (12/11 syllables) totally alters the manner of Menecrates'
correction of Pompey's optimism, creating a blurt where Ff originally suggest caution (6/10/7)

W 2 Ff = 'wand', most modern texts = 'wan'd', one gloss = 'wan'

PCT 3 though Ff's punctuation makes perfect sense, some modern texts advance the comma five words, viz. ', in a
Field of feasts/Keepe'

W 4 F1-2 = 'neere', F3-4 = 'near', yet some modern texts amend this to the exact opposite, 'ne'er'

720	**Menas}** [1]	I cannot hope,
		Cæsar and Anthony shall well greet [2] together;
		His Wife that's dead, did trespasses to Cæsar,
		His Brother wan'd [3] upon him, although I thinke
		Not mov'd by Anthony.
725	**Pompey**	I know not Menas,
		How lesser Enmities may give way to greater, [4]
		Were't not that we stand up against them all:
		'Twer pregnant they should square between themselves,
		For they have entertained cause enough
730		To draw their swords: but how the feare of us
		May Ciment their divisions, and binde up
		The petty difference, we yet not know:
		Bee't as our Gods will have't; it onely stands
		Our lives upon, to use our strongest hands [5]
735		Come Menas.

L 345 - b

ENTER ENOBARBUS AND LEPIDUS
[Most modern texts create a new scene here, Act Two Scene 2]

	Lepidus	Good Enobarbus, 'tis a worthy deed,
		And shall become you well, to intreat your Captaine
		To soft and gentle speech.
	Enobarbus	I shall intreat him
740		To answer like himselfe: if Cæsar move him,
		Let Anthony looke over Cæsars head,
		And speake as lowd as Mars.
		By Jupiter,
		Were I the wearer of Anthonio's [6] Beard,
745		I would not shave't to day.
	Lepidus	'Tis not a time ° for private stomacking.
	Enobarbus	Every time ° serves for the matter that is then
		borne in't. °[7]

[P][1] see footnote #2, page 25

[W][2] Ff = 'greet', some modern texts = ' 'gree'

[W][3] F1 = 'wan'd', F2 and most modern texts = 'warr'd'

[PCT][4] Ff set a comma allowing the thought to flow on: some modern texts replace this with a period

[PCT][5] F1 sets no punctuation, and F2-3 a comma, allowing the thought to flow straight into the command to Menas: F4 sets a colon, while some modern texts set a period thus completely curtailing the flow

[W][6] Ff = 'Anthonio's', most modern texts = 'Anthonius'

[LS/VP][7] Enobarbus' Ff response is a 13 syllable line, which could be either verse or prose; if it is verse the style of the scene is maintained, if prose, this repeats an already seen verbal characteristic of Enobarbus - that of slipping out of verse momentarily to comment upon the action: most modern texts remove the choice by reworking the 'metrical split' created by Lepidus' earlier speech (see also footnotes #1 and #2, next page)

	Lepidus	But small to greater matters must give way.
750	**Enobarbus**	Not if the small come first.
	Lepidus	Your speech is passion:° but pray you stirre No Embers up. Heere comes ° the Noble Anthony. [1]

ENTER ANTHONY AND VENTIDIUS

	Enobarbus	And yonder Cæsar.

ENTER CÆSAR, MECENAS, AND AGRIPPA

	Anthony	If we compose well heere, to Parthia: Hearke Ventidius.
755		
	Cæsar	I do not know ° Mecenas, aske Agrippa.
	Lepidus	Noble Friends:° [2]

760		That which combin'd us was most great, and let not
		A leaner action rend us.
		             What's amisse,
		May it be gently heard.
		             When we debate
		Our triviall difference loud, we do commit
		Murther in healing wounds.
		           Then Noble Partners,
		The rather for I earnestly beseech,
		Touch you the sowrest points with sweetest tearmes,
		Nor curstnesse grow to'th'matter.

765		
770	**Anthony**	'Tis spoken well: Were we before our Armies, and to fight, I should do thus. [3]

[Flourish]

R 345 - b : 2.2.11 -27

[SP] [1] this is the second of five examples where modern texts restructure F1 page 345, right column, in an attempt to avoid the 'metrical splits' created by Ff setting a short (first line of a) speech of less than ten syllables: here F1 creates a potentially splendid theatrical pause as Enobarbus' terse comment marks the differences between the two Roman camps (6/9/12 syllables): once again most modern texts restructure as shown, removing the all-telling moment of silence (11/10)

[SP] [2] Ff's short opening line for Lepidus gives the character great influence in a tiny moment, allowing minute hesitations before and/or after essentially calling the meeting to order (4 or 5/11/3 syllables) : most modern texts rework the passage as shown, (8 or 9/10), removing one of the pauses

[SD] [3] at least one modern text suggests that here Anthony and Cæsar embrace

	Cæsar	Welcome to Rome.
	Anthony	Thanke you.
775	Cæsar	Sit.
	Anthony	Sit sir.
	Cæsar	Nay then.
	Anthony	I learne, you take things ill, which are not so :
		Or being, concerne you not.
780	Cæsar	I must be laught at,° if or for nothing, or a little, I °¹
		Should say my selfe offended, and with you
		Chiefely i'th'world.
		More laught at, that I should
		Once name you derogately : when to sound your name
785		It not concern'd me.
	Anthony	My being in Egypt Cæsar,° what was't to you? °²
	Cæsar	No more then my reciding heere at Rome
		Might be to you in Egypt : yet if you there
		Did practise on my State, your being in Egypt
790		Might be my question.
	Anthony	How intend you, practis'd?
	Cæsar	You may be pleas'd to catch at mine intent,
		By what did heere befall me.
		Your Wife and Brother
795		Made warres upon me, and their contestation
		Was Theame ³ for you, you were the word of warre.
	Anthony	You do mistake your ⁴ busines, my Brother never

SP 1   R345-b : 2. 2. 28 -45

the fourth example of metrical split: here Ff's short line (6 or 7 syllables) for Anthony followed by Cæsar's long opening line (15) deftly creates for Cæsar a moment of (attempted) self-control before spilling into an (over-passionate?) reply: most modern texts rework the opening as shown and lose the potential of both moments

W 2   the fifth example of metrical split: here the short line for Cæsar ('It not concern'd me.', 5 syllables) followed by an overly full line from Anthony ('My being in Egypt Cæsar, what was't to you?', 11 or 12) unequivocally gives Anthony the hesitation before speaking: unlike the other four examples in this passage the modern texts do not create metrical balance but only reverse the imbalance, suggesting Anthony should piggy-back off Cæsar's line, ('It not concern'd me./My being in Egypt Cæsar,') and giving him a second short line('what was't to you?'): this gives Cæsar the pause before reply, as he did a moment earlier: yet Ff setting suggests the exact opposite, that this time Anthony is affected by Cæsar's argument and he is the one that must exert self-control

W 3   though most modern texts agree with Ff and set 'Theame', suggested glosses have included 'theam'd' and 'then'

W 4   Ff = 'your', one modern gloss = 'the'

Did urge me in his Act : I did inquire it,
And have my Learning from some true reports
800 That drew their swords with you, did he not rather
Discredit my authority with yours,
And make the warres alike against my stomacke,
Having alike your cause.
Of this, my Letters
805 Before did satisfie you.
If you'l patch a quarrell,
As matter whole you have ¹ to make it with,   R 345 - b
It must not be with this.

Cæsar	You praise your selfe,° by laying defects of judge-
810	ment to me :° but you patcht up your excuses.
Anthony	Not so, not so :° ²

I know you could not lacke, I am certaine on't,
Very necessity of this thought, that I
Your Partner in the cause 'gainst which he fought,
815 Could not with gracefull ³ eyes attend those Warres
Which fronted mine owne peace.
As for my wife,
I would you had her spirit, in such another,
The third oth'world is yours,†⁴ which with a Snaffle,
820 You may pace easie, but not such a wife.

Enobarbus   Would we had all such wives, that the men
might go to Warres with the women.

Anthony   So much uncurbable, her Garboiles (Cæsar)
Made out of her impatience :   which not wanted
825 Shrodenessc of policie to :   I greeving grant,
Did you too much disquiet, for that you must,⁵

---

^W ₁
some modern texts totally reverse Ff's statement by adding 'not', setting 'As matter whole you have not to make
it with' instead of Ff's perfectly acceptable 'As matter whole you have to make it with'

^{VP} ₂
presumably arguing that in moving from quire 'xx3' (Compositor B) to quire 'yy' (Compositor E), B had under-
estimated the available space and thus had to crowd text together, most modern texts alter Ff's prose to verse as
shown: (in this left-hand column, Folio page 346 there are two more Ff prose speeches (both Cæsar's) and a
passage of four lines which modern texts similarly alter): however, if the Ff setting is allowed to stand as is, it
shows Cæsar momentarily slipping into prose; Anthony careful to maintain the (grace and dignity of) verse, and a
pause to enable him to make sure he doesn't lose control

^W ₃
though most modern texts agree with Ff and set 'gracefull', one gloss = 'grateful'

^{PCT} ₄
F1 sets a misplaced mark which could be punctuation: F2/most modern texts set a comma

^{PCT} ₅
this 'need-to-breathe-for-self-control' comma is rarely set by modern texts

30

	But say I could not helpe it.
Cæsar	I wrote to you,° when rioting in Alexandria you ° 1

830

Did pocket up my Letters : and with taunts
Did gibe my Misive out of aùdience.

Anthony	Sir,² he fell upon me, ere admitted, then :

Three Kings I had newly feasted, and did want
Of what I was i'th'morning : but next day
I told him of my selfe, which was as much

835

As to have askt him pardon.
                                    Let this Fellow
Be nothing of our strife : if we contend
Out of our question wipe him.

Cæsar	You have broken ° the Article of your oath,

840

which you shall never ° have tongue to charge me with.° 3

Lepidus	Soft Cæsar.
Anthony	No Lepidus, let him speake, ⟩

The Honour is Sacred which he talks on now,
Supposing that I lackt it : but on Cæsar,

845

The Article of my oath.

Cæsar	To lend me Armes, and aide when I requir'd
	them,° the which you both denied.
Anthony	Neglected rather :° 4

And then when poysoned houres had bound me up

850

From mine owne knowledge,⁵ as neerely as I may,
Ile play the penitent to you.

LS 1 this Ff line structure repeats an earlier moment when a final short line from Anthony gives Cæsar a moment of hesitation before an overlylong opening line reply (7/14 or 15 syllables): as before, most modern texts remove the irregularity by restructuring as shown (11/10 or 11)

LS 2 though Cæsar's last line can easily be scanned/spoken as ten syllables by giving 'au/di/ence' its full value, most modern texts suggest Anthony spring-board off it by setting 'Sir' as a split line: in addition to removing Cæsar's over-articulateness (in itself a possibly useful psychological clue), this alteration reduces Anthony's apparent (11 syllable) strain to regularity

VP 3 Cæsar's Ff prose reply is the second speech in this column which most modern texts alter to verse as shown: if the Ff setting is maintained, the seriousness of the charge could be thus enhanced by Cæsar's slip from verse, which, according to Ff, is more than momentary since his next Ff speech (next footnote) is in prose too

VP 4 as Cæsar spells out the 'article of your oath' that Anthony is supposed to have broken, F1 maintains his prose: once more most modern texts reduce this contrast between his state of behaviour and the others around him by setting it as verse (the style of the others) as shown

PCT 5 Ff set a comma, suggesting Anthony is running the excuse and the apology together: most modern texts establish a more formal break between the two by setting a colon

But mine honesty,
Shall not make poore my greatnesse, nor my power
Worke without it.
855   Truth is, that Fulvia,
To have me out of Egypt, made Warres heere,
For which my selfe, the ignorant motive, do
So farre aske pardon, as befits mine Honour
To stoope in such a case.
)

860 **Lepidus**   'Tis Noble spoken.

     Mecenas   If it might please you, to enforce no further
                       The griefes betweene ye : to forget them quite,
                       Were to remember : that the present neede,
                       Speakes to attone you.
)
865 **Lepidus**   Worthily spoken Mecenas.

     Enobarbus   Or if you borrow one anothers Love for the
                       instant, you may when you heare no more words of
                       Pompey returne it againe : you shall have time to wrangle
                       in, when you have nothing else to do.

870 **Anthony**   [1] Thou art a Souldier,[2] onely speake no more.

     Enobarbus   That trueth should be silent, I had almost for-
                       got.

     Anthony   You wrong this presence, therefore speake no
                       more.

875 **Enobarbus**   Go too then : your Considerate stone.

     Cæsar   I do not much dislike the matter, but
                       The manner of his speech : for't cannot be,   L 346 - e
                       We shall remaine in friendship, our conditions
                       So diffring in their acts.
880   Yet if I knew,
                       What Hoope should hold us staunch from edge to edge

---

L 346 - e / R 346 - e : 2. 2. 93 - 115

VP 1
these Ff four lines could be either prose or verse (especially the middle two, with the lines too long for the
column width, forcing the last words to spill onto a separate line): if prose, it might suggest that Enobarbus'
interruption and subsequent arguing creates more of a problem for Anthony than he would care to admit: certainly,
the prose would stand out in great contrast against Cæsar's subsequent Ff comment, in which he returns to verse for
the first time in three speeches

PCT 2
most modern texts transfer the comma until after 'only', thus rendering the line as a very public insult and
rebuke: by maintaining the Ff comma, Anthony could be seen to be trying to maintain self-control by reminding
Enobarbus much more politely about his rank and the need for his silence

	Ath'world:[1] I would persue it.
Agrippa	Give me leave Cæsar.
Cæsar	Speake Agrippa.[2]

885

Agrippa	Thou hast a Sister by the Mothers side, admir'd Octavia:[3] Great Mark Anthony ° is now a widdower.
Cæsar	Say not, say[4] Agrippa; ° if Cleopater heard you, your proofe[5] ° were well deserved of rashnesse.°
Anthony	I am not marryed Cæsar: let me heere ° Agrippa

890 further speake.[6]

Agrippa　　To hold you in perpetuall amitie,
　　　　　To make your Brothers, and to knit your hearts
　　　　　With an un-slipping knot, take Anthony,
　　　　　Octavia to his wife: whose beauty claimes

895

No worse a husband then the best of men:° whose[7] Vertue, and whose generall graces, speake °

That which none else can utter.
　　　　　　　　　　　　By this marriage,
All little Jelousies which now seeme great,

900　　　And all great feares, which now import their dangers,
Would then be nothing.
　　　　　　　　　Truth's[8] would be tales,
Where now halfe tales be truth's: her love to both,
Would each to other, and all loves to both

905　　　Draw after her.

PCT 1 though the Ff reading (' Yet if I knew,/What Hoope should hold us staunch from edge to edge/Ath'world: I would persue it' makes perfect sense, some texts remove this punctuation and add an earlier comma, viz. 'Yet if I knew,/What Hoope should hold us staunch, from edge to edge/Ath'world I would persue it.'

LS 2 the actor has choice as to which two of these three short lines may be joined as one line of split verse

PCT 3 the reproductions of the First Folio show a blur which is some form of punctuation: F2 - 4 set a question mark: most modern texts set a period

W 4 Ff = 'Say not, say', most modern texts = 'Say not so'

W 5 Ff = 'proofe', most modern texts = 'reproof'

VP 6 in the right-hand column of page 346 this is the only passage Ff set as prose, which, in company with the rest of the scene, most modern texts recast as verse, even though doing so creates a short (6 syllable) final line for Anthony, something most modern texts strive to avoid: if the Ff prose setting stands it might suggest that all three characters, Agrippa, Cæsar and Anthony, are very carefully handling the first mention of the subtext of much of the scene, the divisiveness between Cæsar and Anthony, Anthony's relationship with Cleopatra

LS 7 most modern texts follow F2-4 and transfer 'whose' to the start of the next line, setting up two ten syllable lines: F1's irregularity (11/9 syllables) gently illustrates how carefully Agrippa is handling this most explosive of proposals

W 8 in this and the following line, F1-2 = 'Truth's', F3/most modern texts = 'Truths'

33

		Pardon what I have spoke,
		For 'tis a studied not a present thought,
		By duty ruminated.
	Anthony	Will Cæsar speake? ⟩
910	Cæsar	Not till he heares how Anthony is toucht,
		With what is spoke already. ⟩
	Anthony	What power is in Agrippa,
		If I would say Agrippa, be it so,

		To make this good? → [1]
915	Cæsar	The power of Cæsar,°
		And his power, unto Octavia. →
	Anthony	May I never °

		(To this good purpose, that so fairely shewes)
		Dreame of impediment: let me have thy hand [2]
920		Further this act of Grace: and from this houre,
		The heart of Brothers governe in our Loves,
		And sway our great Designes. ⟩
	Cæsar	There's my hand:
		A Sister I bequeath you, whom no Brother
925		Did ever love so deerely.
		Let her live
		To joyne our kingdomes, and our hearts, and never
		Flie off our Loves againe. ⟩
	Lepidus	Happily, Amen.
930	Anthony	I did not think to draw my Sword 'gainst Pompey,
		For he hath laid strange courtesies, and great
		Of late upon me.
		I must thanke him onely,
		Least my remembrance, suffer ill report:
935		At heele of that, defie him. ⟩
	Lepidus	Time cals upon's,
		Of us must Pompey presently be sought,

R 346 - e : 2. 2. 136 - 158

LS 1 these four short Ff lines mark a huge moment in the play, as both Anthony and Cæsar come close to agreement on what apparently seems to be Anthony's complete personal betrayal of Cleopatra: the words are simple, but the moment, with its potential hesitations is huge, and Ff offer a very skillful, economical, way of speaking/playing it: most modern texts combine the four short Ff lines into two split verse lines as shown

PCT 2 Ff's lack of punctuation at this point makes good sense as Anthony drives home the need for Cæsar's personal commitment to the marriage of convenience: at least one modern text destroys the flow by setting a period

		Or else he seekes out us.
	Anthony	Where lies he?
940	**Cæsar**	About the Mount-Mesena. [1]
	Anthony	What is his strength by land?
	Cæsar	Great, and encreasing: [2]

But by Sea ° he is an absolute Master.

	Anthony	So is the Fame, °
945		Would we had spoke together.

       Hast we for it,
Yet ere we put our selves in Armes, dispatch we
The businesse we have talkt of.
         }

	Cæsar	With most gladnesse,
950		And do invite you to my Sisters view, R 346 - e

		[3] Whether straight Ile lead you.
	Anthony	Let us Lepidus ° not lacke your companie.
	Lepidus	Noble Anthony,° not sickenesse should detaine me.°

[Flourish. Exit omnes]
MANET ENOBARBUS, AGRIPPA, MECENAS

955	**Mecenas**	Welcome from Ægypt Sir.
	Enobarbus	Halfe the heart of Cæsar, worthy Mecenas.

         My
honourable Friend Agrippa.

	Agrippa	Good Enobarbus.
960	**Mecenas**	We have cause to be glad, that matters are so well disgested : you staid well by't in Egypt.
	Enobarbus	I Sir, we did sleepe day out of countenaunce : and made the night light with drinking.

R 346 - e / L 347 - e : 2. 2. 159 - 178

N 1
 most modern texts set 'Misena'

ALT 2
 most modern texts follow Ff and set '<u>Anthony</u>: What is his strength by land? <u>Cæsar</u>: Great, and encreasing:', though one text follows an early commentator and sets '<u>Anthony</u>: What is his strength? <u>Cæsar</u>: By land/Great, and encreasing:': the actor has choice how the five short lines may be joined together: some modern texts regularise the following lines as shown, instead of allowing Ff's irregularity to underscore the seriousness of the current situation

LS 3
 the Ff opening of a short (six syllable) line suggests that Cæsar (whether deliberately or no) ignores Lepidus as he begins to lead Anthony away, and Anthony (for whatever reason) remedies the situation: the modern texts' restructuring removes both parts of the incident

	Mecenas	Eight Wilde-Boares rosted whole at a break-
965		fast : and but twelve persons there.

                                             Is this true?

Enobarbus   This was but as a Flye by an Eagle : we had much
more monstrous matter of Feast, which worthily deserved noting.

970   **Mecenas**   She's a most triumphant Lady, if report be
square to her.

Enobarbus   When she first met Marke Anthony, she purst
up his heart upon the River of Sidnis. [1]

   Agrippa   There she appear'd indeed : or my reporter de-
975   vis'd well for her.

Enobarbus   I will tell you,
The Barge she sat in, like a burnisht Throne
Burnt on the water : the Poope was beaten Gold,
Purple the Sailes : and so perfumed that
980   The Windes were Love-sicke. →[2]

With them the Owers were Silver,
Which to the tune of flutes kept strokc, and made
The water which they beate, to follow faster;
As amorous of their strokes.
985   For her owne person,
It beggerd all discription, she did lye
In her Pavillion, cloth of Gold, of Tissue,
O're-picturing that Venus,[3] where we see
The fancie out-worke Nature.
990   On each side her,
Stood pretty Dimpled Boyes, like smiling Cupids,
With divers coulour'd Fannes[4] whose winde did seeme,
To glove[5] the delicate cheekes which they did coole,
And what they undid did.

995   **Agrippa**   Oh rare for Anthony.

L 347 c : 2. 2. 179 - 205

[N1] F1 = 'Sidnis', F2 and most modern texts = 'Cydnus'

[SP2] Ff's two short lines (5/7 or 8 syllables) allow Enobarbus a moment of personal recollection before continuing
the new sentence: most modern texts set two of the Ff lines as one, remove the period so that there are no longer
two sentences, and rephrase by altering the placing of the punctuation, viz. 'That/The Windes were love-sicke with
them; the Owers [i.e. oars] were Silver

[N3] F2 and most modern texts = 'Venus', F1 = 'Venns'

[W4] F1 = 'Fa nnes', F2/most modern texts = 'Fannes'

[W5] though most modern texts agree with Ff and set 'glove', one interesting gloss = 'glow'

Enobarbus	Her Gentlewoman,¹ like the Nereides,
	So many Mer-maides tended her i'th'eyes,
	And made their bends adornings.
	At the Helme.²
1000	A seeming Mer-maide steeres : The Silken Tackle,
	Swell with the touches of those Flower-soft hands,
	That yarely frame the office.
	From the Barge
	A strange invisible perfume hits the sense
1005	Of the adjacent Wharfes.
	The Citty cast
	Her people out upon her : and Anthony
	Enthron'd i'th'Market-place, did sit alone,
	Whistling to'th'ayre : which but for vacancie,
1010	Had gone to gaze on Cleopater too,
	And made a gap in Nature.
	}
Agrippa	Rare Egiptian.
Enobarbus	Upon her landing, Anthony sent to her,
	Invited her to Supper : she replyed,
1015	It should be better, he became her guest :
	Which she entreated, our Courteous Anthony,
	Whom nere the word of no woman hard speake,
	Being barber'd ten times o're, goes to the Feast ;
	And for his ordinary, paies his heart,
1020	For what his eyes eate onely.
	}
Agrippa	Royall Wench : L 347 - e
	She made great Cæsar lay his Sword to bed,
	He ploughed her, and she cropt.
	}
Enobarbus	I saw her once
1025	Hop forty Paces through the publicke streete,†³
	And having lost her breath, she spoke, and panted,
	That she did make defect, perfection,

L 347 - e / R 347 - e : 2. 2. 206 - 231

▼₁ F1 = 'Gentlewoman', F2 and most modern texts = 'Gentlewomen'

PCT₂ in the photostatted reproductions of F1 there appears to be a period set after 'Helme', though it could be
an unrelated ink mark: F2 sets it as a period: most modern texts either omit it or follow F3 and set a comma: if F1's
period stands, it would suggest Enobarbus' recollection of the appearance of the powerful mythical creature (the
'Mer-maide') is so strong it momentarily makes him lose focus

PCT₃ F1's punctuation is slightly blurred, but looks like a comma: F2/most modern texts set a comma

> And breathlesse powre breath forth. [1]

Mecenas	Now Anthony,° must leave her utterly.
1030 Enobarbus	Never he will not:° [2]

Age cannot wither her, nor custome stale
Her infinite variety: other women cloy
The appetites they feede, but she makes hungry,
Where most she satisfies.
1035   For vildest things
Become themselves in her, that the holy Priests
Blesse her, when she is Riggish.

Mecenas	If Beauty, Wisedome, Modesty, can settle[†3]
	The heart of Anthony: Octavia is
1040	[4] A blessed Lottery to him.
Agrippa	Let us go.°
	Good Enobarbus, make your selfe
	my guest,° whilst you abide heere.
Enobarbus	Humbly Sir I thanke you.°

[Exeunt]
ENTER ANTHONY, CÆSAR, OCTAVIA BETWEENE [†5] THEM
[Most modern texts create a new scene here, Act Two Scene 3]

1045 Anthony	[6] The world, and my great office, will
	Sometimes ° devide me from your bosome.
Octavia	All which time,° before the Gods my knee shall
	bowe my prayers ° [†7] to them for you.

R 347 - e : 2. 2. 232 - 2. 3. 4

[PCT 1] some modern texts add two explanatory commas 'And, breathlesse, powre breath forth.'

[LS 2] the irregularity of F1's three lines (6/10/5) allows for a hesitation before the unthinkable is voiced, and before
it is denied: most modern texts remove the quiet enormity of the moment by setting two lines (10/11 as shown)

[W 3] F1 = 'sett le', F2/most modern texts = 'settle'

[VP 4] after Enobarbus' outpouring about Cleopatra and the subsequent discussion of her, Ff's setting suggests that
once the subject of Octavia is broached the verse slips from verse to prose, a nice twist: most modern texts reset the
passage as verse as shown

[W 5] F1 = 'betw eene them', F2 = 'betweenethem', F3/most modern texts = 'between them'

[LS/VP 6] Ff set a very interesting opening for the top of the scene where the patterns of speech inform the actor/
reader as much or even more than the content of what is being said: there are two short verse lines (8/9 syllables)
from Anthony, a prose reply from Octavia, followed by Anthony's over-the-page short line awkward switch of focus
from Octavia to Cæsar (7 or 8): (this irregularity is so set even though arguably there is room for Octavia's reply to be
set as verse:) most modern texts remove the three awkward moments by resetting the passage as almost regular verse
as shown (10/10/10 or 11/11 or 12)

[W 7] F2 and most modern texts = 'prayers', F1 = 'ptayers'

38

Anthony	Goodnight Sir.
1050	My Octavia °

Read not my blemishes in the worlds report :
I have not kept my square, but that to come
Shall all be done by th'Rule : good night deere Lady :
Good night Sir. [1]

| 1055 | **Cæsar** | Goodnight. |

[Exit]

ENTER SOOTHSAIER

| **Anthony** | Now sirrah : you do wish your selfe in Egypt? |

Soothsayer	[2] Would I had never come from thence, nor you ° thither.
Anthony	If you can, your reason?
1060	**Soothsayer**	I see it in ° my motion : have it not in my tongue, But yet ° hie you to Egypt againe.
Anthony	Say to me,° whose Fortunes shall rise higher Cæsars or mine? °
Soothsayer	Cæsars.°
1065	Therefore (oh Anthony) stay not by his side ° [3]

Thy Daemon that [4] thy spirit which keepes thee, is
Noble, Couragious, high [5] unmatchable,
Where Cæsars is not.
                But neere him, thy Angell
1070   Becomes a feare : [6] as being o're-powr'd, therefore
Make space enough betweene you.

| **Anthony** | Speake this no more. |

---

[1] F2/some modern texts assign 'Good night Sir' to Octavia, others follow F1 and leave it with Anthony

[2] following Ff's earlier pattern for the Soothsayer, pages 5 - 6 this text, once more his interchange starts unusually, first in prose and then irregular verse, as if the blunt immediacy of his responses to Anthony's very direct questions initially cause him problems: most modern texts regularise the passage as shown

[3] F1-2 sets no punctuation at the end of the Soothsayer's first line, as if the enormity of the response forces him to rush on to the next point: most modern texts follow F3 and print a period

[4] though most modern texts agree with F1 and set 'that', at least one follows F2 and sets 'that's'

[5] some modern texts follow F3 and add a comma, others stay with F1-2 and set no punctuation

[6] Ff = 'feare:', most modern texts = 'feared' as well as replacing Ff's colon with a comma: if any heavier punctuation is set (; or :) modern texts usually do so after 'o're-powr'd'

39

Soothsayer	To none but thee no more but: ¹ when to thee,
	If thou dost play with him at any game,
1075	Thou art sure to loose: And of that Naturall lucke,
	He beats thee 'gainst the oddes.

                                              Thy Luster thickens,
When he shines by: I say againe, thy spirit
Is all affraid to governe thee neere him:
1080 But he alway ² 'tis Noble.
)

Anthony Get thee gone:
Say to Ventigius ³ I would speake with him.

[Exit]

He shall to Parthia, be it Art or hap,
He hath spoken true.
1085   The very Dice obey him,
And in our sports my better cunning faints,
Under his chance, if we draw lots he speeds,
His Cocks do winne the Battaile, still of mine,
When it is all to naught: and his Quailes ever
1090 Beate mine (in hoopt) at odd's.
                      I will to Egypte: R 347 - e
And though I make this marriage for my peace,
I'th'East my pleasure lies.
                      Oh come Ventigius.

ENTER VENTIGIUS

1095 You must to Parthia, your Commissions ready:
Follow me, and recive't.

[Exeunt]
ENTER LEPIDUS, MECENAS, AND AGRIPPA
[Most modern texts create a new scene here, Act Two Scene 4]

Lepidus	⁴ Trouble your selves no further: pray you
	hasten ° your Generals after.

RT ₁ F1 sets two peculiar pieces of punctuation in this speech: the first here, highlighting 'but . . .', could suggest the Soothsayer is emphasising he still reserves the right to talk to Anthony when he oversteps himself vis-a-vis Cæsar: F2 modifies the problem by removing the colon and placing a comma before the second 'but', viz. 'To none but thee no more, but': most modern texts unsatisfactorily modify the passage even more, viz. 'To none but thee; no more but when to thee.', (also setting a period at the end of the line)

W ₂ F1 = 'he alway 'tis', F2 - 4 = 'he alway is', one modern gloss = 'he away'

N/P ₃ F1 sets 'Ventigius' throughout: F2 and most modern texts = 'Ventidius'

VP ₄ with the possible exception of Lepidus' second speech, Ff set this whole interchange in prose, a fair indication that the scene is one of relaxed farewells among familiars: most modern texts reset the passage in (formal) verse as shown

40

Agrippa	Sir, Marke Anthony,° will e'ne but kisse Octavia, and weele follow.°	
Lepidus	Till I shall see you in your Souldiers dresse,° Which will become you both : Farewell.	
Mecenas	We shall :° ¹ as I conceive the journey, be at ² Mount ° before you Lepidus.	
Lepidus	Your way is shorter,° my purposes do draw me much about,° you'le win two dayes upon me.	
Both	Sir good successe.°	
Lepidus	Farewell.°	

1100

1105

[Exeunt]
ENTER CLEOPATER, ³ CHARMIAN, IRAS, AND ALEXAS
[Most modern texts create a new scene here, Act Two Scene 5]

Cleopatra	Give me some Musicke : Musicke, moody foode of ° ⁴ us that trade in Love.
Omnes	The Musicke, hoa.°

1110

ENTER MARDIAN THE EUNUCH

Cleopatra	Let it alone, let's to Billiards : ⁺⁵ come Charmian.
Charmian	My arme is sore, best play with Mardian.

Cleopatra	⁶ As well a woman with an Eunuch plaide,° as with a woman. Come you'le play with me Sir?°

1115

Mardian	⁷ As well as I can Madam.°
Cleopatra	And when good will is shewed, Though't come to short °

PCT ₁ F2 and most modern texts set a comma, F1 a colon

W ₂ F2 and most modern texts = 'at the Mount' suggesting a place; F1 = 'at Mount', perhaps suggesting his group will be on horseback quicker than Lepidus

W ₃ F1 = 'Cleopater', F2 and most modern texts = 'Cleopatra'

VP ₄ though Ff set a small 'o' in 'of', suggesting Cleopatra is sufficiently disturbed (by Anthony's absence?) not to speak verse at the top of the scene, most modern texts create a two line verse opening for her by setting 'Of'

W ₅ F2 and most modern texts = 'billiards', F1 = 'billards'

VP ₆ Ff show Cleopatra still speaking prose (see footnote #4 above), most modern texts reset it as verse

VP/SP ₇ as Cleopatra turns to verse, by setting two short lines for the start of her speech F1 gives her a wonderfully wicked pause before the second line, referring to Mardian's lack of complete male genitalia: by resetting as shown most modern texts move the pause to just before she starts to speak, which is hardly as mischievous

41

1120		The Actor may pleade pardon.
		Ile none now,
		Give me mine Angle, weele to'th'River ¹ there
		My Musicke playing farre off.
		I will betray
1125		Tawny fine fishes,² my bended hooke shall pierce
		Their slimy jawes: and as I draw them up,
		Ile thinke them every one an Anthony,

And say, ah ha; y'are caught.

1130	Charmian	³ 'Twas merry when ° you wager'd on your Ang- ling, when your diver ° did hang a salt fish on his hooke which he ° with fervencie drew up.
	Cleopatra	That time?
		Oh times:° ⁴

		I laught him out of patience: and that night
1135		I laught him into patience, and next morne,
		Ere the ninth houre, I drunke him to his bed:
		Then put my Tires and Mantles on him, whilst
		I wore his Sword Phillippan.
		Oh from Italie,

ENTER A MESSENGER

1140		Ramme ⁵ thou thy fruitefull tidings in mine eares,
		That long time have bin barren.
	Messenger	Madam, Madam.

	Cleopatra	⁶ Anthonyo's dead,
1145		If thou say so Villaine,° thou kil'st thy Mistris:
		But well and free,° if thou so yeild him.
		There is Gold, and heere °

My blewest vaines to kisse: a hand that Kings
Have lipt, and trembled kissing.

L 348 · e : 2. 5. 9 · 30

PCT ₁ at least one modern text removes the period from the following line and resets it after 'to'th'River'

W ₂ most modern texts = 'Tawny-finn'd fishes', Ff = 'Tawny fine fishes'

VP ₃ Ff set the passage in prose, perhaps suggesting Charmian is so overcome with laughter she cannot keep to the verse structure: most modern texts reset the passage as verse as shown

PCT ₄ most modern texts alter Ff's colon to an exclamation mark

W ₅ though most modern texts agree with Ff and set 'Ramme', one gloss = 'Rain'

LS ₆ Ff's highly irregular opening gives Cleopatra two wonderfully theatrical moments, a pause after uttering the first dreadful thought, then a sentence break and pause as she (presumably) hunts for gold, perhaps removing jewelry to give the Messenger (4/11/9/5 syllables): most modern texts regularise the passage as shown (10/9/10)

Messenger	First Madam, he is well.
1150	Cleopatra	Why there's more Gold.

But sirrah marke, we use [1]
To say, the dead are well: bring it to that,
The Gold I give thee, will I melt and powr
Downe thy ill uttering throate.

1155	Messenger	Good Madam heare me.	L 348 - e
	Cleopatra	Well, go too I will: [2]

But there's no goodnesse in thy face [3] if Anthony
Be free and healthfull; so tart a favour
To trumpet such good tidings.
1160   If [†4] not well,
Thou shouldst come like a Furie crown'd with Snakes,
Not like a formall man.

	Messenger	Wilt please you heare me?
	Cleopatra	I have a mind to strike thee ere thou speak'st:
1165		Yet if thou say Anthony lives, 'tis [5] well,

Or friends with Cæsar, or not Captive to him,
Ile set thee in a shower of Gold, and haile
Rich Pearles upon thee.

	Messenger	Madam, he's well.
1170	Cleopatra	Well said.
	Messenger	And Friends with Cæsar.
	Cleopatra	Th'art an honest man.
	Messenger	Cæsar, and he, are greater Friends then ever.
	Cleopatra	Make thee a Fortune from me.
1175	Messenger	But yet Madam.

L 348 - e / R 348 - e : 2. 5. 31 - 49

LS 1
     yet again Ff, in setting four irregular (short) lines (7/6/4/6 syllables) creates some very understandable
hesitations as the Messenger hedges and Cleopatra attempts to discover the truth: most modern texts create two split
          lines from Ff's four, (13/10), thus removing any pauses: however, see *The Arden Shakespeare, Anthony and
          Cleopatra*, op. cit., page 73, footnote to lines 31,32 which argues that it was simply too narrow a column on the
          First Folio page that caused Ff to be set thus

LS 2
     the actor has choice as to which two of these three short lines may be joined as one line of split verse

PCT 3
     F1's lack of punctuation makes good emotional sense even if not grammatically tidy: F2 - 4 add a comma,
     some modern texts unnecessarily set a period

W 4
     F2 and most modern texts = 'If', F1 = 'I f'

W 5
     Ff/some modern texts = 'tis', some modern texts = 'is'

43

Cleopatra	I do not like but yet, it does alay
	The good precedence, fie upon but yet,
	But†1 yet is as a Jaylor to bring foorth
	Some monstrous Malefactor.

1180

Prythee Friend,
Powre out the packe of matter to mine eare,
The good and bad together: he's friends with Cæsar,
In state of health†2 thou saist, and thou saist, free.

Messenger	Free Madam, no: I made no such report,

1185

He's bound unto Octavia.

Cleopatra	For what good turne?
Messenger	For the best turne i'th'bed.
Cleopatra	I am pale Charmian.
Messenger	Madam, he's married to Octavia.

1190

Cleopatra	The most infectious Pestilence upon thee.

[Strikes him downe]

Messenger	Good Madam patience.
Cleopatra	What say you?

[Strikes him]

Hence horrible Villaine, or Ile spurne thine eyes
Like balls before me: Ile unhaire thy head,

[She hales him up and downe]

1195

Thou shalt be whipt with Wyer, and stew'd in brine,
Smarting in lingring pickle.

Messenger	Gratious Madam,
	I that do bring the newes, made not the match.
Cleopatra	Say 'tis not so, a Province I will give thee,

1200

And make thy Fortunes proud: the blow thou had'st
Shall make thy peace, for moving me to rage,
And I will boot thee with what guift beside
Thy modestie can begge.

Messenger	He's married Madam.

▼1 F1 = 'Bur', F2/most modern texts = 'But'

▼2 F1 = 'heal th', F2/most modern texts = 'health'

| 1205 | Cleopatra | Rogue, thou hast liv'd too long. |

[Draw a knife]

| | Messenger | Nay then Ile runne: |
| | | What meane you Madam, I have made no fault. |

[Exit]

| | Charmian | Good Madam keepe your selfe within your selfe, |
| | | The man is innocent. |

1210	Cleopatra	Some Innocents scape not the thunderbolt:
		Melt Egypt into Nyle: and kindly creatures
		Turne all to Serpents.
		Call the slave againe,
		Though I am mad, I will not byte him: Call?

| 1215 | Charmian | He is afeard to come. |

	Cleopatra	I will not hurt him,[1]
		These hands do lacke Nobility, that they strike
		A meaner then my selfe: since I my selfe
		Have given my selfe the cause.
1220		Come hither Sir.

ENTER THE MESSENGER AGAINE

		Though it be honest, it is never good
		To bring bad newes: give to a gratious Message	R 348 - e
		An host of tongues, but let ill tydings tell
		Themselves, when they be felt.

| 1225 | Messenger | I have done my duty. |
| | Cleopatra | Is he married?[2] |

| | | I cannot hate thee worser then I do, |
| | | If thou againe say yes. |

| | Messenger | He's married Madam. |

| 1230 | Cleopatra | The Gods confound thee, →[3] |
| | | Dost thou hold there still? |

[SD 1] some modern texts add stage directions for Charmian, first that she exit now to bring back the Messenger, and then that she accompanies his return in three lines time

[L3 2] the actor has choice as to which two of these three short lines may be joined as one line of split verse

[SP 3] the two (short) line Ff setting (5/5 syllables) allows Cleopatra moments to react to the inevitability of the Messenger's unequivocal reply: most modern texts join the two short lines together

	Messenger	Should I lye Madame?

    Cleopatra   Oh, I would thou didst :)
So halfe my Egypt were submerg'd and made

1235   A Cesterne for scal'd Snakes.
                    Go get thee hence,
Had'st thou Narcissus in thy face to me,
Thou would'st appeere most ugly : He is married?

    Messenger   I crave your Highnesse pardon.
)

1240   **Cleopatra**   He is married?

    Messenger   Take no offence,that I would not offend you,
To punnish me for what you make me do
Seemes much unequall, he's married to Octavia.

    Cleopatra   Oh that his fault should make a knave of thee,

1245   That art [1] not what th'art sure of.
                          Get thee hence,
The Marchandize which thou hast brought from Rome

Are all too deere for me :
Lye they upon thy hand,° and be undone by em. [2]

1250   **Charmian**   Good your Hignesse patience.°

    Cleopatra   In praysing Anthony, I have disprais'd Cæsar. °

    Charmian   Many times Madam.

    Cleopatra   I am paid for't now :° lead me from hence,° [3]

I faint, oh Iras, Charmian : 'tis no matter.

1255   Go to the Fellow, good Alexas bid him
Report the feature of Octavia : her yeares,
Her inclination, let him not leave out
The colour of her haire. [4]
                    Bring me word quickly,

1260   Let him for ever go, let him not Charmian,
Though he be painted one way like a Gorgon,
The other wayes a Mars.

L 349 - e : 2. 5. 93 - 117

W 1 most commentators, dissatisfied with Ff phrasing, have suggested several word alternatives, the most
interesting of which replaces Ff's 'art' with either 'say'st' or 'act'

SD 2 most modern texts provide a stage direction for the Messenger's exit

LS 3 the irregular Ff setting (6/12/6/12/5/9 syllables) creates one hesitation for Cleopatra before the curse on the
luckless Messenger, and two more between herself and Charmian, possibly after each of Charmian's replies: most
modern texts in restructuring the passage, reduce Ff's six irregular lines to five, but cannot solve the irregularities
(12/12/12/10/4 syllables), and thus only remove the hesitations

SD 4 most modern texts set an exit for Alexas

[1] Bid you Alexas
Bring me word, how tall she is : pitty me Charmian,
1265   But do not speake to me.
                     Lead me to my Chamber.

[Exeunt]

**FLOURISH. ENTER POMPEY, AT ONE DOORE WITH DRUM AND TRUM-
PET: AT ANOTHER CÆSAR, LEPIDUS, ANTHONY, ENOBARBUS, ME-
CENAS, AGRIPPA, MENAS [2] WITH SOULDIERS MARCHING**
[Most modern texts create a new scene here, Act Two Scene 6]

Pompey	Your Hostages I have, so have you mine :
	[3] And we shall talke before we fight.
Cæsar	Most meete ° that first we come to words,
1270	And therefore have we °

              Our written purposes before us sent,
              Which if thou hast considered, let us know,
              If't will tye up thy discontented Sword,
              And carry backe to Cicelie much tall youth,
1275   That else must perish heere.
                         }

Pompey   To you all three,
              The Senators alonc of this great world,
              Chiefe Factors for the Gods. [4]
                         I do not know,
1280   Wherefore my Father should revengers want,
              Having a Sonne and Friends, since Julius Cæsar,
              Who at Phillipi the good Brutus ghosted,
              There saw you labouring for him.
                         What was't
1285   That mov'd pale Cassius to conspire?
                         And what
              Made [5] all-honor'd, honest, Romaine Brutus,[6]
              With the arm'd rest, Courtiers of beautious freedome,

---

L 349 - c : 2. 5. 117 - 2. 6. 17

WHO [1] most modern texts indicate this is spoken to Mardian

SD [2] most modern texts alter the stage direction, placing Menas with Pompey and sometimes omitting Agrippa
altogether: see *The Arden Shakespeare, Anthony and Cleopatra*, op. cit., page 80, footnote to the stage direction

LS [3] in view of the rather blunt opening from Pompey, Ff's three short lines (8/8/5 syllables), suggesting surprise and
care as Cæsar replies, are theatrically understandable: most modern texts restructure the passage as shown (10/11)

PCT [4] Ff set a period, emphasising the formal greeting of the opening of Pompey's second speech, a great contrast
to the way in which he started the scene: most modern texts set a comma or colon

W [5] F2/most modern texts add 'the' (even though it extends the metrics of the line): the word is not set in F1

W [6] F1 = 'honest, Romaine Brutus', F2-4 = 'honest Romaine Brutus', most modern texts = 'honest Roman, Brutus'

		To drench the Capitoll, but that they would
1290		Have one man but a man, and that his it [1]
		Hath made me rigge my Navie.
		At whose burthen,
		The anger'd Ocean fomes, with which I meant

L 349 - e

To scourge th'ingratitude, that despightfull Rome

1295   Cast on my Noble Father.

         ❭

Cæsar   Take your time.

Anthony   Thou can'st not feare us Pompey with thy sales.

     Weele speake with thee at Sea.

                   At land thou know'st

1300   How much we do o're-count thee.

         ❭

Pompey   At Land indeed

     Thou dost orecount me of my Fatherrs[†2] house :

     But since the Cuckoo buildes not for himselfe,

     Remaine in't as thou maist.

         ❭

1305   **Lepidus**   Be pleas'd to tell us,

     (For this is from the present now you take) [3]

     The offers we have sent you.

         ❭

Cæsar   There's the point.

Anthony   [4] Which do not be entreated too,

1310   But waigh what it is worth imbrac'd [5]

Cæsar   And what may follow ° to try a larger Fortune.

Pompey   You have made me offer °

     Of Cicelie,[6] Sardinia : and I must

     Rid all the Sea of Pirats.

315   Then, to send

     Measures of Wheate to Rome : this greed upon,

L 349 - e / R 349 - e : 2. 6. 18 -37

▼[1] F1-2 = 'his it', F3/most modern texts = 'is it'

▼[2] F2 and most modern texts = 'fathers', F1 = 'Fatherrs'

▼[3] F1 = '(For this is from the present now you take)', F2-4 = '(For this is from the present now you talk)', most modern texts = '(For this is from the present) how you take'

LS[4] since everyone's future on-stage depends upon Pompey's reply, the four Ff irregular lines (7/8/12/6 syllables) are hardly surpr   ising, since they allow Pompey a moment before beginning the final stages of discussion: the same pattern is to be found at the start of his next speech, line 1320, next page: in both cases most modern texts restructure the passages to more overwrought verse as shown, (here 7/13/13)

PCT[5] F1 = no punctuation (possibly as if Cæsar interrupted him), F2 and most modern texts print a period

N[6] most modern texts follow F2 and set 'Sicily' throughout, F1 = 'Cicelie'

		To part with unhackt edges, and beare backe
		Our Targes undinted.
	Omnes	That's our offer.
1320	**Pompey**	Know then ° I came before you heere,[1]
		A man prepar'd °
		To take this offer.
		But Marke Anthony,
		Put me to some impatience: though I loose
1325		The praise of it by telling.[2]
		You must know
		When Cæsar and your Brother were at blowes,
		Your Mother came to Cicelie, and did finde
		Her welcome Friendly.
1330	**Anthony**	I have heard it Pompey.
		And am well studied for a liberall thanks,
		Which I do owe you.
	Pompey	Let me have your hand:
		I did not thinke Sir, to have met you heere,[3]
335	**Anthony**	The beds i'th'East are soft, and thanks to you,
		That cal'd me timelier then my purpose hither:
		For I have gained by't.
	Cæsar	Since I saw you last,° ther's a change upon you.
	Pompey	Well, I know not,° [4]
340		What counts harsh Fortune †[5] cast's upon my face,
		But in my bosome shall she never come,
		To make my heart her vassaile.
	Lepidus	Well met heere.

R 349 - c : 2. 6. 38 - 56

LS [1] see footnote #4 previous page

PCT [2] Ff set a period here, seeming to mark Pompey as having so much difficulty in controlling his inner feelings that his speech patterns become abrupt and disjointed (all of which match the linear peculiarities and abrupt opening already footnoted in this scene): most modern texts alter this to a comma

PCT [3] F1-2 set a comma, as if either Pompey tails the sentence away without finishing, or Anthony interrupts him: F3/most modern texts set a period

W [4] Ff set three irregular lines with two possible hesitations, the first perhaps as if no one knows how to follow up Anthony's not so oblique reference at not being too displeased at leaving Octavia, the second as if Pompey is weighing up how to respond to Cæsar's less than tactful comment

W [5] F1 = 'Fotune cast's', F3/most modern texts = 'Fortune casts'

	Pompey	I hope so Lepidus, thus we are agreed:
1345		I crave our composion [1] may be written
		And seal'd betweene us, [2]
	Cæsar	That's the next to do.
	Pompey	Weele feast each other, ere we part, and lett's
		Draw lots who shall begin.
1350	**Anthony**	That will I Pompey.

	Pompey	No Anthony take the lot: but first or last,
		your fine Egyptian cookerie shall have ° the fame, I have
		heard that Julius Cæsar,° grew fat with feasting there.
	Anthony	You have heard much.° [3]

1355	**Pompey**	I have faire meaning [4] Sir.
	Anthony	And faire words to them.
	Pompey	Then so much have I heard,

		And I have heard Appolodorus carried ———
	Enobarbus	No more [5] that: he did so.
1360	**Pompey**	What I pray you?
	Enobarbus	A certaine Queene to Cæsar in a Matris.
	Pompey	I know thee now, how far'st thou Souldier?
	Enobarbus	Well,[6] and well am like to do, for I perceive R 349 - c
		Foure Feasts are toward.
365	**Pompey**	Let me shake thy hand,
		I never hated thee: I have seene thee fight,
		When I have envied thy behaviour.

[1] F2 and most modern texts = 'composition', F1 = 'composion'

[2] F1-2 set a comma (possibly as if Pompey interrupts him), F3-4/most modern texts print a period

[3] arguing too much text for too little space at the bottom of the page, most modern texts turn Ff's three line prose speech into four lines of verse as shown: if the Ff setting stands it could show once more Pompey's blunt and disjointed verbal style - after all he is making a public joke about (the very proper) Octavius Cæsar's uncle: this might also explain Ff's possible hesitations (or run-on's as split lines), and the four short lines that follow

[4] Ff = 'meaning', most modern texts = 'meanings'

[5] F3 and most modern texts set 'of', F1-2 do not show the word

[6] for metrical propriety most modern texts add 'Well' from the top of this speech, and 'Sir' from the start of Enobarbus' next to the end of the preceding speeches, so as to form two ten-syllable split lines: however, in both cases the Ff slightly short lines from Pompey (if 'Souldier' and behaviour' are spoken in their shorter form of two and three syllables respectively) allow Enobarbus a moment before each reply, perhaps an attempt by Enobarbus at a public snubbing or humiliation of Pompey

Enobarbus		Sir,[1] I never lov'd you much, but I ha'prais'd ye,
		When you have well deserv'd ten times as much,
1370		As I have said you did.
Pompey		Injoy thy plainnesse,
		It nothing ill becomes thee:
		Aboord my Gally, I invite you all.
		Will you leade Lords?
1375	**All**	Shew's the way, sir.
Pompey		Come.

[Exeunt. Manet Enob{arbus} & Menas]

Menas	[2]	Thy Father Pompey would ne're have made this
		Treaty.
		You, and I have knowne sir.
1380	**Enobarbus**	At Sea, I thinke.
Menas		We have Sir.
Enobarbus		You have done well by water.
Menas		And you by Land.
Enobarbus		I will praise any man that will praise me, thogh
1385		it cannot be denied what I have done by Land.
Menas		Nor what I have done by water.
Enobarbus		Yes some-thing you can deny for your owne
		safety: you have bin a great Theefe by Sea.
Menas		And you by Land.
1390	**Enobarbus**	There I deny my Land service: but give mee
		your hand Menas, if our eyes had authority, heere they
		might take two Theeves kissing.
Menas		All mens faces are true, whatsomere their hands
		are.
1395	**Enobarbus**	But there is never a fayre Woman, ha's a true
		Face.

LS [1] see footnote #6, previous page

A/VP [2] most modern texts indicate the first sentence is spoken as an aside, the second to Enobarbus: surprisingly, though F1 shows the scene moving from formal verse into more casual prose; at least one modern text maintains the opening two speeches as verse

	Menas	No slander, they steale hearts.
	Enobarbus	We came hither to fight with you.
1400	Menas	For my part, I am sorry it is turn'd to a Drink- ing. Pompey doth this day laugh away his Fortune.
	Enobarbus	If he do, sure he cannot weep't backe againe.
	Menas	Y'have said Sir, we look'd not for Marke An- thony heere, pray you, is he married to Cleopatra?
1405	Enobarbus	Cæsars Sister is call'd Octavia.
	Menas	True Sir, she was the wife of Caius Marcellus.
	Enobarbus	But she is now the wife of Marcus Anthonius.
	Menas	Pray ye sir.
	Enobarbus	'Tis true.
1410	Menas	Then is Cæsar and he, for ever knit together.
	Enobarbus	If I were bound to Divine of this unity, I wold not Prophesie so.
	Menas	I thinke the policy of that purpose, made more in the Marriage, then the love of the parties.
1415	Enobarbus	I thinke so too. But you shall finde the band that seemes to tye their friendship together, will bee the very strangler [1] of their Amity: Octavia is of a holy, cold, and still conversation.
1420	Menas	Who would not have his wife so?
25	Enobarbus	Not he that himselfe is not so: which is Marke Anthony: he will to his Egyptian dish againe: then shall the sighes of Octavia blow the fire up in Cæsar, and (as I said before) that which is the strength of their Amity, shall prove the immediate Author of their variance. An- thony will use his affection where it is. Hee married but his occasion heere.

---

[1] F2 = 'stranger', F1 and most modern texts = 'strangler'

52

Menas	And thus it may be.	
1430	Come Sir, will you aboord?	
	I have a health for you.	
Enobarbus	I shall take it sir: we have us'd our Throats in Egypt.	
Menas	Come, let's away.	

[Exeunt]

L 350 - b

MUSICKE PLAYES
ENTER TWO OR THREE SERVANTS WITH A BANKET
[Most modern texts create a new scene here, Act Two Scene 7]

1435   **1st. Servant**   Heere they'l be man: some o'their[†1] Plants are ill rooted already, the least winde i'th'world will blow them downe.

2nd. Servant   Lepidus is high Conlord.[2]

1st. Servant   They have made him drinke Almes drinke.

1440   **2nd. Servant**   As they pinch one another by the dispositon, hee cries out, no more; reconciles them to his entreatie, and himselfe to'th'drinke.

1st. Servant   But it raises the greater[†3] warre betweene him & his discretion.

1445   **2nd. Servant**   Why this is to have a name in great mens Fellowship: I had a live[4] have a Reede that will doe me no service, as a Partizan I could not heave.

1st. Servant   To be call'd into a huge Sphere, and not to be seene to move in't, are the holes where eyes should bee, which
1450   pittifully disaster the cheekes.

A SENNET SOUNDED
ENTER CÆSAR, ANTHONY, POMPEY, LEPIDUS, AGRIPPA, MECENAS,
ENOBARBUS, MENES, WITH OTHER CAPTAINES [5]

L 350 - b / R 350 - b : 2. 6. 132 - 2. 7. 16

[1] F2 and most modern texts = 'o'their', F1 = 'o'th'their'

[2] F2 and most modern texts = 'high colourd', F1 = 'high Conlord'

[3] F2 and some modern texts = 'greater', other modern texts = 'greatest': F1 = 'greatet'

[4] F1-2 = 'live', F3 = 'lieve', most modern texts = 'lief'

[SD 5] because of Enobarbus' line 'the Boy shall sing', line 1566 this text, some modern texts add the Boy to the entry, though he could just as easily enter after Enobarbus' line: also the 'Menes' of the direction is known as 'Menas'

Anthony	[1]	Thus do they Sir : they take the flow o'th'Nyle
		By certaine scales i'th'Pyramid : they know
		By'th'height, the lownesse, or the meane : If dearth
		Or Foizon follow.
1455		The higher Nilus swels,
		The more it promises : as it ebbes, the Seedsman
		Upon the slime and Ooze scatters his graine,
		And shortly comes to Harvest.

Lepidus   Y'have strange Serpents there?

1460   **Anthony**   I Lepidus.

Lepidus   Your Serpent of Egypt, is bred now of your mud
by the operation of your Sun : so is your Crocodile.

Anthony   They are so.

Pompey   Sit, and some Wine : [2] A health to Lepidus.

1465   **Lepidus**   I am not so well as I should be : → [3]
But Ile ne're out.

Enobarbus   Not till you have slept : I feare me you'l bee in
till then.

Lepidus   Nay certainly, I have heard the Ptolomies Pyra-
1470   misis are very goodly things : without contradiction I
have heard that.

Menas   [4] Pompey, a word.

Pompey   Say in mine eare, what is't.

Menas   Forsake thy seate I do beseech thee Captaine,
1475   And heare me speake a word.

Pompey   Forbeare me till anon.

[Whispers in's Eare]

This Wine for Lepidus.

Lepidus   What[†5] manner o'thing is your Crocodile?

R 350 - b : 2. 7. 17 - 41

WHO [1] most modern texts indicate this is addressed to Cæsar

SD [2] some modern texts suggest some of the on-stage characters sit at Pompey's request

SP [3] the Ff two short line setting (9/4 syllables) beautifully captures Lepidus' (wine-induced?) lack of coherence:
most modern texts join the lines together

A [4] most modern texts indicate this and the next four lines are spoken as asides

W [5] it would be a fine conceit to think F1's 'Whar' is a deliberate scene of Lepidus being unable to hold his drink,
but is more than likely a Compositor B accidental: F2/most modern texts = 'What'

Anthony	It is shap'd sir like it selfe, and it is as broad as it	
1480	hath bredth; It is just so high as it is, and mooves with it	
	owne organs.	
	It lives by that which nourisheth it, and	
	the Elements once out of it, it Transmigrates.	
Lepidus	What colour is it of?	
1485 **Anthony**	Of it owne colour too.	
Lepidus	'Tis a strange Serpent.	
Anthony	'Tis so, and the teares of it are wet.	
Cæsar	Will this description satisfie him?	
Anthony	With the Health that Pompey gives him, else heý	
1490	is a very Epicure.	
Pompey	Go hang sir, hang : tell me of that?	
	Away :	
	Do as I bid you.	
	Where's this Cup I call'd for?	

```
1495 Menas      ¹ If not for the sake of Merit thou wilt heare mee,°   R 350 - b
                  Rise from thy stoole.

     Pompey       I thinke th'art mad :   the matter? ° ²

     Menas        I have ever held my cap off to thy Fortunes.°

     Pompey       Thou hast serv'd me with much faith :   what's
1500               else to say? °
                             Be jolly Lords.

     Anthony      These Quicke-sands Lepidus,°
```

Keepe off, them ³ for you sinke.

Menas   Wilt thou be Lord of all the world?

}

R 350 - b / L 351 - e : 2. 7. 42 - 61

A/VP ₁ most modern texts indicate all the ensuing dialogue between Menas and Pompey are spoken just for each
other as a private dialogue, with the exception of Pompey's single sentence 'Be jolly Lords' at the end of his
second speech: also, though Ff show Menas starting in verse, and the scene slipping into prose, some modern
texts set the whole passage as verse as shown

SD ₂ to separate Menas and Pompey from the rest, most modern texts suggest here Pompey rises and goes aside,
followed by Menas

W ³ F2 and most modern texts = 'keep off them,' F1 sets the peculiar 'keep off, them': though F1 is almost
certainly a compositor error, it could be fun to explore Anthony being almost as drunk as Lepidus and needing to
take a pause in the 'wrong' place

| 1505 | **Pompey** | What saist thou? |

	Menas	[1] Wilt thou be Lord of the whole world?
		That's twice.°
	Pompey	How should that be?
	Menas	But entertaine it,° and though thou thinke me
1510		poore, I am the man ° will give thee all the world.
	Pompey	Hast thou drunke well.°

	Menas	No Pompey, I have kept me from the cup,
		Thou art if thou dar'st be, the earthly Jove :
		What ere the Ocean pales, or skie inclippes,
1515		Is thine, if thou wilt ha't.
	Pompey	Shew me which way?
	Menas	These three World-sharers, these Competitors
		Are in thy vessell.
		Let me cut the Cable,
1520		And when we are put off, fall to their throates :
		All there [2] is thine.
	Pompey	Ah, this thou shouldst have done,
		And not have spoke on't.
		In me 'tis villanie,
1525		In thee't had bin good service : thou must know,
		'Tis not my profit that does lead mine Honour :
		Mine Honour it, Repent that ere thy tongue,
		Hath so betraide thine acte.
		Being done unknowne,
1530		I should have found it afterwards well done,
		But must condemne it now : desist, and drinke. [3]

[LS] [1] as Menas begins to bear down on Pompey with the proposed treachery, Ff set an irregular passage, which can
be split into three sections
a) three short lines, (8/2+4 syllables as a split line) which could be seen as a form of
skirting the issue
b) Menas slipping into prose as he states he is capable of doing what he claims, the prose
suggesting a falling from grace as Menas moves into the highly personal
c) a short verse response from Pompey questioning Menas' drunkenness, which, possibly startles
Menas back into verse (4 syllables)
presumably arguing too much text for a little space was responsible for the original setting, most modern texts regularise
the passage as verse as shown

[W] [2] though most modern texts agree with Ff and set 'there', one interesting gloss = 'theirs'

[SD] [3] most modern texts add a stage direction for Pompey to return to the others, leaving Menas alone

Menas		For this, Ile never follow → [1]
		Thy paul'd Fortunes more,
		Who seekes and will not take, when once 'tis offer'd,
1535		Shall never finde it more.
Pompey		This health to Lepidus.
Anthony		Beare him ashore, → [2]
		Ile pledge it for him Pompey.
Enobarbus		Heere's to thee Menas.
1540	**Menas**	Enobarbus, welcome.
Pompey		Fill till the cup be hid.
Enobarbus		There's a strong Fellow Menas. [3]
Menas		Why?
Enobarbus		A beares the third part of the world man : seest
1545		not?
Menas		The third part, then he is drunk : [4] would it were
		all, that it might go on wheeles.
Enobarbus		Drinke thou : encrease the Reeles.
Menas		Come.
1550	**Pompey**	This is not yet an Alexandrian Feast.
Anthony		It ripen's towards it : strike the Vessells hoa.
		[5] Heere's to Cæsar.
Cæsar		I could well forbear't,° it's monstrous labour
		when I wash my braine,° and it grow fouler.

[SP 1] the Ff setting of two short lines allows time for Menas to ensure Pompey is out of earshot before he decides to leave Pompey's service, and take a hesitation before uttering his maxim: most modern texts either combine the two lines, or just provide a single gap by setting 'For this,/I'll never follow thy paul'd Fortunes more'

[SP 2] most modern texts combine Ff's two short lines (4/7 syllables), though the Ff setting would allow for business as others attempt to comply with Anthony's order

[SD 3] most modern texts suggest Anthony is pointing to the one single Attendant who is carrying Lepidus out

[W 4] Ff = 'The third part, then he is drunk', most modern texts leave out 'he' and set the speech as verse, viz. 'The third part then, is drunk would it were all,/That it might go on wheeles.'

[VP 5] the Ff prose setting illustrates exactly what Cæsar hints at, that he cannot carry his drink well, for in saying he would rather fast than drink, he slips from verse to prose: this is in marked contrast to Anthony, who, in the Ff setting, reestablishes the verse

1555	Anthony	Be a Child o'th'time.°
	Cæsar	Possesse it, Ile make answer:° but I had rather fast from all, foure dayes,° then drinke so much in one.
	Enobarbus	[1] Ha my brave Emperour,° shall we daunce now the Egyptian Backenals,° and celebrate our drinke?
1560	Pompey	Let's ha't good Souldier.°

	Anthony	Come, let's all take hands, Till that the conquering Wine hath steep't our sense, In soft and delicate Lethe.
	Enobarbus	All take hands:[†2]
1565		Make battery to our eares with the loud Musicke, L 351 - e The while, Ile place you, then the Boy shall sing.
		The holding every man shall beate [3] as loud, As his strong sides can volly.

MUSICKE PLAYES. ENOBARBUS PLACES THEM HAND IN HAND

The Song [4]

Come thou Monarch of the Vine,
1570   *Plumpie Bacchus, with pinke eyne:*

In thy Fattes [5] our Cares be drown'd,
With thy Grapes our haires be Crown'd.

Cup us till the world go round,
Cup us till the world go round.

1575	Cæsar	What would you more? →[6]
		Pompey goodnight. Good Brother Let me request you of[7] our graver businesse Frownes at this levitie.

[WHO 1] most modern texts indicate this is addressed to Anthony

[W 2] F1 = 'h ands', F2/most modern texts = 'hands'

[W 3] Ff and some modern texts = 'beate', presumably to the rhythm of the music: other modern texts = 'bear',
presumably referring to the amount of drink they are carrying

[SPD 4] most modern texts indicate this is sung by a the Boy referred to in Enobarbus' speech three lines earlier

[W 5] though most modern texts agree with Ff and set 'Fatts', one gloss = 'vats'

[SP 6] Ff's two short lines (4/7 syllables) allow for reaction to Cæsar's comment before he breaks up the party: most
modern texts join the two lines as one

[PCT 7] for clarification, most modern texts set 'Let me request you off' and set a colon before starting the next phrase

1580   Gentle Lords let's part,
You see we have burnt our cheekes.
                         Strong Enobarbe
Is weaker then the Wine, and mine owne tongue
Spleet's what it speakes :   the wilde disguise hath almost
1585   Antickt us all.
                 What needs more words? goodnight.

Good Anthony your hand.

Pompey   Ile try you on the shore.)

Anthony	[1] And shall Sir, gives your hand.
Pompey	Oh Anthony,° you have my Father [2] house.
	But what, we are Friends? °
	Come downe into the Boate.

1590 (line marker at Pompey)

Enobarbus   [3] Take heed you fall not Menas : Ile not on shore,
No to my Cabin :   these Drummes,
1595   These Trumpets, Flutes : what
Let Neptune heare, we bid aloud [4] farewell
To these great Fellowes.
               Sound and be hang'd, sound out.

[Sound a Flourish with Drummes]

Enobarbus   Hoo saies a there's my Cap.

600   **Menas**   Hoa, Noble Captaine, come.)

R 351 - e : 2. 7. 121 - 135

LS [1] as Pompey admitted earlier, recently he has not felt cordial towards Anthony, so the Ff setting of three short lines out of four offers some interesting possibilities in their (drunken) farewells (6/10/5/6 syllables): Anthony's short line offer to shake hands allows Pompey a moment of realising the gesture, before offering an equally enormous one in return, (via a normal line), to billet Anthony in his father's house: the two short lines that follow allow Anthony to indicate a silent yes, or no, or non-committal shrug, or nothing at all, to Pompey's question about friendship, with Pompey awaiting some (possibly vocal) response before continuing with his final line: most modern texts restructure the passage to regular verse as shown, combining Pompey's last line as a split line with the first part of the restructured Enobarbus speech (see footnote #3 below)

W [2] F2 and most modern texts = 'Fathers', F1 = 'Father'

ALT [3] arguing that since the cabin referred to is in fact Menas', most modern texts reassign (and restructure) this passage as follows

Enobarbus   Take heed you fall not.   [Exeunt all but Enobarbus and Menas]
                      Menas: Ile not on shore.
Menas   No to my Cabin.
                      These Drummes, these Trumpets, Flutes: what
                      Let Neptune heare, we bid aloud farewell
                      To these great Fellowes.
                          Sound and be hang'd, sound out.

for further details see *The Arden Shakespeare, Anthony and Cleopatra*, op. cit., page 98-9, footnotes to lines 128 - 129

W [4] F1-2 = 'aloud', F3 and most modern texts = 'a loud'

R 351 - e : 3. 1. 1 - 24

[Exeunt]

**ENTER VENTIDIUS AS IT WERE IN TRIUMPH, THE DEAD BODY OF PACO-
RUS BORNE BEFORE HIM** [1]
[Most modern texts create a new scene here, Act Three Scene 1]

Ventidius		Now darting Parthya art thou stroke, and now
		Pleas'd Fortune does of Marcus Crassus death
		Make me revenger.
		Beare the Kings Sonnes body,
1605		Before our Army thy Pacorus Orades,[2]
		Paies this for Marcus Crassus.
Romaine[3]		Noble Ventidius,
		Whil'st yet with Parthian blood thy Sword is warme,
		The Fugitive Parthians follow.
1610		Spurre through Media,
		Mesapotamia, and the shelters, whether[4]
		The routed flie.
		So thy grand Captaine Anthony
		Shall set thee on triumphant Chariots, and
1615		Put Garlands on thy head.
Ventidius		Oh Sillius, Sillius,
		I have done enough.
		A lower [5] place note well
		May make too great an act.
620		For learne this Sillius,
		Better to leave undone, then by our deed
		Acquire too high a Fame, when him we serves away.
		Cæsar and Anthony, have ever wonne
		More in their officer, then person.
625		Sossius
		One of my place in Syria, his Lieutenant,
		For quicke accomulation of renowne,
		Which he atchiv'd by'th'minute, lost his favour.
		Who does i'th'Warres more then his Captaine can,
630		Becomes his Captaines Captaine : and Ambition
		(The Souldiers vertue) rather makes choise of losse
		Then gaine, which darkens him.

SD/P [1]
    since in the top of his second speech Ventidius addresses the character Ff refer to as a 'Romaine' as Silius, most modern texts add Silius to the entry together with Roman Officers and/or Soldiers, and change the prefix 'Romaine' to 'Silius' throughout

N [2] most modern texts spell this 'Orodes', Ff = 'Orades'

P [3] see footnote #1 above

W [4] F1 = 'whether', F2 and most modern texts = 'whither'

W [5] F2 and most modern texts = 'A lower', F1 = 'Alower'

I could do more to do Anthonius good,
But 'twould offend him.

1635   And in his offence,   R 351 - e
Should my performance perish.

Romaine   ¹ Thou hast Ventidius that,° without the which a
Souldier and his Sword ° graunts scarce distinction : thou
wilt write to Anthony.°

1640 **Ventidius**   Ile humbly signifie what in his name,
That magicall word of Warre we have effected,
How with his Banners, and his well paid ranks,
The nere-yet beaten Horse of Parthia,
We have jaded out o'th'Field.

1645 **Romaine**   Where is he now?

Ventidius   He purposeth to Athens, whither with what hast
The waight we must convay with's, will permit :
We shall appeare before him.
                      On there, passe along.

[Exeunt]
ENTER AGRIPPA AT ONE DOORE, ENOBARBUS AT ANOTHER
[Most modern texts create a new scene here, Act Three Scene 2]

1650 **Agrippa**   What are the Brothers parted?

Enobarbus   They have dipatcht with Pompey, he is gone,
The other three are Sealing.
                      Octavia weepes
To part from Rome :   Cæsar is sad, and Ledipus
1655 Since Pompey's feast, as Menas saies, is troubled
With the Greene-Sicknesse.

Agrippa   'Tis a Noble Lepidus.

Enobarbus   A very fine one :   oh, how he loves Cæsar.

Agrippa   Nay but how deerely he adores Mark Anthony.

1660 **Enobarbus**   Cæsar? why he's the Jupiter of men.

{Agrippa} ²   What's Anthony, the God of Jupiter?

R 351 - e / L 352 - e : 3. 1. 25 - 3. 2. 10

ᵛᴾ₁ presumably arguing too much text for too little a space, most modern texts set Ff's prose as highly irregular
verse (13 or 14/10/12 syllables): should the Ff setting stand it might suggest even talking about honour causes the
Romaine Silius some problems

ᴾ₂ most modern texts assign the speech to Agrippa, Ff (peculiarly, since he is not in the scene) to Anthony

Enobarbus	Spake you of Cæsar?
	How, the non-pareill?
Agrippa	Oh Anthony, oh thou Arabian Bird!
1665 **Enobarbus**	Would you praise Cæsar, say Cæsar go no further.
Agrippa	Indeed he plied them both with excellent praises.
Enobarbus	But he loves Cæsar best, yet he loves Anthony:
	Hoo, Hearts, Tongues, Figure,[1] →[2]
	Scribes, Bards, Poets, cannot
1670	Thinke speake, cast, write, sing, number: hoo,
	His love to Anthony.
	But as for Cæsar,
	Kneele downe, kneele downe, and wonder.
	}
Agrippa	Both he loves.
1675 **Enobarbus**	They are his Shards, and he their Beetle, so:[3]
	This is to horse: Adieu, Noble Agrippa.
Agrippa	Good Fortune worthy Souldier, and farewell.

ENTER CÆSAR, ANTHONY, LEPIDUS, AND OCTAVIA.

Anthony	No further Sir.
Cæsar	You take from me a great part of my selfe:
1680	Use me well in't.
	Sister, prove such a wife
	As my thoughts make thee, and as my farthest Band
	Shall passe on thy approofe: most Noble Anthony,
	Let not the peece of Vertue which is set
1685	Betwixt us, as the Cyment of our love
	To keepe it builded, be the Ramme to batter
	The Fortresse of it: for better[4] might we
	Have lov'd without this meane, if on both[†5] parts
	This be not cherisht.
1690 **Anthony**	Make me not offended,° in your distrust.

L 352 - e : 3. 2. 11 - 33

[W1] most modern texts = 'figures', F1 = 'Figure'

[SP2] as Enobarbus' mockery of Lepidus reaches its height, Ff set two short lines, (5/5 syllables), possibly suggesting fun with the sound of 'Hoo' at the top of the first: most modern texts combine the two lines as one

[SD3] referring to Enobarbus' following line, 'This is to horse', most modern texts add an offstage trumpet call

[W4] though most modern texts agree with Ff and set 'for better', one gloss = 'far, far better'

[W5] F1 = 'onboth', F2/most modern texts = 'on both'

Cæsar	I have said.
Anthony	You shall not finde,° ¹

Though you be therein curious, the lest cause
For what you seeme to feare, so the Gods keepe you,
1695 And make the hearts of Romaines serve your ends :
We will heere part.

Cæsar	Farewell my deerest Sister, fare thee well,
	The Elements be kind to thee, and make
	Thy spirits all of comfort : fare thee well.
1700 **Octavia**	My Noble Brother.
Anthony	The Aprill's in her eyes, it is Loves spring,
	And these the showers to bring it on : be cheerfull. L 352 - e
Octavia	Sir, looke well to my Husbands house : and ___
Cæsar	What Octavia?
1705 **Octavia**	Ile tell you in your eare. ⁾
Anthony	Her tongue will not obey her heart, nor can
	Her heart informe her tongue. †² → ³

The Swannes downe feather
That stands upon the Swell at the ⁴ full of Tide :
1710 ⁵ And neither way inclines.

Enobarbus	⁶ Will Cæsar weepe?
Agrippa	He ha's a cloud in's face.
Enobarbus	⁷ He were the worse for that were he a Horse,° so is
	he being a man.
715 **Agrippa**	Why Enobarbus :°

When Anthony found Julius Cæsar dead,
He cried almost to roaring : And he wept,
When at Phillippi he found Brutus slaine.

ᴸˢ₁
Anthony's word of caution amid Cæsar's public farewells, and Cæsar's refusal to back down is neatly offset by the pauses of Ff's four irregular lines (5/10/3/4 syllables): most modern texts restructure to two long lines (11/11)

ᵂ₂
F1 = 'tougue' (the 'n' having truned upside down in the tray), F2/most modern texts = 'tongue'

ˢᴾ₃
Ff set two short lines (6/5 syllables) allowing Anthony a moment of reflection as he looks at Octavia: most modern texts join the two lines together

ᵂ₄
since F1 sets an 11 syllable line, some modern texts follow F2 and omit 'the'

ᴸˢ₅
the actor has choice as to which two of these three short lines may be joined as one line of split verse

ᴬ₆
most modern texts indicate the next five speeches between Enobarbus and Agrippa are spoken as asides

ⱽᴾ₇
throughout the play, Ff set the more outrageous of Enobarbus' remarks as prose, as here, perhaps suggesting a particular dead-pan, throw-away delivery: most modern texts, as here, reset the lines as verse

Enobarbus That year indeed,†[1] he was trobled with a rheume,
What willingly he did confound, he wail'd,
Beleev't till I weepe too.[2]

Cæsar No sweet Octavia,
You shall heare from me still: the time shall not
Out-go my thinking on you.

Anthony Come Sir, come,
Ile wrastle with you in my strength of love,
Looke heere I have you, thus I let you go,
And give you to the Gods.

Cæsar Adieu, be happy.

Lepidus Let all the number of the Starres give light
To thy faire way.

Cæsar Farewell, farewell.

[Kisses Octavia]

Anthony Farewell.

[Trumpets sound. Exeunt]
ENTER CLEOPATRA, CHARMIAN, IRAS, AND ALEXAS
[Most modern texts create a new scene here, Act Three Scene 3]

Cleopatra [3] Where is the Fellow?

Alexas Halfe afeard to come.°

Cleopatra Go too, go too: Come hither Sir.

ENTER THE MESSENGER AS BEFORE

Alexas Good Majestie:° Herod of Jury dare not looke
upon you, but when you ° are well-pleas'd.

Cleopatra That Herods head,° Ile have: but how?
When
Anthony is gone,° through whom I might commaund it:
Come thou neere.°

R 352 - e : 3. 2. 57 - 3. 3. 6

W [1] F2 and most modern texts = 'year indeed', F1 = 'yearindeed'

W [2] Ff = 'Beleev't till I weepe too.', most modern texts = 'Beleev't, till I wept too.'

VP/LS [3] in what is a textually crowded page, Ff seem to set the first 21 lines of the scene in a mixture of prose and a series of short lines which could be either verse or prose: most modern texts set the passage in verse as shown: however, if the Ff setting stands, then Cleopatra's shift to verse comes at an interesting moment, as she realises her rival Octavia is short, line 1750 this text

	Messenger	Most gratious Majestie.
	Cleopatra	Did'st thou behold ° Octavia?
1745	**Messenger**	I dread Queene.
	Cleopatra	Where?
	Messenger	Madam in Rome,° I lookt her in the face : and saw her led ° betweene her Brother, and Marke Anthony.°
	Cleopatra	Is she as tall as me?
1750	**Messenger**	She is not Madam.°

	Cleopatra	Didst heare her speake? → [1] Is she shrill tongu'd or low?
	Messenger	Madam, I heard her speake, she is low voic'd.
	Cleopatra	That's not so good : he cannot like her long.
1755	**Charmian**	Like her? Oh Isis : 'tis impossible.
	Cleopatra	I thinke so Charmian : dull of tongue, & dwarfish [2] What Majestie is in her gate,[3] remember

		If ere thou look'st on Majestie.
1760	**Messenger**	She creepes :° her motion, & her station are as one. [4] ° [5]

		She shewes a body, rather then a life, A Statue, then a Breather. }
	Cleopatra	Is this certaine?

	Messenger	Or I have no observance.
765	**Charmian**	Three in Egypt ° cannot make better note.

R 352 - e : 3. 3. 7 - 23

SP/VP [1] this is the possible Ff shift to verse: the two short lines (4/6 syllables) suggest the Messenger doesn't understand that Cleopatra's initial question refers to the quality of Octavia's voice: most modern texts join the two lines

PCT [2] F1-2 = no punctuation (possibly as if Cleopatra runs one idea into the next, though F1 two lines below sets
a strange comma to the far right of the word 'Majestie' totally unrelated to any text there): F3 and most modern texts
print a period

W [3] F1-2= 'gate', which for clarity F3/most modern texts set as 'gait'

PCT [4] F1' s punctuation is a little blurred, and could be either a period or the bottom part of a colon: F2 sets a
colon, and most modern texts either a colon or semi-colon

LS [5] Ff's irregular two lines (8/12 syllables) allow for a wonderful hesitation before the Messenger tries to avoid
being attacked again, and then a slight blurt as he starts: most modern texts readjust the lines to normal pentameter
as shown

Cleopatra	He's very knowing,° I do perceiv't,
	There's nothing in her yet.° R 352 - e
	The Fellow ha's good judgement.
Charmian	Excellent.°
Cleopatra	Guesse at her yeares, I prythee.
Messenger	Madam,° she was a widdow.
Cleopatra	Widdow?
	Charmian, hearke.°
Messenger	And I do thinke she's thirtie. [1]

| Cleopatra | Bear'st thou her face in mind? is't long or round? |
| Messenger | Round, even to faultinesse. |

Cleopatra	For the most part too, they are foolish that are
	so.°
	Her haire what colour? [2]
Messenger	Browne Madam : and her forehead
	As low as she would wish it.
	}
Cleopatra	There's Gold for thee,
	Thou must not take my former sharpenesse ill,
	I will employ thee backe againe : I finde thee
	Most fit for businesse.
	Go, make thee ready,
	Our Letters are prepar'd. [3]
	}
Charmian	A proper man.

Line numbers: 1770, 1775, 1780, 1785

R 352 - e / L 353 - e : 3. 3. 23 - 38

[LS 1]
the irregularities in this Ff ten line passage could beautifully mark off five stages in the grilling of the
Messenger, viz. (with 'a' and 'b' set at the bottom of the previous page)
    a) a single 7 syllable line from the Messenger, about his powers of observation, elicits no
          response from Cleopatra, which could be bad for all on stage, so
    b) Charmian leaps in with a full length line of support and reassurance about his powers
    c) Cleopatra via three short lines (8/6/7 syllables) finally accepts his news at face value
          leading Charmian to add, as a split line to Cleopatra's final '7', 'Excellent'
    d) at the beginning of a short (7 syllable) line everyone relaxes, until Cleopatra starts
          questioning on a new topic, Octavia's age
    e) in a short (7 syllable reply) the Messenger squirms before answering vaguely about
          Octavia's widowhood, which leads to a final triumphant overlong (12 or 13 syllables)
      split verse line combining Cleopatra's joy and the Messenger's final assessment
most modern texts regularise the passage, reducing Ff's ten lines to seven as shown

[VP 2]
Ff set this speech as prose, showing Cleopatra momentarily sinking back into the starting mood of the scene;
most modern texts set it as verse (joining the second line to the Messenger's first line of reply as a twelve syllable
split line) as shown

[SD 3]
most modern texts set an exit here for the Messenger

66

Cleopatra	Indeed he is so : I repent me much	
1790	That so I harried him.	
		Why me think's by him,
	This Creature's no such thing.	
	}	
Charmian	Nothing Madam.	
Cleopatra	The man hath seene some Majesty, and should	
1795	know.	

> Charmian ¹ Hath he seene Majestie?
> Isis else defend :° and
> serving you so long.°
>
> Cleopatra I have one thing more to aske him yet good
> 1800 Charmian :° but 'tis no matter, thou shalt bring him to me °
> where I will write ; all may be well enough.°
>
> Charmian I warrant you Madam.

[Exeunt]

ENTER ANTHONY AND OCTAVIA

[Most modern texts create a new scene here, Act Three Scene 4]

Anthony	Nay, nay Octavia, not onely that,
	That were excusable, that and thousands more
1805	Of semblable import, but he hath wag'd
	New Warres 'gainst Pompey.
	Made his will, and read it,

> To publicke eare,° spoke scantly of me,
> When perforce he could not °
> 1810 But pay me tearmes of Honour : cold and sickly
> He vented then most narrow measure : lent me,
> When the best hint was given him : he not look't,
> Or did it from his teeth. ²

L 353 - e : 3. 3. 39 - 3. 4. 10

VP ₁ Ff set the remainder of the scene in prose (perhaps including Cleopatra's previous line) as if the potential
storm of anger has passed and all the court can now relax: most modern texts reset the passage in (sometimes
LS ₂ awkward) verse as shown
this passage has been subject to much examination and revision: notably
a) Ff's first two short lines (9/6 syllables) are often restructured, with little advantage, (to 4/11 syllables) as shown
b) there has been much repunctuation and rephrasing, the most common of which is
> To publicke eare:
> Spoke scantly of me: when perforce he could not
> But pay me tearmes of Honour, cold and sickly
> He vented them*; most narrow measure lent me:
> When the best hint was given him, he not took't*,
> Or did it from his teeth.
c) as the * show, there have been two word substitutions, 'them' for Ff's 'then', and 'not took't' for F1's 'not
look't': while the modern alterations serve both to clarify and tidy the passage grammatically, Ff's setting could
suggest Anthony being so upset he is unable to talk clearly about the situation

Octavia   Oh my good Lord,

1815   Beleeve not all, or if you must beleeve,

    Stomacke not all.

             A more unhappie Lady,

    If this devision chance, ne're stood betweene

    Praying for both parts:

1820   The good Gods wil mocke me presently,

    When I shall pray: Oh blesse my Lord, and Husband,

    Undo that prayer, by crying out as loud,

    Oh blesse my Brother.

             Husband winne, winne Brother,

1825   Prayes, and distroyes the prayer, no midway

    'Twixt these extreames at all.

Anthony   Gentle Octavia,

    Let your best love draw to that point which seeks

    Best to preserve it; if I loose mine Honour,

1830   I loose my selfe: better I were not yours

    Then yours[†1] so branchlesse.

             But as you requested,

    Your selfe shall go between's, the meane time Lady,

    Ile raise the preparation of a Warre

1835   Shall staine your Brother, make your soonest hast,

    So your desires are yours.

Octavia   Thanks to my Lord,

    The Jove of power make me most weake, most weake,

    You[†2] reconciler: Warres 'twixt you twaine would be,

1840   As if the world should cleave, and that slaine men

    Should soader[3] up the Rift.   L 353 - e

Anthony   When it appeeres to you where this begins,

    Turne your displeasure that way, for our faults

    Can never be so equall, that your love

845   Can equally move with them.

             Provide your going,[†4]

    Choose your owne company, and command what cost

    Your heart has[†5] mind too.

[Exeunt]

L 353 - e / R 353 - e : 3. 4. 10 -38

[†1] F2 and most modern texts = 'yours', F1 = 'your'

[†2] F2 and most modern texts = 'Your', F1 = 'You'

[3] Ft = 'soader' , most modern texts = 'solder'

[†4] F1 = 'yourgoing', F2/most modern texts = 'your going'

[†5] F2 and most modern texts = 'has', F1 = 'hes'

ENTER ENOBARBUS, AND EROS
[Most modern texts create a new scene here, Act Three Scene 5]

Enobarbus	How now Friend Eros?	
1850	Eros	Ther's strange Newes come Sir.
	Enobarbus	What man?
	Eros	Cæsar & Lepidus have made warres upon Pompey.
	Enobarbus	This is old, what is the successe?
	Eros	Cæsar having made use of him in the warres
1855		'gainst Pompey: presently denied him rivality, would not
		let him partake in the glory of the action, and not resting
		here, accuses him of Letters he had formerly wrote to
		Pompey.
		Upon his owne appeale seizes him, so the poore
1860		third is up, till death enlarge his Confine.

> **Enobarbus** ¹ Then would ² thou hadst a paire of chaps no†³ more,°
> and throw betweene them all the food thou hast, °they'le
> grinde the other. ⁴
>   Where's Anthony? °

1865	Eros	He's walking in the garden thus, and spurnes
		The rush that lies before him.
		Cries Foole Lepidus,
		And threats the throate of that his Officer,
		That murdred Pompey. }
1870	Enobarbus	Our great Navies rig'd.
	Eros	For Italy and Cæsar, more Domitius,
		My Lord desires you presently: my Newes

> I might have told heareafter.
>
> **Enobarbus** 'Twill be †⁵ naught,° but let it be: bring me to Anthony.
> 1875 **Eros** Come Sir,⁶ °⁷

ᵛᵖ ₁ Ff set the opening of the scene as prose, including the following speech: most modern texts follow Ff until this point, but set this Enobarbus speech in verse, even though he has shown throughout the play so far the characteristic of speaking prose about things close to Anthony or himself

ᵂ ₂ Ff = 'would', most modern texts = 'world'

ᵂ ₃ F2 and most modern texts = 'chaps no', F1 = 'chapsn o'

ᵂ ₄ Ff = 'grinde the other': for clarity most modern texts expand the phrase to 'grinde th'one the other'

ᵂ ₅ F2 and most modern texts = ' 'Twill be', F1 = ''Twillbe'

ᴾᶜᵀ ₆ F1 sets a comma as if either Enobarbus' reaction or Eros' own inner thoughts cause him to break off: F2/most modern texts set a period

ᴸˢ ₇ Ff's irregular lines (7/13/2 syllables) suggest the news has had great impact on both characters: most modern texts restructure to two lines as shown

69

[Exeunt]
ENTER AGRIPPA, MECENAS, AND CÆSAR
[Most modern texts create a new scene here, Act Three Scene 6]

Cæsar	Contemning Rome he ha's done all this, & more
	In Alexandria: heere's the manner oft:
	I'th'Market-place on a Tribunall silver'd,
	Cleopatra and himselfe in Chaires of Gold
1880	Were publikely enthron'd: at the [1] feet, sat
	Cæsarion whom they call my Fathers Sonne,
	And all the unlawfull issue, that their Lust
	Since then hath made betweene them.
	Unto her,
1885	He gave the stablishment of Egypt, made her
	Of lower Syria, Cyprus, Lydia,° absolute Queene.
Mecenas	This in the publike eye?° [2]

Cæsar	I'th'common shew place, where they exercise,
	His Sonnes hither [3] proclaimed the King of Kings,[4]
1890	Great Media, Parthia, and Armenia
	He gave to Alexander.
	To Ptolomy he assign'd,
	Syria, Silicia, and Phœnetia: she
	In th'abiliments of the Goddesse Isis
1895	That day appeer'd, and oft before gave audience,
	[5] As 'tis reported so. [6]
Mecenas	Let Rome be thus ° inform'd.
Agrippa	Who queazie with his insolence ° already,
	Will their good thoughts call from him. °
1900	Cæsar The people knowes it,
	And have now receiv'd ° his accusations.
Agrippa	Who does he accuse? °

R353-e : 3.6.1-23

[W] [1] though most modern texts agree with Ff and set 'the', one gloss = 'their'

[LS] [2] the Ff irregular two lines (13 to 15/6 syllables) illustrate both Cæsar's overlong indignation and Mecenas' pausing before asking a key question

[W] [3] Ff = 'thither', most modern texts = 'he there'

[W] [4] Ff = 'King of Kings', most modern texts = 'Kings of Kings'

[LS] [5] the fact of Ff twice setting short lines surrounding a normal one suggests Cæsar's care in responding to both of Agrippa's questions, and Agrippa's equal care in posing the question as to who is accused: the modern text's resetting removes these possibilities

[W] [6] F1 = 'reported so', F2 and most modern texts = 'reported, so'

Cæsar	Cæsar, and that having in Cicilie [1]

Sextus Pompeius spoil'd, we had not rated him
1905 His part o'th'Isle.
Then does he say, he lent me
Some shipping unrestor'd..
Lastly, he frets

[2] That Lepidus of the Triumpherate,° should be depos'd,
1910 And being that, we detaine ° all his Revenue.

Agrippa Sir, this should be answer'd.°

Cæsar 'Tis done already, and the Messenger gone:
I have told him Lepidus was growne too cruell, R 353 - e
That he his high Authority abus'd,
1915 And did deserve his change: for what I have conquer'd,
I grant him part: but then in his Armenia,

And other of his conquer'd Kingdoms, I ° demand the like [3]

Mecenas Hee'l never yeeld to that.° [4]

Cæsar Nor must not then be yeelded to in this.

ENTER OCTAVIA WITH HER TRAINE

1920 **Octavia** Haile Cæsar, and my L. [5] haile most deere Cæsar.

Cæsar That ever I should call thee Cast-away.

Octavia You have not call'd me so, nor have you cause.

Cæsar Why have you stoln upon us thus? you come not
Like Cæsars Sister.
1925 The wife of Anthony
Should have an Army for an Usher, and
The neighes of Horse to tell of her approach,
Long ere she did appeare.
The trees by th'way
1930 Should have borne men, and expectation fainted,
Longing for what it had not.

R 353 - c / L 354 - b : 3. 6. 24 - 48

[N] [1] F2/most modern texts = 'Sicily', F1 = 'Cicelie'

[LS] [2] the Ff setting of two long and one short lines (14/11 or 12/6 syllables) allows for both Cæsar's indignation and Agrippa's care in suggesting to Cæsar a course of action: modern texts offer a much more normal setting (10/10 or 11/11 syllables)

[PCT] [3] F1-3 = no punctuation, probably because of lack of column width (for it is hardly likely that Mecenas would interrupt Cæsar): F4 and most modern texts print a period

[LS] [4] Ff set a long and a short line (14/6 syllables) perhaps suggesting Cæsar's indignation once more, and Mecenas (diplomatically) taking care in offering an opinion counter to that of Cæsar: most modern texts regularise the passage as shown

[AB] [5] most modern texts expand Ff's 'L.' to 'lords'

		Nay, the dust
		Should have ascended to the Roofe of Heaven,
		Rais'd by your populous Troopes: But you are come
1935		A Market-maid to Rome, and have prevented
		The ostentation of our love; which left unshewne,
		Is often left unlov'd: we should have met you
		By Sea, and Land, supplying every Stage
		With an augmented greeting.
		}
1940	**Octavia**	Good my Lord,
		To come thus was I not constrain'd, but did it
		On my free-will.
		My Lord Marke Anthony,
		Hearing that you prepar'd for Warre, acquainted
1945		My greeved eare withall: whereon I begg'd
		His pardon for returne.
		}
	Cæsar	Which soone he granted,
		Being an abstract ¹' tweene his Lust, and him.
	Octavia	Do not say so, my Lord.
		}
1950	**Cæsar**	I have eyes upon him,
		And his affaires come to me on the wind:° wher is he now?
	Octavia	My Lord, in Athens.° ²
	Cæsar	No my most wronged Sister, Cleopatra
		Hath nodded him to her.
1955		He hath given his Empire
		Up to a Whore, who now are levying
		The Kings o'th'earth for Warre.
		He hath assembled,
		Bochus the King of Lybia, Archilaus
1960		Of Cappadocia, Philadelphos King
		Of Paphlagonia: the Thracian King Adullas,
		King Mauchus of Arabia, King of Pont,
		Herod of Jewry, Mithridates King
		Of Comageat, Polemen and Amintas,
1965		The Kings of Mede and Licoania,
		With a more larger List of Scepters. ³

L 354 - b : 3. 6. 49 - 76

ᵂ₁
ᴸˢ₂ though some modern texts agree with Ff and set 'abstract', one gloss = 'obstruct'

Ff's setting of two irregular lines (14/5 syllables) could allow both for Cæsar's anger (over Anthony's disloyalty to Octavia, Cæsar's sister) to explode, as well as for her hesitation in responding to his question about Anthony's
ᴺ₃ whereabouts, and his hesitation before disabusing her: most modern texts regularise the passage as shown of the various names in this speech, modern texts correct Ff as follows (the correction is shown first each time): 'Archelaus' for 'Archilaus'; 'Manchus' for 'Mauchus'; 'Comagene' for 'Comageat'; 'Polemon' for 'Polemen'; 'Amyntas' for 'Amintas; and F2's 'Lyaconia' corrects F1's 'Licoania'

Octavia		Aye me most wretched,
		That have my heart parted betwixt two Friends,
		That does afflict each other.
1970	**Caesar**	Welcom hither :° your Letters did with-holde our breaking forth[†][°][1]
		Till we perceiv'd both how you were wrong led,
		And we in negligent danger :[2] cheere your heart,
		Be you not troubled with the time, which drives
		O're your content, these strong necessities,
1975		But let determin'd things to destinie
		Hold unbewayl'd their way.

Welcome to Rome,

Nothing more deere to me : You are abus'd
Beyond the marke of thought : and the high Gods
1980 To do you Justice, makes his[3] Ministers
Of us, and those that love you.

Best of comfort,

And ever welcom to us.   **Agrippa** Welcome Lady.

Mecenas		Welcome deere Madam,
1985		Each heart in Rome does love and pitty you,
		Onely th'adulterous Anthony, most large L 354 - b
		In his abhominations, turnes you off,
		And gives his potent Regiment to a Trull
		That noyses it against us.
		}
1990	**Octavia**	Is it so sir?
	Cæsar	Most certaine : Sister welcome : pray you
		Be ever knowne to patience.

My deer'st Sister.

[Exeunt]
ENTER CLEOPATRA, AND ENOBARBUS
[Most modern texts create a new scene here, Act Three Scene 7]

Cleopatra	I will be even with thee, doubt it not.
1995 **Enobarbus**	But why, why, why?
Cleopatra	Thou hast forespoke my being in these warres,
	And say'st it is[†4] not fit.

LS [1] modern texts regularise Ff's short/long line pairing (7/14 syllables): the Ff setting could suggest Cæsar
▼ [2] initially doesn't know how to respond to Octavia's distress, but when he does he overdoes it
▼ [3] though most modern texts agree with Ff and set 'negligent danger', one gloss = 'danger negligent'
[3] F1 = 'makes his Ministers', most modern texts set 'make their Ministers' ('make' from F2, 'their' as a modern gloss)
▼ [4] F2 and most modern texts = 'it is' F1 = 'it it'

73

Enobarbus	Well: is it, is it. }

Cleopatra	[1] If not, denounc'd against us,[2] why should not
	we ° be there in person.
Enobarbus	[3] Well, I could reply:° if wee should serve with
	Horse and Mares together,° the Horse were meerly lost:
	the Mares would beare ° a Soldiour and his Horse.
Cleopatra	What is't you say? °

Enobarbus	Your presence needs must puzle Anthony,
	Take from his heart, take from his Braine, from's time,
	What should not then be spar'd.
	He is already
	Traduc'd for Levity, and 'tis said in Rome,
	That Photinus an Eunuch, and your Maides
	Mannage this warre.
Cleopatra	Sinke Rome, and their tongues rot }
	That speake against us.
	A Charge we beare i'th'Warre,
	And as the president of my Kingdome will
	Appeare there for a man.
	Speake not against it,

I will not stay behinde.

ENTER ANTHONY AND CAMIDIAS [5]

Enobarbus	Nay I have done,° here comes the Emperor.
Anthony	Is it not strange Camidius,°

That from Tarrentum, and Brandusium,[6]
He could so quickly cut the Ionian Sea,
And take in Troine.[7]
You have heard on't (Sweet?)

R 354 - b : 3. 7. 4 - 23

[VP 1] in this quarrel between Cleopatra and Enobarbus, Ff set at least these three speeches (and possibly the first two at the top of the scene) in prose, as if there were no time for the elegance of verse: most modern texts set the passage as verse as shown

[W 2] Ff = 'If not, denounc'd against us,': most modern texts = 'Is't not denounc'd against us,'

[A 3] most modern texts indicate this is spoken as an aside

[LS 4] the small hesitations of Ff's irregular setting (6/10/7 or 8 syllables) allow not only the entry more weight, but provide a silent moment between the often adversarial Enobarbus and Cleopatra: most modern texts set two lines, the second one rushed (10/13 or 14) to no particular advantage

[N/P 5] the entry refers to the character as Camidias: in dialogue Anthony refers to him as Camidius: most modern texts correct the spelling throughout to Canidius, as he is named in *North's Plutarch* of 1579

[N 6] F2 and most modern texts = 'Brundusium', F1 = 'Brandisium'

[N 7] F2 and most modern texts = 'Toryne', F1 = 'Troine'

2025	Cleopatra	Celerity is never more admir'd,
		Then by the negligent.

Anthony
A good rebuke,
Which might have well becom'd the best of men
To taunt at slacknesse.
2030   Camidius, wee
Will fight with him by Sea.

Cleopatra   By Sea, what else?

Camidus   Why will my Lord, do so?

Anthony   For that he dares us too't.

2035   Enobarbus   So hath my Lord, dar'd him to single fight.

Camidus   I, and to wage this Battell at Pharsalia,
Where Cæsar fought with Pompey.
                                       But these offers
Which serve not for his vantage, he shakes off,
2040   And so should you.

Enobarbus   Your Shippes are not well mann'd,
Your Marriners are Militers,[1] Reapers, people
Ingrost by swift Impresse.
                            In Cæsars Fleete,
2045   Are those, that often have 'gainst Pompey fought,
Their shippes are yare, yours heavy: no disgrace
Shall fall you for refusing him at Sea,
Being prepar'd for Land.

Anthony   By Sea, by Sea.

2050   Enobarbus   Most worthy Sir, you therein throw away
The absolute Soldiership you have by Land,
Distract your Armie, which doth most consist
Of Warre-markt-footmen, leave unexecuted
Your owne renowned knowledge, quite forgoe
2055   The way which promises assurance, and
Give up your selfe meerly to chance and hazard,
From firme Securitie.

Anthony   Ile fight at Sea.   R 354-b

Cleopatra   I have sixty Sailes, Cæsar none better.

R 354-b / L 355-b : 3. 7. 24 - 49

[1] F2 and most modern texts = 'Muliters', (viz. 'muleteers'): F1 = 'Militers'

2060	**Anthony**	Our over-plus of shipping will we burne,
		And with the rest full mann'd, from th'head of Action [1]
		Beate th'approaching Cæsar.
		But if we faile,
		We then can doo't at Land.

[Enter a Messenger] [2]

2065		Thy Businesse?
	Messenger	The Newes is true, my Lord, he is descried,
		Cæsar ha's taken Toryne.
	Anthony	Can he be there in person?
		'Tis impossible
2070		Strange, that his power should be.
		Camidius,
		Our nineteene Legions thou shalt hold by Land,
		And our twelve thousand Horse.
		Wee'l to our Ship,
2075		Away my Thetis.

ENTER A SOLDIOUR

		How now worthy Souldier?
	Souldier	Oh Noble Emperor,[†3] do not fight by Sea,
		Trust not to rotten plankes : Do you misdoubt
		This Sword, and these my Wounds ; let th'Egyptians
2080		And the Phoenicians go a ducking : wee
		Have us'd to conquer standing on the earth,
		And fighting foot to foot.
	Anthony	Well, well, away.

[exit Ant{ony} Cleo{patra} & Enob{arbus}]

	Souldier	By Hercules I thinke I am i'th'right.
2085	**Camidius**	Souldier thou art : but his whole action growes
		Not in the power on't : so our Leaders leade,[4]

L 355 - b : 3. 7. 50 - 69

[N]1 F2 and most modern texts = 'Actium', F1 = 'Action'

[UE]2 with the entry being unusually set alongside the text instead of being centred on a separate line, this is presumably one added by the Playhouse rather than specified in Shakespeare's manuscript: in terms of action, it could be that fear of the anger of Cleopatra and Anthony is widespread, and that in entering, the Messenger is trying to interrupt as little as possible

[PCT]3 F1 sets what could be a blurred comma or perhaps a period: F2/most modern texts set a comma

[W]4 Ff = 'Leaders leade', most modern texts = 'Leaders led'

	And we are Womens men.
Souldier	[1] You keepe by Land ° the Legions and the Horse whole, do you not? °

2090	{**Camidius**} [2]	Marcus Octavius, Marcus Justeus, Publicola, and Celius, are for Sea : But we keepe whole by Land.
		This speede of Cæsars Carries beyond beleefe.
2095	**Souldier**	While he was yet in Rome,[3] } His power went out in such distractions, As [4] beguilde all Spies.
	Camidius	Who's his Lieutenant, heare you? }
	Souldier	They say, one Towrus.
2100	**Camidius**	Well, I know the man. }

ENTER A MESSENGER

	Messenger	The Emperor cals Camidius.

Camidius	With Newes the times with Labour, And throwes forth ° each minute, some.° [5]

[exeunt]

ENTER CÆSAR [6] WITH HIS ARMY, MARCHING

[Most modern texts create a new scene here, Act Three Scene 8]

	Cæsar	Towrus?
2105	**Towrus**	My Lord.
	Cæsar	Strike not by land, → [7] Keepe whole, provoke not Battaile °

L 355 - b : 3. 7. 70 - 3. 8. 3

VP [1] Ff set the Souldier's speech in prose, perhaps suggesting that the criticism of the campaign, most unusually voiced by an officer to a non-ranking soldier, has momentarily knocked him out of verse: most modern texts set the speech as verse as shown

P [2] Ff set this speech for Ventidius, though he is not present: most modern texts reassign it to Canidius/Camidius

PCT [3] F1 sets a blurred mark which could be either a comma or period: most modern texts follow F2 and omit any form of punctuation

LS [4] to try to balance the metric structure, some modern texts transfer 'As' to the end of the previous line

LS [5] Ff's two short (7 syllable) lines suggest the abrupt summoning causes some personal reaction in Camidius:

SD [6] most modern texts restructure as shown

SP [7] most modern texts add Towrus (which they usually spell as 'Taurus') to the entry

most modern texts set Ff's two short lines (4/7 syllables) as one: the Ff setting shows Cæsar in some thought as he makes his plans, not, as the modern texts suggest, just giving orders

Till we have done at Sea.

2110

          Do not exceede
The Prescript of this Scroule: Our fortune lyes
Upon this jumpe.

[exit]

ENTER ANTHONY, AND ENOBARBUS
[Most modern texts create a new scene here, Act Three Scene 9]

Anthony

Set we our Squadrons on yond side o'th'Hill,
In eye of Cæsars battaile, from which place
We may the number of the Ships behold,

2115

And so proceed accordingly.

[exit]

**CAMIDIUS MARCHETH WITH HIS LAND ARMY ONE WAY OVER THE
STAGE, AND TOWRUS THE LIEUTENANT OF CÆSAR THE OTHER WAY:
AFTER THEIR GOING IN, IS HEARD THE NOISE OF A SEA-FIGHT.**

ALARUM. ENTER ENOBARBUS AND SCARUS
[Most modern texts create a new scene here, Act Three Scene 10]

Enobarbus

Naught, naught, al naught, I can behold no longer:
Thantoniad, the Egyptian Admirall,
With all their sixty flye, and turne the Rudder:

L 355 - b

To see't, mine eyes are blasted.

ENTER SCARRUS

2120 **Scarrus**

Gods, & Goddesses,° all the whol synod of them!

Enobarbus

What's thy passion.° 1

Scarrus

The greater Cantle of the world, is lost
With very ignorance, we have kist away
Kingdomes, and Provinces.

2125 **Enobarbus**

How appeares the Fight?

Scarrus

On our side, like the Token'd Pestilence,
Where death is sure.
        Yon ribaudred ² Nagge of Egypt,
(Whom Leprosie o're-take) i'th'midst o'th'fight,

L 355 - b / R 355 - b : 3. 8. 4 - 3. 10. 11

LS 1 Ff set three irregular lines (7/12/4 syllables) possibly highlighting a silent entry before Scarrus lets loose: most modern texts set two longer lines (12/11 syllables) suggesting Scarrus speaks as she enters

W 2 the description 'ribaudred Nagge' has been subject to much speculation, though no truly satisfactory alternative has yet been offered apart from, perhaps, 'ribauld': for details see *The Arden Shakespeare, Anthony and Cleopatra*, op. cit., page 128, footnote to line 10, and *William Shakespeare: A Textual Companion*, op. cit., page 551, footnote to 3.10.10/1674

2130   When vantage like a payre of Twinnes appear'd
    Both as the same, or rather ours the elder;
    (The Breeze upon her) like a Cow in Inne,[1]
    Hoists Sailes, and flyes.

Enobarbus   That I beheld:
2135   Mine eyes did sicken at the sight, and could not
    Indure a further view.

Scarrus   She once being looft,[2]
    The Noble ruine of her Magicke, Anthony,
    Claps on his Sea-wing, and (like a doting Mallard)
2140   Leaving the Fight in heighth, flyes after her:
    I never saw an Action of such shame;
    Experience, Man-hood, Honor, ne're before,
    Did violate so it selfe.

Enobarbus   Alacke, alacke.

ENTER CAMIDIUS

2145   **Camidius**   Our Fortune on the Sea is out of breath,
    And sinkes most lamentably.
                    Had our Generall
    Bin what he knew himselfe, it had gone well:
    Oh his[3] ha's given example for our flight,
2150   Most grossely by his owne.

Enobarbus   I, are you thereabouts?
                    Why then goodnight °
    indeede.

Camidius   Toward Peloponnesus are they fled.°

2155   **Scarrus**   'Tis easie toot,
    And there I will attend ° what further comes.

Camidius   To Cæsar will I render °[4]

R 355 - b : 3. 10. 12 - 32

w 1
w 2 F2 and most modern texts = 'June', F1 = 'Inne'
w 3 modern texts usually set Ff's 'looft', a sailing term, in its more modern form 'luff'd
ls 4 F1 = 'his', F2 and most modern texts = 'he'
    this short passage speaks volumes as to the characteristics of each of the men facing military disaster: the Ff irregular passage offers
    a) Enobarbus in his accustomed prose often spoken at an important/critical moment
    b) a possibly slightly short line from Camidius as he assesses where their fleeing leaders have gone
    c) two speeches starting with short lines as Camidius and Enobarbus succinctly lay open
        their intentions (Camidius will surrender, Enobarbus will fight on)
    and the Ff irregularities underline each character's inner struggle: most modern texts restructure the passage in somewhat more regular verse as shown (10/12/10/11 syllables)

My Legions and my Horse, sixe Kings alreadie
Shew me the way of yeelding.
}

2160   **Enobarbus**   Ile yet follow
The wounded chance of Anthony, though my reason
Sits in the winde against me.

1

ENTER ANTHONY WITH ATTENDANTS
[Most modern texts create a new scene here, Act Three Scene 11]

        Anthony   Hearke, the Land bids me tread no more upon't,
It is asham'd to beare me.
2165   Friends, come hither,
I am so lated in the world, that I
Have lost my way for ever.
                                      I have a shippe,
Laden with Gold, take that, divide it :   flye,
2170   And make your peace with Cæsar.
                                      }

        Omnes   Fly?
        Not wee.

        Anthony   I have fled my selfe, and have instructed cowards
To runne, and shew their shoulders.
2175   Friends be gone,
I have my selfe resolv'd upon a course,
Which has no neede of you.
                                      Be gone,
My Treasure's in the Harbour.
2180   Take it :   Oh,
I follow'd that I blush to looke upon,
My very haires do mutiny :   for the white
Reprove the browne for rashnesse, and they them
For feare, and doting.
2185   Friends be gone, you shall
Have Letters from me to some Friends, that will
Sweepe your way for you.
                                      Pray you looke not sad,
Nor make replyes of loathnesse, take the hint
2190   Which my dispaire proclaimes.
                                      Let them [2] be left
Which leaves it selfe, to the Sea-side straight way ;
I will possesse you of that ship and Treasure.   R 355 - b

R 355 - b :   3. 10. 33 - 3. 11. 21

SD [1] most modern texts set an exit for all on-stage

▼ [2] Ff = 'them', most modern texts = 'that'

Leave me, I pray a little : pray you now,
2195 Nay do so : for indeede I have lost command,
Therefore I pray you, Ile see you by and by.

[Sits downe]

ENTER CLEOPATRA LED BY CHARMIAN AND EROS [1]

Eros	Nay gentle Madam, to him, comfort him.°
Iras	Do most deere Queene.
Charmian	Do, why, what else?
Cleopatra	Let me sit downe :° Oh Juno.
Anthony	No, no, no, no, no.°
Eros	See you heere, Sir?
Anthony	Oh fie, fie, fie.
Charmian	Madam.°
Iras	Madam, oh good Empresse.
Eros	Sir, sir.° [2]

Anthony   Yes my Lord, yes ; he at Phillipi kept
His sword e'ne like a dancer, while I strooke
The leane and wrinkled Cassius, and 'twas I
2210 That the mad Brutus ended : he alone
Dealt on Lieutenantry, and no practise had
In the brave squares of Warre : yet now : no matter.

Cleopatra   Ah stand by.

Eros	[3] The Queene my Lord, the Queene.
Iras	Go to him,° Madam, speake to him, Hee's [4] unqualited ° with very shame.
Cleopatra	Well then, sustaine me : Oh.°

L 356 - b : 3. 11. 22 - 45

SD [1] many texts alter the entry to have Cleopatra led on by her closest women, Charmian and Iras: as M.R.Ridley points out in *The Arden Shakespeare, Anthony and Cleopatra*, op. cit., page 132, footnote to lines 24-5, this undermines the simple fact that it is Eros who speaks first: those who leave the opening of Ff's entry as is usually suggest Iras is in close attendance

LS [2] most modern texts set these ten Ff ambiguous lines as originally set, very awkward prose, natural under the circumstances: if awkward verse were required instead, one possible solution is shown by the symbols °

LS [3] some modern texts set Ff's four short lines (6 - possibly forming a shared verse line with the previous Cleopatra line - 8/9/6 syllables) allowing for the difficulty of the situation: at least one modern text crams the text into three almost regular lines (9/10/10) thus running roughshod over the delicate hesitations Ff offer

W [4] some modern texts set 'He is' for Ff's 'Hee's' so as to expand the line to ten syllables

Eros	Most Noble Sir arise, the Queene approaches,
	Her head's declin'd, and death will cease [1] her, but
2220	Your comfort makes the rescue.
Anthony	I have offended Reputation,
	A most unnoble swerving.
	⟩
Eros	Sir, the Queene.
Anthony	Oh whether hast thou lead me Egypt, see
2225	How I convey my shame, out of thine eyes,
	By looking backe what I have left behinde
	Stroy'd in dishonor.
	⟩
Cleopatra	Oh my Lord, my Lord,
	Forgive my fearfull sayles, I little thought
2230	You would have followed.
Anthony	Egypt, thou knew'st too well,
	My heart was to thy Rudder tyed by'th'strings,
	And thou should'st stowe [2] me after.
	O're my spirit
2235	The [3] full supremacie thou knew'st, and that
	Thy becke, might from the bidding of the Gods
	Command mee.
	⟩
Cleopatra	Oh my pardon.
	⟩
Anthony	Now I must
2240	To the young man send humble Treaties, dodge
	And palter in the shifts of lownes, who
	With halfe the bulke o'th'world plaid as I pleas'd,
	Making, and marring Fortunes.
	You did know
2245	How much you were my Conqueror, and that
	My Sword, made weake by my affection, would
	Obey it on all cause.
	⟩
Cleopatra	Pardon, pardon.
Anthony	Fall not a teare I say, one of them rates
2250	All that is wonne and lost: Give me a kisse,
	Even this repayes me.
	We sent our Schoolemaster,° is a come backe?

---

[1] F1 = 'cease', F2 and most modern texts = 'seize'

[2] Ff = 'stowe', most modern texts = 'tow'

[3] Ff = 'The', most modern texts = 'Thy'

2255	Love I am full of Lead:° some Wine Within there, and our Viands: Fortune knowes,° [1] We scorne her most, when most she offers blowes.

[Exeunt]
ENTER CÆSAR, AGRIPPA, AND DOLLABELL{A}, [t2] WITH OTHERS [3]
[Most modern texts create a new scene here, Act Three Scene 12]

Cæsar	Let him appeare that's come from Anthony. Know you him.	L 356 - b

Dolabella	Cæsar, 'tis his Schoolemaster,
	An argument that he is pluckt, when hither
2260	He sends so poore a Pinnion of his Wing,
	Which had superfluous Kings for Messengers,
	Not many Moones gone by.

ENTER AMBASSADOR FROM ANTHONY

Cæsar	Approach and speake.

Ambassador	Such as I am, I come from Anthony:
2265	I was of late as petty to his ends,
	As is the Morne-dew on the Mertle leafe
	To his grand Sea.

Cæsar	Bee't so, declare thine office. }

Ambassador	Lord of his Fortunes he salutes thee, and
2270	Requires to live in Egypt, which not granted
	He Lessons [4] his Requests, and to thee sues
	To let him breath betweene the Heavens and Earth
	A private man in Athens: this for him.

	Next, Cleopatra does confesse thy Greatnesse,
2275	Submits her to thy might, and of thee craves
	The Circle of the Ptolomies for her heyres,
	Now hazarded to thy Grace. }

Cæsar	For Anthony,
	I have no eares to his request.

[LS] [1] Ff's irregular setting (5 or 6/10/8/9 or 10 syllables) is a masterly setting for Anthony, the first short line allowing time for the kiss's effect before continuing, the second to realise the depths of his own depression before telling her of his feelings: most modern texts regularise (not particularly successfully) the passage as shown (11 or 12/10/11 or 12 syllables), basically substituting one set of irregularities for another

[W] [2] F2 and most modern texts = 'Dolabella', F1 = 'Dolabello'

[SD] [3] since he speaks later in the scene, most modern texts name Thidias as one of the 'Others'

[W] [4] F2 and most modern texts = 'Lessens', which removes the potential of F1's 'Lessons'

2280	The Queene,
	Of Audience, nor Desire shall faile, so thee
	From Egypt drive her all-disgraced Friend,
	Or take his life there.
	This if shee performe,
2285	She shall not sue unheard.
	So to them both.
Ambassador	Fortune pursue thee.
Cæsar	Bring him through the Bands: [1]
	[2] To try thy Eloquence, now 'tis time, dispatch,
2290	From Anthony winne Cleopatra, promise
	And in our Name, what she requires, adde more
	From thine invention, offers. [3]
	Women are not
	In their best Fortunes strong ; but want will perjure
2295	The ne're touch'd Vestall.
	Try thy cunning Thidias,
	Make thine owne Edict for thy paines, which we
	Will answer as a Law.
	}
Thidias	Cæsar, I go.
2300	**Cæsar**	Observe how Anthony becomes his flaw,
	And what thou think'st his very action speakes
	In every power that mooves.
	}
Thidias	Cæsar, I shall.

[Exeunt]
ENTER CLEOPATRA, ENOBARBUS, CHARMIAN, & IRAS
[Most modern texts create a new scene here, Act Three Scene 13]

Cleopatra	What shall we do, Enobarbus?
	}
2305	**Enobarbus**	Thinke, and dye.
Cleopatra	Is Anthony, or we in fault for this?
Enobarbus	Anthony onely, that would make his will
	Lord of his Reason.
	What though you fled,
2310	From that great face of Warre, whose severall ranges
	Frighted each other?
	Why should he follow?

SD [1] most modern texts set an exit for the Ambassador

WHO [2] most modern texts indicate this is addressed to Thidias

W [3] Ff = 'From thine invention, offers.': one modern gloss = 'As thine invention offers.'

The itch of his Affection should not then
Have nickt his Captain-ship, at such a point,
2315 When halfe to halfe the world oppos'd, he being
The meered ^{1} question?
                         'Twas a shame no lesse
Then was his losse, to course your flying Flagges,
And leave his Navy gazing.
                          }
2320 **Cleopatra** Prythee peace.

ENTER THE AMBASSADOR, WITH ANTHONY

Anthony	^{2} Is that his answer?	**Ambassador**	I my Lord.
Anthony	The Queene shall then have courtesie, So she ° will yeeld us up.		
Ambassador	He sayes so.		
Anthony	Let her know't.°		

2325

To the Boy Cæsar send this
grizled head,° and he will fill thy wishes to the brimme,°
With Principalities.

Cleopatra	That head my Lord? °

R 356 - b

2330 **Anthony** To him againe, tell him he weares the Rose
Of youth upon him : from which, the world should note
Something particular : His Coine, Ships, Legions,
May be a Cowards, whose Ministers would prevaile
Under the service of a Childe, as soone
2335 As i'th'Command of Cæsar.
                          I dare him therefore
To lay his gay Comparisons ^{3} a-part,
And answer me declin'd, Sword against Sword,
Our selves alone : Ile write it : Follow me. ^{4}

R 356 - b / L 357 - b : 3. 13. 7 - 28

$^{W}_1$ though most modern texts agree with Ff and set 'meered', one gloss = 'mooted', see *The Arden Shakespeare,*
$_{LS\ 2}$ *Anthony and Cleopatra,* op. cit., page 140, footnote to line 10, for further discussion
  arguing too much text for too little space, most modern texts restructure Ff's irregular opening as shown: if
  the Ff setting were to stand, it could suggest
  a) with Anthony and the Ambassador starting with two sets of short lines, (the second pair
      8/9 syllables as a split line) they are taking great care to set up a clear understanding
      of Cæsar's offer
  b) Anthony's mix of verse and prose as he then (angrily?) tells Cleopatra of the offer
  c) Cleopatra's prose or short verse reply, (suggesting perhaps she touches Anthony's head)
$^{W}_3$ though most modern texts agree with Ff and set 'Comparisons', one interesting gloss = 'caparisons'
$^{SD}_4$ most modern texts add two stage directions here, the first for the exit of Anthony and the Ambassador, the
  second suggesting Enobarbus' next speech is an aside

85

2340	Enobarbus	Yes like enough : hye battel'd Cæsar will
		Unstate his happinesse, and be Stag'd to'th'shew
		Against a Sworder.
		I see mens Judgements are
		A parcell of their Fortunes, and things outward
2345		Do draw the inward quality after them
		To suffer all alike,[1] that he should dreame,
		Knowing all measures, the full Cæsar will
		Answer his emptinesse ; Cæsar thou hast subdu'de
		His judgement too.

ENTER A SERVANT

2350	Servant	A Messenger from Cæsar.
	Cleopatra	What no more Ceremony?
		See my Women,
		Against the blowne Rose may they stop their nose,
		That kneel'd unto the Buds.
2355		Admit him sir.[2]

	Enobarbus	Mine honesty, and I, beginne to square,
		The Loyalty well held to Fooles, does make
		Our Faith meere folly : yet he that can endure
		To follow with Allegeance a falne Lord,
2360		Does conquer him that did his Master conquer,
		And earnes a place i'th'Story.

ENTER THIDIAS

	Cleopatra	Cæsars will.
	Thidias	Heare it apart.
	Cleopatra	None but Friends : say boldly.
2365	Thidias	So haply are they Friends to Anthony.
	Enobarbus	He needs as many (Sir) as Cæsar ha's,
		Or needs not us.
		If Cæsar please, our Master
		Will leape to be his Friend : For us you know,
2370		Whose he is, we are, and that is Cæsars.

L 357 - b : 3. 13. 29 - 52

PCT [1] though most modern texts agree with Ff and set a comma, one commentator suggests setting a period

SD [2] most modern texts add two stage directions, the first that the Servant now leaves, and that again Enobarbus' next speech is an aside

Thidias	So. [1]	

      Thus then thou most renown'd, Cæsar intreats,
Not to consider in what case thou stand'st
Further then he is Cæsars. [2]

2375 **Cleopatra**   Go on, right Royall. }

Thidias   He knowes that you embrace [3] not Anthony
As you did love, but as you feared him.

Cleopatra   Oh. }

Thidias   The scarre's upon your Honor, therefore he
2380   Does pitty, as constrained blemishes,

[4] Not as deserved.

Cleopatra   He is a God,
And knowes ° what is most right.
                Mine Honour
2385   Was not yeelded,° but conquer'd meerely.

Enobarbus   [5] To be sure of that,° I will aske Anthony.

Sir, sir, thou art so leakie °

That we must leave thee to thy sinking, for
Thy deerest quit thee.

[Exit Enob.{arbus}]

2390 **Thidias**   Shall I say to Cæsar,
What you require of him :   for he partly begges
To be desir'd to give.
                  It much would please him,
That of his Fortunes you should make a staffe
2395   To leane upon.
                But it would warme his spirits

L 357 - b : 3. 13. 52 - 69

LS [1] some modern texts transfer this to the end of Enobarbus' speech as completion of a split line

W [2] F1 = 'Cæsars', F2/most modern texts = 'Cæsar'

W [3] Ff = 'embrace', some modern texts = 'embrac'd'

LS [4] Ff's irregular setting might suggest the following

  a) a split line (4 + 4 syllables), allowing Cleopatra to take stock before answering

  b) two 9 syllables lines from Cleopatra, allowing her to be careful in her equivocal speech
      of seeming agreement

  c) a slightly long line paired with a short one (11/7 syllables) as Enobarbus, seemingly
      taking Cleopatra's speech at face value, is appalled by the turn of events and moved
      to leave unbidden

the modern texts restructuring (4 + 4 + 2/11/10/13 syllables) wipes out the possible three Ff steps, and sets a totally different mood for the exiting Enobarbus

A [5] most modern texts indicate this is spoken as an aside

87

To heare from me you had left Anthony,
And put your selfe under his shrowd,° the universal Landlord† . ¹

| Cleopatra | What's your name?° |

2400 **Thidias** My name is Thidias.

Cleopatra Most kinde Messenger,
Say to great Cæsar this in disputation,²   L 357·b
I kisse him conqu'ring hand : Tell him, I am prompt
To lay my Crowne at's feete, and there to kneele. ³

2405 Tell him, from his all-obeying breath, I heare
The doome of Egypt.

Thidias 'Tis your Noblest course :
Wisedome and Fortune combatting together,
If that the former dare but what it can,
2410 No chance may shake it.
                 Give me grace to lay
My dutie on your hand.

Cleopatra Your Cæsars Father oft,
(When he hath mus'd of taking kingdomes in)
2415 Bestow'd his lips on that unworthy place,
⁴ As it rain'd kisses.

ENTER ANTHONY AND ENOBARBUS

Anthony Favours?
       By Jove that thunders.°
             What art thou Fellow?†

2420 **Thidias** One that but performes °
The bidding of the fullest man, and worthiest
To have command obey'd.

Enobarbus ⁵ You will be whipt.

LS ₁ most modern texts regularise the overlylong 15 syllable final line flourish of Thidias by combining the final phrase with the following short Cleopatra question as a split verse line

W ₂ Ff = 'disputation', most modern texts = 'deputation'

PCT/W ₃ Ff set a period plus 'Tell him': most modern texts set no punctuation followed by 'Till, from'

LS ₄ Ff's three irregular lines allow for silence (5 syllables) as Anthony and Enobarbus return (and possibly the kissing of Cleopatra's hand by Thidias), a 12 syllable explosion from Anthony, and a startled pause (5) before Thidias begins his foolhardy reply: most modern texts restructure the text to a two line reply (12/10 syllables)

A ₅ most modern texts indicate this and Enobarbus' next comments are spoken as asides

Anthony	Approch there : ah you Kite.
2425	Now Gods & divels
	Authority melts from me of late.[1]
	When I cried hoa,
	Like Boyes unto a musse, Kings would start forth,
	And cry, your will.
2430	Have you no eares?
	I am Anthony yet.
	Take hence this Jack, and whip him.

ENTER A SERVANT[2]

Enobarbus	'Tis better playing with a Lions whelpe,
	Then with an old one dying.
2435	**Anthony**	Moone and Starres,
	Whip him : wer't twenty of the greatest Tributaries
	That do acknowledge Cæsar, should I finde them
	So sawcy with the hand of she heere, what's her name
	Since she was Cleopatra?
2440	Whip him Fellowes,
	Till like a Boy you see him crindge his face,
	And whine aloud for mercy.
	Take him hence.
Thidias .	Marke Anthony.
2445	**Anthony**	Tugge him away : being whipt
	Bring him againe, the[3] Jacke of Cæsars shall
	Beare us an arrant to him.

[Exeunt with Thidius]

	You were halfe blasted ere I knew you : Ha?
	Have I my pillow left unprest in Rome,
2450	Forborne the getting of a lawfull Race,
	And by a Jem of women, to be abus'd
	By one that lookes on Feeders?
Cleopatra	Good my Lord.

PCT 1
Ff = 'Authority melts from me of late. When I cried hoa', most modern texts = 'Authority melts from me: of late, when I cried hoa'

SD 2
since Anthony has twice called for someone to enter, and since the previous line is an instruction, most modern texts advance the entry one or two lines, even though the Ff entry is equally valid, and (because of Anthony's later line, 'Whip him Fellowes', line 2441 this text) usually indicate that more than one Servant enters

W 3
Ff = 'the', most modern texts = 'this'

	Anthony	You have beene a boggeler ever,
2455		But when we in our viciousnesse grow hard
		(Oh misery on't) the wise Gods seele our eyes
		In our owne filth, drop [1] our cleare judgements, make us
		Adore our errors, laugh at's while we strut
		To our confusion.
2460	**Cleopatra**	Oh, is't come to this?
	Anthony	I found you as Morsell, cold upon
		Dead Cæsars Trencher: Nay, you were a Fragment
		Of Gneius Pompeyes, besides what hotter houres
		Unregistred in vulgar Fame, you have
2465		Luxuriously pickt out.
		For I am sure,
		Though you can guesse what Temperance should be,
		You know not what it is.
	Cleopatra	Wherefore is this?
2470	**Anthony**	To let a Fellow that will take rewards,
		And say, God quit you, be familiar with
		My play-fellow, your hand; this Kingly Seale,
		And plighter of high hearts.
		O that I were
2475		Upon the hill of Basan, to out-roare
		The horned Heard, for I have savage cause,
		And to proclaime it civilly, were like
		A halter'd necke, which do's the Hangman thanke,
		For being yare about him.
2480		Is he whipt?

R 357 - b

ENTER A SERVANT WITH THIDIAS [2]

Servant	Soundly, my Lord.
Anthony	Cried he? and begg'd a Pardon?
Servant	He did aske favour. [3]

	Anthony	If that thy Father live, let him repent
2485		Thou was't not made his daughter, and be thou sorrie
		To follow Cæsar in his Triumph, since
		Thou hast bin whipt.

R 357 - b / L 358 - b : 3. 13. 110 - 137

[1] Ff = 'the wise Gods seele our eyes/In our own filth, drop our . . .', most modern texts unnecessarily add a colon, viz. 'the wise Gods seele our eyes:/In our own filth drop our . . .'

[2] most modern texts advance the entry to just before Anthony's question

[3] the actor has choice as to which two of these three short lines may be joined as one line of split verse

For following him,[1] henceforth
The white hand of a Lady Feaver thee,
2490　　Shake thou to looke on't.
　　　　　　　　Get thee backe to Cæsar,
Tell him thy entertainment : looke thou say
He makes me angry with him.
　　　　　　　　For he seemes
2495　　Proud and disdainfull, harping on what I am,
Not what he knew I was.
　　　　　　　　He makes me angry,
And at this time most easie 'tis to doo't :
When my good Starres, that were my former guides
2500　　Have empty left their Orbes, and shot their Fires
Into th'Abisme of hell.
　　　　　　　　If he mislike,
My speech, and what is done, tell him he has
Hiparchus, my enfranched Bondman, whom
2505　　He may at pleasure whip, or hang, or torture,
As he shall like to quit me.
　　　　　　　　Urge it thou :
Hence with thy stripes, be gone.

[Exit Thid.{ias}]

Cleopatra	Have you done yet?
Anthony	Alacke our Terrene Moone ° is now Eclipst, And it portends alone ° the fall of Anthony.
Cleopatra	I must stay his time? ° [2]

Anthony	To flatter Cæsar, would you mingle eyes With one that tyes his points. }
2515　Cleopatra	Not know me yet?
Anthony	Cold-hearted toward me? }
Cleopatra	Ah (Deere) if I be so, From my cold heart let Heaven ingender haile, And poyson it in the sourse, and the first stone 2520　Drop in my necke : as it determines so Dissolve my life, the next Cæsarian smile,[3]

L 358 - b : 3. 13. 137 - 162

W 1 Ff = 'Thou hast been whipt. For following him, henceforth/The . . .': most modern texts = 'Thou hast been
LS 2 whipt for following him. Henceforth/The . . .'
　　the Ff setting of short lines (4/4 syllables) surrounding Anthony's reply (10/12 syllables) suggests that first
　　Thidias' exit gives Cleopatra pause before she starts to reassure Anthony, and that his response makes her realise
　　just how much she has to do to get him out of his mood: most modern texts regularise the lines as shown
W 3 Ff = 'smile', most modern texts = 'smite'

		Till by degrees the memory of my wombe,
		Together with my brave Egyptians all,
		By the discandering [1] of this pelleted storme,
2525		Lye gravelesse, till the Flies and Gnats of Nyle
		Have buried them for prey. ⟩
	Anthony	I am satisfied :
		Cæsar sets [2] downe in Alexandria, where
		I will oppose his Fate.
2530		Our force by Land,
		Hath Nobly held, our sever'd Navie too
		Have knit againe, and Fleete, threatning most Sea-like.
		Where hast thou bin my heart?
		Dost thou heare Lady?
2535		If from the Field I shall returne once more
		To kisse these Lips, I will appeare in Blood,
		I, and my Sword, will earne our Chronicle,
		There's hope in't yet. ⟩
	Cleopatra	That's my brave Lord.
2540	**Anthony**	I will be trebble-sinewed, hearted, breath'd,
		And fight maliciously : for when mine houres
		Were nice and lucky, men did ransome lives
		Of me for jests : But now, Ile set my teeth,
		And send to darkenesse all that stop me.
2545		Come,
		Let's have one other gawdy night : Call to me
		All my sad Captaines, fill our Bowles once more :
		Let's mocke the midnight Bell. ⟩
	Cleopatra	It is my Birth-day,
2550		I had thought t'have held it poore.
		But since my Lord
		Is Anthony againe, I will be Cleopatra.
	Anthony	We will yet do well. L 358 - b
	Cleopatra	Call all his Noble Captaines to my Lord.

555	**Anthony**	[3] Do so, wee'l speake to them, →
		And to night Ile force °
		The Wine peepe through their scarres. →
		Come on (my Queene) °

L 358 - b / R 358 - b   :   3. 13. 163 - 190

▼ 1   Ff = 'discandering', most modern texts = 'discandying'

▼ 2   Ff = 'sets', most modern texts = 'sits'

LS 3   most modern texts create two full lines from these unusual four short Ff lines (6/4 and 6/4 syllables): however, this marks the final moment of Anthony's recovery, the Ff setting could suggest either his recovery is not quite as easy as it would seem, or that he is overcome at having Cleopatra once more in partnership with him

		There's sap in't yet.
2560		The next time I do fight
		Ile make death love me : for I will contend
		Even with his pestilent Sythe.

[Exeunt]

	Enobarbus	Now hee'l out-stare the Lightning, to be furious
		Is to be frighted out of feare, and in that moode
2565		The Dove will pecke the Estridge ; and I see still
		A diminution in our Captaines braine,
		Restores his heart ; when valour prayes in reason,[1]
		It eates the Sword it fights with : I will seeke
		Some way to leave him.

[Exeunt]

ENTER CÆSAR, AGRIPPA, & MECENAS WITH HIS ARMY,
CÆSAR READING A LETTER
[Most modern texts create a new scene here, Act Four Scene 1]

2570	Cæsar	He calles me Boy, and chides as he had power
		To beate me out of Egypt.
		My Messenger
		He hath whipt with Rods, dares me to personal Combat. [2]

		Cæsar to Anthony : let the old Ruffian know,
2575		I have many other wayes to dye : meane time
		Laugh at his Challenge.
		}

	Mecenas	Cæsar must thinke,
		When one so great begins to rage, hee's hunted
		Even to falling.
2580		Give him no breath, but now
		Make boote of his distraction : Never anger
		Made good guard for it selfe.
		}

	Cæsar	Let our best heads know,
		That to morrow, the last of many Battailes
2585		We meane to fight.
		Within our Files there are,
		Of those that serv'd Marke Anthony but late,
		Enough to fetch him in.
		See it done,
2590		And Feast the Army, we have store to doo't,
		And they have earn'd the waste.
		Poore Anthony.

▼[1] Ff = 'prayes in reason', most modern texts = 'preys on reason'

Ff[2] Ff set a period, most modern texts a comma

[Exeunt]

ENTER ANTHONY, CLEOPATRA, ENOBARBUS, CHARMIAN, IRAS, ALEXAS, WITH OTHERS
[Most modern texts create a new scene here, Act Four Scene 2]

Anthony	He will not fight with me, Domitian? [1]
Enobarbus	No?
2595 **Anthony**	Why should he not?
Enobarbus	He thinks, being twenty times of better fortune, He is twenty men to one.
Anthony	To morrow Soldier, By Sea and Land Ile fight : or I will live, 2600 Or bathe my dying Honor in the blood Shall make it live againe. Woo't thou fight well.
Enobarbus	Ile strike, and cry. Take all.
2605 **Anthony**	Well said, come on : Call forth my Houshold Servants, lets to night

[Enter 3 or 4 Servitors] [2]

	Be bounteous at our meale. Give me thy hand, Thou hast bin rightly honest, so hast thou, 2610 Thou, and thou, and thou : you have serv'd me well, And Kings have beene your fellowes.
Cleopatra	[3] What meanes this?
Enobarbus	'Tis one of those odde tricks which sorow shoots Out of the minde.
615 **Anthony**	And thou art honest too : I wish I could be made so many men, And all of you clapt up together, in An Anthony : that I might do you service, So good as you have done. R 358 - b

R 358 - b : 4. 2. 1 - 19

[N]1 Ff = 'Domitian', most modern texts = 'Domitius'

[SD]2 in view of Anthony's acknowledgements in the next two speeches, one modern text suggests at least six Servitors should enter

[A]3 most modern texts indicate this and the next speech are asides between Cleopatra and Enobarbus

2620	**Omnes**	The Gods forbid.

Anthony Well, my good Fellowes, wait on me tonight:
Scant not my Cups, and make as much of me
As when mine Empire was your Fellow too,
And suffer'd my command.

2625 **Cleopatra** ¹ What does he meane?

Enobarbus To make his Followers weepe.

Anthony Tend me to night;
May be, it is the period of your duty,
Haply you shall not see me more, or if,
2630 A mangled shadow.
                         Perchance to morrow,
You'l serve another Master.
                         I looke on you,
As one that takes his leave.
2635   Mine honest Friends,
I turne you not away, but like a Master
Married to your good service, stay till death:
Tend me to night two houres, I aske no more,
And the Gods yeeld you for't.

2640 **Enobarbus** What meane you (Sir)
To give them this discomfort?
                         Looke they weepe,
And I an Asse, am Onyon-ey'd;   for shame,
Transforme us not to women.

2645 **Anthony** Ho, ho, ho:
Now the Witch take me, if I meant it thus.

Grace grow where those drops fall (my hearty Friends)
You take me in too dolorous a sense,
For I spake to you for your comfort, did desire you
2650 To burne this night with Torches: Know (my hearts)
I hope well of to morrow, and will leade you,
Where rather Ile expect victorious life,
Then death, and Honor.
                        Let's to Supper, come,
655 And drowne consideration.

[Exeunt]
ENTER A COMPANY OF SOLDIOURS
[Most modern texts create a new scene here, Act Four Scene 3]

ᴬ₁ most modern texts indicate this and the next speech are asides between Cleopatra and Enobarbus

1st. Soldier	Brother, goodnight: to morrow is the day.	
2nd. Soldier	It will determine one way: Fare you well.	
	Heard you of nothing strange about the streets.	
1st. Soldier	Nothing: what newes?	
2nd. Soldier	Belike 'tis but a Rumour, good night to you.	
1st. Soldier	Well sir, good night.	

2660

[They meete other Soldiers]

2nd. Soldier	Souldiers, have carefull Watch.
1st. Soldier [1]	And you: Goodnight, goodnight.

[They place themselves in every corner of the Stage]

2665

2nd. Soldier	Heere we: and if to morrow
	Our Navie thrive, I have an absolute hope
	Our Landmen will stand up.
1st. Soldier	'Tis a brave Army,° and full of purpose.

[Musicke of the Hoboyes is under the Stage]

2nd. Soldier	Peace, what noise?
1st. Soldier	List list.° [2]

2670

2nd. Soldier	Hearke.
1st. Soldier	Musicke i'th'Ayre.
3rd. Soldier	Under the earth.
4th. Soldier	It signes well, do's it not?
2nd. Soldier	No.

2675

1st. Soldier	Peace I say: What should this meane?
2nd. Soldier	'Tis the God Hercules, whom Anthony loved,
	Now leaves him.
1st. Soldier	Walke, let's see if other Watchmen

L 359 - b : 4. 4. 1 - 17

[1] to allow for the parting of some of the Soldiers the text seems to indicate, at least one modern text assigns this speech to a 3rd. Soldier, while others reassign some of the following Ff 2nd. Soldier speeches to a 4th Soldier

[2] Ff's four lines (6/10/3/2) allow minute pauses for the uncertainty of the Soldiers, especially once the music starts: most modern texts reset the text as two lines as shown (11/10): also, F2 set a comma between 'List list'

	[1] Do heare what we do? →	
2680	**2nd. Soldier**	How now Maisters?
	[Speak together]	
	Omnes	How now? ° how now do you heare this? →
	1st. Soldier	I, is't not strange? °

2nd. Soldier   Do you heare Masters?
                          Do you heare?

2685 **1st. Soldier**   Follow the noyse so farre as we have quarter.   L 359 - b
                  Let's see how it will give off.

Omnes   Content: 'Tis strange.

[Exeunt]
ENTER ANTHONY AND CLEOPATRA, WITH OTHERS [2]
[Most modern texts create a new scene here, Act Four Scene 4]

Anthony   Eros, mine Armour Eros.

Cleopatra   Sleepe a little.

2690 **Anthony**   No my Chucke.
                          Eros, come mine Armor Eros.

ENTER EROS

Come good Fellow, put thine [3] Iron on,
If Fortune be not ours to day, it is
Because we brave her.
2695   Come.

Cleopatra   Nay, Ile helpe too, Anthony.
                  What's this for?
                              [4] Ah let be, let be, thou art
                  The Armourer of my heart: False, false: This, this,
2700   Sooth-law Ile helpe: Thus it must bee.

Anthony   Well, well,° we shall thrive now.

[LS 1] see the last footnote, previous page
[SD 2] since Charmian speaks at the end of the scene, most modern texts add her to the entry
[W 3] Ff = 'thine', most modern texts = 'mine'
[P/LS 4] though Ff set the whole speech for Cleopatra, most modern texts give these next two lines to Anthony and the final line again to Cleopatra: also, while F1 -2 end line 2699 with a comma, F3/most modern texts set a period

	Seest thou my good Fellow.° 　　　　　　　Go, put on thy defences.
Eros	Briefely Sir.°¹

2705 Cleopatra　Is not this buckled well?
　　　　　　　　　　　}

Anthony　Rarely, rarely:
He that unbuckles this, till we do please
To daft ² for our Repose, shall heare a storme.

Thou fumblest Eros, and my Queenes a Squire
2710　More tight at this, then thou: Dispatch.
　　　　　　　　　　　　　　O Love,
That thou couldst see my Warres to day, and knew'st
The Royall Occupation, thou should'st see
A Workeman in't.

ENTER AN ARMED SOLDIER

2715　Good morrow to thee, welcome,
Thou look'st like him that knowes a warlike Charge:
To businesse that we love, we rise betime,

	And go too't with delight.
Souldier	A thousand Sir,° early though't be, have on their 2720　Riveted trim,° and at the Port expect you.°³

[Showt]
[Trumpets Flourish]
ENTER CAPTAINES, AND SOULDIERS

{Captain} ⁴　The Morne is faire: Good morrow Generall.

All　Good morrow Generall.
　　　　　　　　　　　}

Anthony　'Tis well blowne Lads.

This Morning, like the spirit of a youth
2725　That meanes to be of note, begins betimes.

So, so: Come give me that, this way, well-sed.

R 359 - b : 4. 4. 9 - 28

ᴸˢ ₁ Ff's irregular setting allows Anthony a moment to look at how Cleopatra has dressed him before commenting: most modern texts regularise the passage as shown

ᵂ ₂ most modern texts set 'daff'd' for F1's 'daft', F2 = 'doft'

ᴸˢ ₃ most modern texts readjust the Ff setting as shown (10/11/7 syllables): Ff's opening hesitation (6/11/11) allows the Soldier a moment (of surprise at being addressed by his Commander-in-Chief?) before replying

ᴾ ₄ Ff give this line to Alexas: however, since Alexas is not included in the entry, nor should he be, most modern texts reassign this speech to a Captain

Fare thee well Dame, what ere becomes of me,
This is a Soldiers kisse: rebukeable,[1]
And worthy shamefull checke it were, to stand
On more Mechanicke Complement, Ile leave thee.

2730

Now like a man of Steele,[2] you that will fight,
Follow me close, Ile bring you too't: Adieu.

[Exeunt]

Charmian   Please you retyre to your Chamber?

                                    }

Cleopatra   Lead me:

2735   He goes forth gallantly: That he and Cæsar might
Determine this great Warre in single fight;
Then Anthony; but now.
                       Well on.

[Exeunt]

TRUMPETS SOUND. ENTER ANTHONY, AND EROS [3]
[Most modern texts create a new scene here, Act Four Scene 5]

Eros [4]   The Gods make this a happy day to Anthony.

2740   Anthony   Would thou, & those thy scars had once prevaild
To make me fight at Land.
                        }

Eros   Hadst[†5] thou done so,
The Kings that have revolted, and the Soldier
That has this morning left thee, would have still

745   Followed thy heeles.

Anthony   Whose gone this morning?

Eros   Who?°one ever neere thee, call for Enobarbus, °[6]   R 359 - b

He shall not heare thee, or from Cæsars Campe,

R 359 - b / L 380* - b   :   4. 4. 29 - 4. 5. 8

[SD 1] most modern texts add a stage direction that Anthony kiss Cleopatra

[W 2] Ff = 'Ile leave thee./Now like a man of steele, you that . . .', most modern texts = 'Ile leave thee/Now like a man of steele. You that . . .'

[P 3] as many commentators have pointed out, in this scene there is a need for at least two people with Anthony: Eros must be present since he is named in Anthony's final speech, but it is unlikely he is the character spoken with at the top of the scene even though Ff assign him all the non-Anthony speeches throughout the scene: Anthony's opening speech suggests he is talking with the Soldier who earlier advised him not to fight at sea, lines 2077 - 2082, page 76 this script: thus most modern texts add his character to the entry, see the next footnote

[P 4] because of the argument presented in the previous footnote, most modern texts assign all the non-Anthony speeches in the scene to a character simply called a Soldier with the exception of the one marked *, line 2752 below

[W 5] F1 = 'Had'st', F2/most modern texts = 'Hadst'

[LS 6] very foolishly, some modern texts re-arrange Ff's split short line(9 syllables) and hesitation before an explosive (12 syllable) reply, into a more regular response (10/11 syllables)

		¹ Say I am none of thine.
2750	Anthony	What sayest thou?
	Soldier	Sir ° he is with Cæsar.
	Eros *	Sir, his Chests and Treasure ° he has not with him.
	Anthony	Is he gone?
	Soldier	Most certaine. °

2755   **Anthony**   Go Eros, send his Treasure after, do it,
Detaine no jot I charge thee : write to him,
(I will subscribe) gentle adieu's, and greetings ;
Say, that I wish he never finde more cause
To change a Master.
2760   Oh my Fortunes have
Corrupted honest men.
             Dispatch Enobarbus. ²

[Exit]
**FLOURISH. ENTER AGRIPPA, CÆSAR, WITH ENOBARBUS,
AND DOLLABELLA**
[Most modern texts create a new scene here, Act Four Scene 6]

   Cæsar   Go forth Agrippa, and begin the fight :
Our will is Anthony be tooke alive :
765   Make it so knowne.
                      }
   Agrippa   Cæsar, I shall. ³

   Cæsar   The time of universall peace is neere :
Prove this a prosp'rous day, the three nook'd world
Shall beare the Olive freely.

ENTER A MESSENGER

L 380* - b : 4. 5. 9 - 4. 6. 6

LS/VP ₁
   most modern texts regularise the Ff passage as shown: however, Ff could be set in either verse or prose:
if prose, the shock could have leached all forms of courtesy from the scene momentarily: if irregular verse, the
action might break down as follows
      a) a short (6 syllable) line from the Soldier, allowing Anthony a moment of shock
      b) two short lines forming a split line (4 + 6 syllables) as the Soldier answers Anthony's
             question and a full line from Eros all but confirming Enobarbus' desertion
      c) two short (3 + 3 syllables) lines still allowing Anthony a moment of pause before
             committing himself to one of the most telling acts of the play, the sending on of
             Enobarbus' treasure
RCT ₂
   several attempts have been made to modify the severity of the F1 reading 'Dispatch Enobarbus': the most
sentimental offers 'Despatch. O, Enobarbus', and most modern texts offer a variation on 'Despatch. Enobarbus':
F2 = 'Despatch Eros', F3-4 = 'Despatch, Eros.'
SD ₃
   most modern texts set an exit for Agrippa

2770	**Messenger**	Anthony ° is come into the Field.
	Cæsar	Go charge Agrippa,° ¹

Plant those that have revolted in the Vant,²
That Anthony may seeme to spend his Fury
Upon himselfe.

[Exeunt]

2775   **Enobarbus**   Alexas did revolt, and went to Jewry on
Affaires of Anthony, there did disswade ³
Great Herod to incline himselfe to Cæsar,
And leave his Master Anthony.   For this paines,
2780   Cæsar hath hang'd him :   Camindius ⁴ and the rest
That fell away, have entertainment, but
No honourable trust :   I have done ill,
Of which I do accuse my selfe so sorely,
That I will joy no more†⁵

ENTER A SOLDIER OF CÆSARS

2785   **Soldier**   Enobarbus, Anthony
Hath after thee sent all thy Treasure, with
His Bounty over-plus.   The Messenger
Came on my guard, and at thy Tent is now

790		Unloading of his Mules.
	Enobarbus	I give it you.
	Soldier	Mocke not Enobarbus,⁶

I tell you true :   Best you saf't the bringer
Out of the hoast, I must attend mine Office,
795   Or would have done't my selfe.   Your Emperor
Continues still a Jove.

[Exit]

L 380* - b : 4. 6. 7 - 28

^{LS} ₁   Ff's three short lines (7/9/5 syllables) allow minute pauses for the entry of the Messenger, the news, and
Cæsar's order to have their fullest impact: most modern texts eradicate the pauses by setting two lines (10/11) as
shown

^W ₂   F2 and most modern texts = 'Van', F1 = 'Vant'

^W ₃   though most modern texts agree with Ff and set 'disswade', one gloss = 'persuade'

^N ₄   F2 = 'Camidius', F1 = 'Camindius', most modern texts = 'Canidius'

^W ₅   F2 and most modern texts = 'more' F1 = 'mote'

^{LS} ₆   the actor has choice as to which two of these three short lines may be joined as one line of split verse

101

Enobarbus		I am alone the Villaine of the earth,
		And feele I am so most.
2800		Oh Anthony,
		Thou Mine of Bounty, how would'st thou have payed
		My better service, when my turpitude
		Thou dost so Crowne with Gold.
		This blowes my hart,
2805		If swift thought breake it not: a swifter meane
		Shall out-strike thought, but thought will doo't.
		I feele [1]
		I fight against thee: No I will go seeke
		Some Ditch, wherein to dye: the foul'st best fits
2810		My latter part of life.

[Exit]
[Alarum, Drummes and Trumpets]
ENTER AGRIPPA [2]

Agrippa	Retire, we have engag'd our selves too farre :
	Cæsar himselfe ha's worke, and our oppression
	Exceeds what we expected. [3]

[Exit]   L 380[4] b

ALARUMS.
ENTER ANTHONY, AND SCARRUS WOUNDED
[Most modern texts create a new scene here, Act Four Scene 7]

Scarrus	O my brave Emperor, this is fought indeed,
815	Had we done so at first, we had droven them home
	With clowts about[5] their heads.

[Far off][6]

Anthony	Thou bleed'st apace.
Scarrus	I had a wound heere that was like a T,
	But now 'tis made an H.
20 **Anthony**	They do retyre.

LS [1]
 most modern texts add 'I feele' to the end of the previous sentence, viz. '. . . will doo't, I feele.'

SD/WHO [2]
 most modern texts add 'Others' to the entry so Agrippa is addressing them rather than the audience

W [3]
 F2 and most modern texts = 'we expected', F1 = 'weexpected'

COMP [4]
 if set in correct chronological sequence this page should be numbered as #360: F1 sets #380

W [5]
 F2 and most modern texts = 'clowts about', F1 = 'clowtsabout'

SD [6]
 most modern texts explain this refers to the sound of a retreat, and move the stage direction down three lines to just before Anthony's 'They do retyre,'

	Scarrus	Wee'l beat 'em into Bench-holes, I have yet
		Roome for six scotches more.

ENTER EROS

	Eros	They are beaten Sir, and our advantage serves
		For a faire victory.
2825	Scarrus	Let us score their backes, ⎬
		And snatch 'em up, as we take Hares behinde,¹
		'Tis sport to maul a Runner. ⎬
	Anthony	I will reward thee
		Once for thy sprightly comfort, and ten-fold
2830		For thy good valour.
		Come thee on. ⎬
	Scarrus	Ile halt after.

	Anthony	We have beate him to his Campe: Runne one
		Before,° & let the Queen know of our guests² :³ to morrow °⁴

2835		Before the Sun shall see's, wee'l spill the blood
		That ha's to day escap'd.
		I thanke you all,
		For doughty handed are you, and have fought
		Not as you serv'd the Cause, but as't had beene
2840		Each mans like mine: you have shewne all Hectors.
		Enter the Citty, clip your Wives, your Friends,
		Tell them your feats, whil'st they with joyfull teares
		Wash the congealement from your wounds, and kisse
		The Honour'd-gashes whole.

ENTER CLEOPATRA

2845		⁵ Give me thy hand,
		To this great Faiery, Ile commend thy acts,

R 380* - b : 4. 7. 9 - 4. 8. 11

PCT ₁ Ff = 'Hares behinde,': most modern texts = 'Hares, behinde,'

W ₂ Ff = 'guests', most modern texts set the archaic word for 'deeds', viz. 'gests'

SD ₃ some modern texts add an exit for someone to exit to inform Cleopatra as Anthony bids

LS ₄ Ff's irregular opening (9/13 syllables) allows for a moment of joy before issuing the second overly-long line: most modern texts regularise the passage to two 11 syllable lines as shown

WHO/SP ₅ most modern texts indicate this is addressed to Scarrus: also, Ff set two short lines (perhaps allowing a moment for Scarrus to do as Anthony commands); most modern texts set the two lines as one

Make her thankes blesse thee.

                        Oh thou day o'th'world,

Chaine mine arm'd necke, leape thou, Attyre and all

2850   Through proofe of Harnesse to my heart, and there

Ride on the pants triumphing.

                           }

Cleopatra   Lord of Lords,[1]

Oh infinite Vertue, comm'st thou smiling from

The worlds great snare uncaught.

                          }

2855   **Anthony**   Mine [2] Nightingale,

We have beate them to their Beds. → [3]

What Gyrle, though gray

Do somthing mingle with our yonger brown, yet ha we

A Braine that nourishes our Nerves, and can

2860   Get gole for gole of youth.

                        Behold this man,

Commend unto his Lippes thy savouring [4] hand,

Kisse it my Warriour: He hath fought to day,

As if a God in hate of Mankinde, had

2865   Destroyed in such a shape.

                       }

Cleopatra   Ile give thee Friend

An Armour all of Gold: it was a Kings.

Anthony   He has deserv'd it, were it Carbunkled

Like holy Phoebus Carre.

2870   Give me thy hand,

Through Alexandria make a jolly March,

Beare our hackt Targets, like the men that owe them.

Had our great Pallace the capacity

To Campe this hoast, we all would sup together,

2875   And drinke Carowses to the next dayes Fate   R 380[5] - b

Which promises Royall perill.

                      Trumpetters

With brazen dinne blast you the Citties eare,

Make mingle with our ratling Tabourines,

2880   That heaven and earth may strike their sounds together,

Applauding our approach.

                    [Exeunt]

R 380* - b / L 361 - b : 4. 8. 12 - 39

PCT [1] F1's punctuation is slightly blurred and could be a period or a comma: F2/most modern texts set a comma

W [2] F2 and most modern texts = 'My', F1 = 'Mine'

SP [3] Ff set two short lines, allowing a silent moment for both Anthony and Cleopatra: most modern texts join the two lines together

W [4] Ff = 'savouring', most modern texts = 'favouring'

COMP [5] if set in correct chronological sequence this page should be numbered as #360: F1 sets #380

ENTER A CENTERIE, AND HIS COMPANY, ENOBARBUS FOLLOWES
[Most modern texts create a new scene here, Act Four Scene 9]

Centerie	If we be not releev'd within this houre,
	We must returne to'th'Court of Guard : the night
	Is shiny, and they say, we shall embattaile
2885	By'th'second houre i'th'Morne.
1st. Watch	This last day ° was a shrew'd one too's.
Enobarbus	Oh beare me witnesse night. °
2nd. Watch	What man is this?
1st. Watch	Stand close, and list him. °
2890 Enobarbus	Be witnesse to me (O thou blessed Moone) °
	When men revolted shall upon Record °
	Beare hatefull memory : poore Enobarbus did °
	Before thy face repent.
Centerie	Enobarbus?
2895 2nd. Watch	Peace : ° Hearke further. ° [1]
Enobarbus	Oh Soveraigne Mistris of true Melancholly,
	The poysonous dampe of night dispunge upon me,
	That Life, a very Rebell to my will,
	May hang no longer on me.
2900	Throw my heart
	Against the flint and hardnesse of my fault,
	Which being dried with greefe, will breake to powder,
	And finish all foule thoughts.
	Oh Anthony,
2905	Nobler then my revolt is Infamous,
	Forgive me in thine owne particular,
	But let the world ranke me in Register
	A Master leaver, and a fugitive :
	Oh Anthony!
2910	Oh Anthony! [2]
1st. Watch	Let's speake to him.
Centerie	Let's heare him, for the things he speakes
	May concerne Cæsar.
2nd. Watch	Let's do so, but he sleepes.
2915 Centerie	Swoonds rather, for so bad a Prayer as his

[1] Ff's irregular setting allows for moments of silence, or for dialogue to be spoken on top of each other: most
modern texts readjust both passages to almost regular pentameter as shown

SD [2] most modern texts indicate that here Enobarbus dies

Was never yet for sleepe. }

1st. Watch Go we to him.

2nd. Watch Awake sir, awake, speake to us. }

1st. Watch Heare you sir?

2920 **Centerie** The hand of death hath raught him.

[Drummes afarre off]

Hearke the Drummes ° demurely wake the sleepers :
Let us beare him ° to'th'Court of Guard : he is of note :
Our houre ° is fully out.

2nd. Watch Come on then, he may recover yet. ° 1

[exeunt] 2
ENTER ANTHONY AND SCARRUS, WITH THEIR ARMY
[Most modern texts create a new scene here, Act Four Scene 10]

2925 **Anthony** Their preparation is to day by Sea,
We please them not by Land. }

Scarrus For both, my Lord.

Anthony I would they'ld fight i'th'Fire, or i'th'Ayre,
Weel'd fight there too.
2930 But this it is, our Foote
Upon the hilles adjoyning to the Citty
Shall stay with us.
Order for Sea is given,
They have put forth the Haven : 3
2935 Where their appointment we may best discover,
And looke on their endevour.

[exeunt]

ENTER CÆSUR,4 AND HIS ARMY
[Most modern texts create a new scene here, Act Four Scene 11]

Cæsar But being charg'd, we will be still by Land,
Which as I tak't we shall, for his best force
Is forth to Man his Gallies.
2940 To the Vales, L 361 - b
And hold our best advantage.

SD 1 the irregular Ff setting (7/10/12/6/8 syllables) gives full weight to the drums before the Centerie speaks:
most modern texts restructure the passage as shown (10/11/10/12)

SD 2 most modern texts add they take Enobarbus' body off with them

PCT 3 Ff set a colon emphasising the news of what has already occurred, and where they have to report, most
modern texts replace this with a comma allowing the sequence to flow on unchecked

W/N 4 F1 = 'Cæsur', F2/most modern texts = 'Cæsar'

[exeunt]

[Alarum afarre off, as at a Sea-fight]

ENTER ANTHONY, AND SCARRUS
[Most modern texts create a new scene here, Act Four Scene 12]

Anthony	Yet they are not joyn'd:	
	Where yon'd Pine does stand,° I shall discover all.	
	Ile bring thee word ° straight, how 'tis†¹ like to go.	
	[exit]	
2945 **Scarrus**	Swallowes have built ° ²	

In Cleopatra's Sailes their nests.

The Auguries ³
Say, they know not, they cannot tell, looke grimly,
And dare not speake their knowledge.

2950   Anthony,
Is valiant, and dejected, and by starts
His fretted Fortunes give him hope and feare
Of what he has, and has not.

ENTER ANTHONY

Anthony   All is lost:
2955   This fowle Egyptian hath betrayed me:
My Fleete hath yeelded to the Foe, and yonder
They cast their Caps up, and Carowse together
Like Friends long lost.

Triple-turn'd Whore, 'tis thou
2960   Hast sold me to this Novice, and my heart
Makes onely Warres on thee.

Bid them all flye:
For when I am reveng'd upon my Charme,
I have done all.

2965   Bid them all flye, be gone. ⁴

Oh Sunne, thy uprise shall I see no more,
Fortune, and Anthony part heere, even heere
Do we shake hands?

All come to this?
2970   The hearts
That pannelled ⁵ me at heeles, to whom I gave

ᵂ ₁ F2 and most modern texts = 'tis', F1 = 'ris'

ˢᶠ ₂ the Ff setting allows for a moment of silence before both Anthony and Scarrus speak (5/10/11/4 syllables): most modern texts regularise the opening as shown (10/10/10)

ᵂ ₃ Ff = 'Auguries', most modern texts = 'augurers'

ˢᴰ ₄ most modern texts add a stage direction here for Scarrus' exit

ᵂ ₅ Ff = 'pannelled', most modern texts = 'spaniel'd'

Their wishes, do dis-Candie, melt their sweets
On blossoming Cæsar :   And this Pine is barkt,
That over-top'd them all.

2973   Betray'd I am.

Oh this false Soule of Egypt! this grave Charme,
Whose eye beck'd forth my Wars, & cal'd them home :
Whose Bosome was my Crownet, my chiefe end,
Like a right Gypsie, hath at fast and loose

2980   Beguil'd me, to the very heart of losse.

What Eros, Eros?

ENTER CLEOPATRA

Ah, thou Spell!
                          Avaunt.

Cleopatra   Why is my Lord enrag'd against his Love?

2985   **Anthony**   Vanish, or I shall give thee thy deserving,
And blemish Cæsars Triumph.
                                          Let him take thee,
And hoist thee up to the shouting Plebeians,
Follow his Chariot, like the greatest spot

2990   Of all thy Sex.
                          Most Monster-like be shewne
For poor'st Diminitives, for Dolts, and let
Patient Octavia, plough thy visage up
With her prepared nailes.

[exit Cleopatra]

2995   'Tis well th'art gone,
If it be well to live.
                          But better 'twere
Thou fell'st into my furie, for one death
Might have prevented many.

3000   Eros, hoa?

The shirt of Nessus is upon me, teach me
Alcides, thou mine Ancestor, thy rage.

Let me lodge Licas on the hornes o'th'Moone,
And with those hands that graspt the heaviest Club,

3005   Subdue my worthiest selfe :   The Witch shall die,
To the young Roman Boy she hath sold me, and I fall
Under this plot :   She dyes for't.
                                          Eros hoa?

[exit]

ENTER CLEOPATRA, CHARMIAN, IRAS, MARDIAN
[Most modern texts create a new scene here, Act Four Scene 13]

3010	Cleopatra	Helpe me my women : Oh hee's more mad Then Telamon for his Shield, the Boare of Thessaly

                     [1] Was never so imbost.

Charmian   To'th'Monument,° there locke your selfe,
And send him word you are dead :°   R 361 - b

             The Soule and Body rive not more in parting,
3015   Then greatnesse going off.

Cleopatra   To'th'Monument :
Mardian, go tell him I have slaine my selfe :
Say, that the last I spoke was Anthony,
And word it (prythee) pitteously.
3020   Hence Mardian,
And bring me how he takes my death to'th'Monument. [2]

[Exeunt]
ENTER ANTHONY, AND EROS
[Most modern texts create a new scene here, Act Four Scene 14]

Anthony   Eros, thou yet behold'st me?

Eros   I Noble Lord .

Anthony   Sometime we see a clowd that's Dragonish,
3025   A vapour sometime, like a Beare, or Lyon,
A toward [3] Cittadell, a pendant Rocke,
A forked Mountaine, or blew Promontorie
With Trees upon't, that nodde unto the world,

And mocke our eyes with Ayre .
3030   Thou hast seene these Signes,°
They are blacke Vespers Pageants .

Eros   I my Lord .° [4]

LS [1] the pauses inherent in Ff's three lines (6/8/7) suggest Charmian takes a moment before coming up with the idea, and that Cleopatra does not necessarily agree straightaway: most modern texts remove both these points by setting two lines (10/11) as shown

PCT [2] though most modern texts agree with Ff and set '. . . how he takes my death to'th'Monument.', one gloss = '. . . how he takes my death. To'th'Monument.'

W [3] Ff = 'toward', most modern texts = 'tower'd'

LS [4] the hesitations implied in Ff's irregular setting, Anthony's four short lines (6/5/7/3 syllables) followed by a short reply from Eros, would seem to match Anthony's despair -vocally: most modern texts restructure the passage as shown (11/10)

Anthony That which is now a Horse, even with a thoght
the [1] Racke dislimes,[2] and makes it indistinct
3035   As water is in water.

Eros It does my Lord.

Anthony My good Knave Eros, now thy Captaine is
Even such a body: Heere I am Anthony,
Yet cannot hold this visible shape (my Knave)[3]
3040   I made these warres for Egypt, and the Queene,
Whose heart I thought I had, for she had mine:
Which whil'st it was mine, had annext untoo't
A Million moe, (now lost:) shee Eros has
Packt Cards with Cæsars,[4] and false plaid my Glory
3045   Unto an Enemies triumph.

Nay, weepe not gentle Eros, there is left us
[5] Our selves to end our selves.

ENTER MARDIAN

Oh thy vilde Lady,° she has rob'd me of my Sword.

Mardian No Anthony,°
3050   My Mistris lov'd thee, and her Fortunes mingled °
With thine intirely.

Anthony Hence sawcy Eunuch peace,° she hath betraid me,
And shall dye the death.°

Mardian Death of one person,†[6] can be paide but once,
3055   And that she ha's discharg'd.
                              What thou would'st do
Is done unto thy hand: the last she spake
Was Anthony, most Noble Anthony.

Then in the midd'st a tearing grone did breake
3060   The name of Anthony: it was divided
Betweene her heart, and lips: she rendred life

L 362 - b : 4. 14. 9 - 33

[VP] [1] F1 - 2 set the lower-case 'the', which if not accidental would suggest Anthony slips into prose for a moment:
F3/most modern texts set the indicator of verse, the upper-case 'the'

[W] [2] Ff = 'dislimes', most modern texts = 'dislimns', an archaic word suggesting the opposite of 'paints': one other
gloss suggests 'dis-stains'

[PCT] [3] to clarify the moment some modern texts offer a period where Ff set the second part of a parenthesis

[W] [4] Ff = 'Cæsars', most modern texts = 'Cæsar'

[LS] [5] the irregular Ff setting allows Anthony to explode at Mardian (6/12 syllables); for Mardian to pause before giving
a measured reply (4/11/5); for Anthony to explode once more (11); and before Mardian speaks (5), again to take care
before reply: most modern texts restructure the text to create an overlylong 11/11/11/11/10 as shown

[W] [6] F2 and most modern texts = 'person' F1 = 'parson'

Thy name so buried in her.

Anthony	Dead then?
Mardian	Dead.

3065 Anthony Unarme [1] Eros, the long dayes taske is done,
And we must sleepe: [2] That thou depart'st hence safe
Does pay thy labour richly: Go.

[exit Mardian]

Off, plucke off,
The seven-fold shield of Ajax cannot keepe
3070 The battery from my heart.
                          Oh cleave my sides.

Heart, once be stronger then thy Continent,
Cracke thy fraile Case.
                          Apace Eros, apace;
3075 No more a Soldier: bruised peeces go,
You have bin Nobly borne.
                          From me awhile.

[exit Eros]

I will o're-take thee Cleopatra, and
Weepe for my pardon.
3080   So it must be, for now
All length is Torture: since the Torch is out,
Lye downe and stray no farther.
                          Now all labour   L 362 - b
Marres what it does: yea, very force entangles
3085 It selfe with strength: Seale then and all is done.

Eros?
          I come my Queene.
                          Eros?
                          Stay for me,
3090 Where Soules do couch on Flowers, wee'l hand in hand,
And with our sprightly Port make the Ghostes gaze:
Dido, and her Æneas shall want Troopes,
And all the haunt be ours.
                          Come Eros, Eros.

ENTER EROS

w 1 some modern texts add 'me', Ff omit the word
who 2 most modern texts indicate this is addressed to Mardian

3095	Eros	What would my Lord?
		⟩
	Anthony	Since Cleopatra dyed,
		I have liv'd in such dishonour, that the Gods
		Detest my basenesse.
		I, that with my Sword,
3100		Quarter'd the World, and o're greene Neptunes backe
		With Ships, made Cities; condemne my selfe, to lacke
		The Courage of a Woman, lesse Noble minde
		Then she which by her death, our Cæsar telles
		I am Conqueror of my selfe.
3105		Thou art sworne Eros,
		That when the exigent should come, which now
		Is come indeed: When I should see behinde me

> Th'inevitable prosecution of° disgrace and horror,
> That on my command,° thou then would'st kill me.
>
> 3110 Doo't, the time is come:° Thou strik'st not me,
> 'Tis Cæsar thou defeat'st.°
>   Put colour in thy Cheeke.
>
> Eros   The Gods with-hold me,° ¹

3115		Shall I do that which all the Parthian Darts,
		(Though Enemy) lost ayme, and could not.
	Anthony	Eros,
		Would'st thou be window'd in great Rome, and see
		Thy Master thus with pleacht Armes, bending downe
		His corrigible necke, his face subdu'de
120		To penetrative shame; whil'st the wheel'd seate
		Of Fortune Cæsar drawne before him, branded
		His Basenesse that ensued.
		⟩
	Eros	I would not see't.
	Anthony	Come then: for with a wound I must be cur'd.
125		Draw that thy honest Sword, which thou hast worne
		Most usefull for thy Country.
		⟩
	Eros	Oh sir, pardon me.
	Anthony	When I did make thee free, swor'st ÿ² not then

R 362 - b : 4. 14. 55 - 81

LS ¹ Ff's irregular setting, four lines from Anthony (overly passionate, with a moment of hesitation before beginning the second sentence - 15/10/9/12 syllables), and short line hesitation before beginning to reply for Eros (5 syllables), serves to show the enormity of the struggle within both men as the apparently inevitable need for imminent and honourable death is voiced: most modern texts regularise the lines as shown (10/10/10/10/11)

AB ² F1 = 'ÿ', (printed as such because of lack of column width): F2/most modern texts = 'thou'

	To do this when I bad thee?
3130	Do it at once,
	Or thy precedent Services are all
	But accidents unpurpos'd.
	Draw, and come.
3135	**Eros** Turne from me then that Noble countenance,
	Wherein the worship of the whole world lyes.
	Anthony Loe thee. [1]
	Eros My sword is drawne.
	Anthony Then let it do at once
	The thing why thou hast drawne it.
3140	**Eros** My deere Master,
	My Captaine, and my Emperor.
	Let me say
	Before I strike this bloody stroke, Farwell.
	Anthony 'Tis said man, and farewell.
3145	**Eros** Farewell great Chiefe.
	Shall I strike now?
	Anthony Now Eros.

[Killes himselfe]

Eros	Why there then:
	Thus I do escape the sorrow ° of Anthonies death.
3150 **Anthony**	Thrice-Nobler then my selfe,° [2]

	Thou teachest me: Oh valiant Eros, what
	I should, and thou could'st not, my Queene and Eros
	Have by their brave instruction got upon me
	A Noblenesse in Record.
155	But I will bee
	A Bride-groome in my death, and run intoo't
	As to a Lovers bed.
	Come then, and Eros,
	Thy Master dies thy Scholler; to do thus
160	I learnt of thee. [3]

R 362 - b : 4. 14. 82 - 103

SD [1] most modern texts indicate Anthony turns his face away from Eros

LS [2] the first short Ff line (3 syllables) would allow for the blow before speaking; the second long line (13) would
be his final comment; the third, short, line (6) allows for Anthony's reaction before speaking: most modern texts
both fail to regularise the passage (11/11), and often delay the stage direction until after Eros has finished speaking

SD [3] most modern texts add the stage direction that Anthony falls on his sword

How, not dead?

Not dead?

The Guard, how? [1]

Oh dispatch me.

R 362 · b

ENTER A GUARD [2]

3165 | **1st. Guard** | What's the noise?

Anthony [3]	I have done my worke ill Friends:
	Oh make an end ° of what I have begun.
2nd. Guard	The Starre is falne.°
1st. Guard	And time is at his Period.
All	Alas,° and woe.
Anthony	Let him that loves me, strike me dead.°

3170 (All)

1st. Guard	Not I.
2nd. Guard	Nor I.
3rd. Guard	Nor any one.

[exeunt]

3175 | **{Dercetius}** [4] | Thy death and fortunes bid thy folowers fly [5] |
|---|---|
| | This sword but shewne to Cæsar with this tydings, |
| | Shall enter me with him. |

ENTER DIOMEDES

Diomedes	Where's Anthony?
{Decretas}	There Diomed there.
Diomedes	Lives he :° wilt thou not answer man? ° [6]

3180

W [1] Ff = 'how', most modern texts = 'ho'

P/N [2] since before the next entry involving Diomedes the character F2-4 refers to as 'Decre.' speaks, most modern texts set an entry for Decretas here, accompanying the members of the Guard

LS [3] with the Guards' first line being combined with Anthony's call for help, the Ff setting allows for a slight pause (for the Guards to discover or attempt to help him?) before Anthony speaks: most modern texts prefer to restructure as shown

P/N [4] Fl alone uses the prefix 'Dercetius' here, and then just 'Decre.' for his next speech: F2-4 refer to 'Decre.', and both texts set 'Dec.' in what modern texts term Act Five Scene 1, page 120 this script: however, at the top of the page, Ff set the stage direction 'Enter Decretas with the Sword of Anthony' and he names himself as 'Decretius', line 3348, on the same page

PCT [5] F1-2 set no punctuation as if the two thoughts run into each other, F3 and most modern texts print a period

SD [6] most modern texts indicate Decretas now exits with Anthony's sword

114

Anthony	Art thou there Diomed?
	Draw thy sword, and give mee,° ¹
	Suffising strokes for death.
	⟩
Diomedes	Most absolute Lord:
	My Mistris Cleopatra sent me to thee.
Anthony	When did shee send thee?
	⟩
Diomedes	Now my Lord.
	⟩
Anthony	Where is she?
Diomedes	Lockt in her Monument: she had a Prophesying feare†
	Of what hath come to passe: for when she saw
	(Which never shall be found) you did suspect
	She had dispos'd with Cæsar, and that your rage
	Would not be purg'd, she sent you ² word she was dead:
	But fearing since how it might worke, hath sent
	Me to proclaime the truth, and I am come
	I dread, too late.
Anthony	Too late good Diomed: call my Guard I prythee.
Diomedes	³ What hoa: the Emperors Guard,
	The Guard, what hoa?°
	Come, your Lord calles.°

3185

3190

3195

3200

ENTER 4 OR 5 OF THE GUARD OF ANTHONY

Anthony	Beare me good Friends where Cleopatra bides,
	'Tis the last service that I shall command you.
1st. Guard	Woe, woe are we sir, you may not live to weare
	All your true Followers out.
	⟩
All	Most heavy day.

3205

L 363 - b : 4. 14. 116 - 134

LS ¹ starting on the previous page, the Ff irregular setting allows for the following
     a) two short lines from Diomedes and Decretas (4 + 5 syllables) allowing a moment for
        Diomedes to move to Anthony
     b) a short (8 syllable) line for Diomedes, split into 'Lives he', Decretas' non reply,
        then 'wilt thou not answer man?'
     c) a short (6 syllable) line from Anthony, spoken after Decretas' exit
     d) a short line from Anthony spoken in pain after Diomedes tries to aid him
  most modern texts regularise the passage as shown

W ² at least one modern text omits 'you' so as to maintain the pentameter

LS ³ the Ff setting's first, short (7 syllables), line allows Diomedes to call and for there to be no immediate
response, so he has to call again (8): in elongating the first line (11) most modern texts remove the dreadful pause
when the audience/Diomedes fears perhaps everyone has fled and no one is left to come

115

Anthony	Nay good my Fellowes, do not please sharp fate
	To grace it with your sorrowes.
	Bid that welcome
	Which comes to punish us, and we punish it
3210	Seeming to beare it lightly.
	Take me up,
	I have led you oft, carry me now good Friends,
	And have my thankes for all.

[Exit bearing Anthony] [1]

**ENTER CLEOPATRA, AND HER MAIDES ALOFT, WITH
CHARMIAN & IRAS**

[Most modern texts create a new scene here, Act Four Scene 15]

Cleopatra	Oh Charmian, I will never go from hence.
3215 Charmian	Be comforted deere Madam.
	}
Cleopatra	No, I will not:
	All strange and terrible events are welcome,
	But comforts we dispise; our size of sorrow
	Proportion'd to our cause, must be as great
3220	As that which makes it.

ENTER DIOMED [2]

	How now? is he dead?
Diomedes	His death's upon him, but not dead.
	Looke out o'th other side your Monument,
	His Guard have brought him thither.

ENTER ANTHONY, AND THE GUARD.   L 363 - b

225 Cleopatra	Oh Sunne,
	Burne the great Sphere thou mov'st in, darkling stand

      [3] The varrying shore o'th'world.

                             O Antony,° Antony, Antony [4]

      Helpe Charmian, / helpe Iras helpe:° helpe Friends

230   Below, / let's draw him hither.°

SD [1] most modern texts indicate they carry out Eros too

SD [2] most modern texts indicate the 'non-Cleopatra and her women' action occurs 'below', i.e. at normal stage level

LS [3] Ff's irregular setting (17/10/7 syllables) allows Cleopatra a huge release on Anthony's name: the attempt by most modern texts attempt to regularise the passage still sets up other peculiar less concentrated irregularities, (for example, 11/14/9 syllables as shown by the symbol °)

PCT [4] F1 - 2 set no punctuation which could suggest that Cleopatra runs her cries into the appeals for help: however, since the letter 'h' is removed from the normal setting of Anthony's name, probably the period was omitted for lack of room: F3/most modern texts set a period

116

Anthony	[1] Peace, Not Cæsars Valour hath o'rethrowne Anthony, But Anthonie's/ hath Triumpht on it selfe.
Cleopatra	So it should be, / That none but Anthony ° should conquer Anthony. / But woe 'tis so. °

3235

Anthony   I am dying Egypt, dying;   onely
                 I heere importune death a-while, untill
                 Of many thousand kisses, the poore last

3240   I lay upon thy lippes.

Cleopatra   I dare not Deere,
                 Deere my Lord pardon: I dare not,[2]
                 Least I be taken: nor th'Imperious shew
                 Of the full-Fortun'd Cæsar, ever shall

3245   Be brooch'd with me, if Knife, Drugges, Serpents have
                 Edge, sting, or operation.
                           I am safe:
                 Your Wife Octavia, with her modest eyes,
                 And still Conclusion, shall acquire no Honour

3250   Demuring upon me: but come, come Anthony,
                 Helpe me my women, we must draw thee up:
                 Assist good Friends.

Anthony   Oh quicke, or I am gone.

Cleopatra   Heere's sport indeede: → [3]
3255   How heavy weighes my Lord?

                 Our strength is all gone into heavinesse,
                 That makes the waight.
                           Had I great Juno's powcr,
                 The strong wing'd Mercury should fetch thee up,

3260   As set thee by Joves side.
                           Yet come a little,
                 Wishes were ever Fooles.
                        Oh comc, come, come,[4]

[LS 1] Ff's six irregular lines (1/11/11/4/12/4 syllables) allow for breaks and silences within Cleopatra's speech supporting and enlarging Anthony's view of his death: most modern texts regularise the passage in one of two ways as shown by the symbols ° and /

[LS 2] the ending of this short (8 syllable) line has been subject to much conjecture: commentators have suggested adding 'descend' or 'open', though most modern texts leave the Ff setting alone

[SD 3] from both the dialogue and these two short Ff lines (4/6 syllables) it seems the attempt to raise Anthony to the upper level has begun: surprisingly, most modern texts place the direction after 'Oh come, come, come' (which seems to be the end of the lifting, not the beginning: not so surprisingly they also join the two short lines together

[SD 4] most modern texts indicate that this is when Anthony is lifted up to Cleopatra (see the previous footnote)

117

[They heave Anthony aloft to Cleopatra]

And welcome, welcome.
3265   Dye when thou hast liv'd,
Quicken with kissing :   had my lippes that power,
Thus would I weare them out.

All   A heavy sight.

Anthony   I am dying Egypt, dying. [1]

3270   Give me some Wine, and let me speake a little.

Cleopatra   No, let me speake, and let me rayle so hye,
That the false Huswife Fortune, breake her Wheele,
Provok'd by my offence.

Anthony   One word (sweet Queene)
3275   Of Cæsar seeke your Honour, with your safety.
                                                    Oh.

Cleopatra   They do not go together.

Anthony   Gentle heare me,
None about Cæsar trust, but Proculeius.

3280 Cleopatra My Resolution, and my hands, Ile trust,
None about Cæsar.

Anthony   The miserable change now at my end,
Lament nor sorrow at :   but please your thoughts
In feeding them with those my former Fortunes
3285   Wherein I lived. [2]
                        The greatest Prince o'th'world,
The Noblest :   and do now not basely dye,
Not Cowardly put off my Helmet to
My Countreyman.
3290   A Roman, by a Roman
Valiantly vanquish'd.
                        Now my Spirit is going,
I can no more. [3]

Cleopatra   Noblest of men, woo't dye?

[LS 1] the actor has choice as to which two of these three short lines may be joined as one line of split verse

[PCT 2] most modern texts alter Ff's period to a colon: the Ff setting could indicate a strong need to pause (the pain perhaps?)

[SD 3] there is no Ff indication as to when Anthony actually dies: modern texts indicate various spots from here throughout Cleopatra's next speech: the most frequent suggestion is just after her line 'Oh see my women:/The Crowne o'th'earth doth melt'

3295

Hast thou no care of me, shall I abide
In this dull world, which in thy absence is
No better then a Stye?
                    Oh see my women :
The Crowne o'th'earth doth melt.

3300
                                        My Lord?

Oh wither'd is the Garland of the Warre,   R 363 - b
The Souldiers pole is falne :   young Boyes and Gyrles
Are levell now with men :   The oddes is gone,
And there is nothing left remarkeable

3305
                    ¹ Beneath the visiting Moone. ²

Charmian	Oh quietnesse, Lady.
Iras	She's dead too, our Soveraigne.
Charmian	Lady.
Iras	Madam.
3310 Charmian	Oh Madam, Madam, Madam.
Iras	Royall Egypt : Empresse.
Charmian	Peace, peace, Iras. ³

Cleopatra

No more but in ⁴ a Woman, and commanded
By such poore passion, as the Maid that Milkes,

3315
And doe's the meanest chares.
                                    It were for me,
To throw my Scepter at the injurious Gods,
To tell them that this World did equall theyrs,
Till they had stolne our Jewell.

3320
                                        All's but naught :
Patience is sottish, and impatient does
Become a Dogge that's mad :   Then is it sinne,
To rush into the secret house of death,
Ere death dare come to us.

3325
                                    How do you Women?
What, what ⁵ good cheere?
                    Why how now Charmian?

R 363 - b / L 364 - b   :   4. 15. 60 - 83

LS ₁
there are various combinations for the eight ambiguous (short) Ff lines; one of the most common is shown here,
but the text, verse or prose, could be grouped in several permutations, and sometimes spoken one on top of
another

SD ₂
most modern texts indicate that here Cleopatra faints

SD ₃
most modern texts indicate this is spoken because Cleopatra has begun to move

▼ ₄
Ff = 'in', most modern texts = 'e'en'

▼ ₅
most modern texts add a comma here, viz 'What, what, good cheer', Ff = 'What, what good cheere'

> My Noble Gyrles?
>   Ah Women, women!
>   Looke
> Our Lampe is spent, it's out.
>   Good sirs, take heart,
> Wee'l bury him: And then, what's brave, what's Noble,
> Let's doo't after the high Roman fashion,
> And make death proud to take us.
>   Come, away,
> This case of that huge Spirit now is cold.
>
> Ah Women, Women!
>   Come, we have no Friend
> But Resolution, and the breefest end.

3330

3335

3340

[Exeunt, bearing of Anthonies[+1] body]
ENTER CÆSAR, AGRIPPA, DOLLABELLA, MENAS,[2] WITH
HIS COUNSELL OF WARRE
[Most modern texts create a new scene here, Act Five Scene 1]

Cæsar	Go to him Dollabella, bid him yeeld, Being so frustrate, tell him, He[3] mockes ° the pawses that he makes.
Dolabella	Cæsar, I shall. ° [4] [5]

ENTER DECRETAS WITH THE SWORD OF ANTHONY

Cæsar	Wherefore is that? And what art thou that dar'st Appeare thus to us?
Decretas	I am call'd Decretas, Marke Anthony I serv'd, who best was worthie Best to be serv'd: whil'st he stood up, and spoke He was my Master, and I wore my life To spend upon his haters. If thou please To take me to thee, as I was to him,

3345

3350

[W1] F1 = 'Authonies', F2/most modern texts = 'Anthonies'

[SD2] most modern texts alter and expand the entry: since one set of Ff prefixes refers to 'Mec.' not 'Me.' or 'Men.' they replace Menas with Mecenas: they add Proculeius (who speaks in this scene) and Gallus (whom Cæsar orders to accompany Proculeius later in the scene)

[W3] Ff = 'He mockes', some modern texts add 'but', viz. 'He but mockes' to maintain the pentameter

[SD4] most modern texts indicate Dolabella now leaves

[LS5] the irregular Ff opening (10/7/8 syllables) might suggest Cæsar is having difficulty maintaining self-control: as ever, most modern texts regularise the text as shown, often adding an extra word to maintain normal pentameter (see footnote #3 above)

3355

> Ile be to Cæsar: if ÿ¹ pleasest not,° I yeild thee up my life.
>
> Cæsar   What is't thou say'st? °²

Decretas   I say (Oh Cæsar) Anthony is dead.

Cæsar   The breaking of so great a thing, should make
A greater cracke.

3360   The round³ World
Should have shooke Lyons into civill streets,
And Cittizens to their dennes.
                    The death of Anthony
Is not a single doome, in the⁴ name lay

3365   A moity of the world.

Decretas   He is dead Cæsar,
Not by a publike minister of Justice,
Nor by a hyred Knife, but that selfe-hand
Which writ his Honor in the Acts it did,

3370   Hath with the Courage which the heart did lend it,
Splitted the heart.
                    This is his Sword,
I robb'd his wound of it: behold it stain'd
With his most Noble blood.

3375   Cæsar   Looke you sad Friends,⁵   L 364 - b
The Gods rebuke me, but it is Tydings⁶
To wash the eyes of Kings.

{Dolabella}⁷   And strange it is,
That Nature must compell us to lament

3380

> ⁸ Our most persisted deeds.
>
> Mecenas   His taints and Honours,° wag'd⁹ equal with him.
>
> {Dolabella}   A Rarer spirit never °

L 364 - b / R 364 - b : 5. 1. 11 - 31

AB ¹ F1 = ÿ, (printed as such because of lack of column width), F2/most modern texts = thou

LS ² the Ff irregularity (16/4 syllables) suggests that Decretas' final over-long statement is very passionate, and that
Cæsar is momentarily puzzled and silenced by the offer: most modern texts regularise the passage as shown (10/10)

W ³ Ff = 'round': the most used modern gloss = 'ruin'd', though one interesting gloss = 'reaved'

W ⁴ though most modern texts agree with Ff and set 'the', one gloss = 'its'

W ⁵ F1-2 = 'Looke you sad Friends', F3 = 'Looke you, sad Friends', one modern gloss = 'Looke you sad, Friends'

W ⁶ F1 = 'it is Tydings', F2 and most modern texts = 'it is a Tydings'

P ⁷ Ff set a problem, for shortly after these two speeches Cæsar asks where Dolabella might be, then remembers
he has already sent him away on a task (lines 3930 - 34 his script): thus, most modern editors assign the two Ff
Dolabella speeches to Agrippa

LS ⁸ the Ff irregular setting (6/10/6 or 7 syllables) seems to suggest the Agrippa/Dolabella character at a loss for
words, and that Mecenas offers a word of help: most modern texts regularise the passage as shown (11/11 or 12)

W ⁹ though some modern texts agree with Ff and set 'wag'd', others use the gloss 'weigh'd'

	Did steere humanity: but you Gods will give us
	Some faults to make us men.
3385	Cæsar is touch'd.

Mecenas   When such a spacious Mirror's set before him,
He needes must see himselfe.

}

Cæsar   Oh Anthony,
I have followed thee to this, but we do launch [1]
3390   Diseases in our Bodies.
I must perforce
Have shewne to thee such a declining day,
Or looke on thine: we could not stall together,
In the whole world.
3395   But yet let me lament
With teares as Soveraigne as the blood of hearts,
That thou my Brother, my Competitor,
In top of all designe; my Mate in Empire,
Friend and Companion in the front of Warre,
3400   The Arme of mine owne Body, and the Heart
Where mine his thoughts did kindle; that our Starres
Unreconciliable, should divide ° our equalnesse to this.
Heare me good Friends,° [2]
But I will tell you at some meeter Season,
3405   The businesse of this man lookes out of him,
Wee'l heare him what he sayes.

ENTER AN ÆGYPTIAN

Whence are you?

Ægyptian   A poore Egyptian yet, the Queen my mistris
Confin'd in all, she has her Monument [3]
3410   Of thy intents, desires, instruction, [4]
That she preparedly may frame her selfe
To'th'way shee's forc'd too. [5]

Cæsar   Bid her have good heart,

R 364-b : 5. 1. 32 -56

[1] though some modern texts agree with Ff and set 'launch', others accept the gloss 'lance'

[2] the Ff irregular setting (15/4) shows a rhetorically shaken Cæsar: most modern texts readjust to show much more self-control (9/10 syllables)

[3] Ff — 'A poore Egyptian yet, the Queen my mistris/Confin'd in all, she has her Monument'; most modern texts modify the two commas to make more sense, vlz. 'A poore Egyptian yet; the Queen my mistris/Confin'd in all she has, her Monument': however, it could be that the Egyptian is nervous, and, as with Peter Quince's Prologue in Act Five of *A Midsommer Nights Dreame*, the peculiar punctuation might give spoken evidence of his nerves: see also footnote #3, next page

[4] Ff = 'desires, instruction', most modern texts = 'desires instruction'

[5] F1 = 'too', F2 and most modern texts = 'to'

3415

                                    }
                      She soone shall know of us, by some of ours,
                      How honourable, and how kindely Wee

        ¹   Determine for her.

                                    For Cæsar cannot leave °² to be ungentle ³

Ægyptian   So the Gods preserve thee.°

[Exit]

Cæsar   Come hither Proculeius.

3420   Go and say
                      We purpose her no shame: give her what comforts
                      The quality of her passion shall require;
                      Least in her greatnesse, by some mortall stroke
                      She do defeate us.

3425   For her life in Rome,
                      Would be eternall in our Triumph: Go,
                      And with your speediest bring us what she sayes,
                      And how you finde of her.

Proculeius   Cæsar I shall.   }

[Exit Proculeius]

3430 **Cæsar**   ⁴ Gallus, go you along:⁵ where's Dolabella,° to se-
                      cond Proculeius?

      All   Dolabella.°

      Cæsar   Let him alone: for I remember now
                      How hee's imployed: he shall in time be ready.

3435   Go with me to my Tent, where you shall see
                      How hardly I was drawne into this Warre,
                      How calme and gentle I proceeded still
                      In all my Writings.
                                    Go with me, and see
3440   What I can shew in this.

R 364 - b : 5. 1. 57 -77

LS ₁
F1 sets for Cæsar a final 16 syllable line, which if allowed to stand is a wonderful indication of the self -indulgent
pomposity that Cæsar sometimes reveals: this would make the potential interruption by the Egyptian (see footnote
#3) even funnier

W ₂
Ff = 'leave', most modern texts = 'live': one modern gloss = 'learn'

PCT ₃
most modern texts add a period, while Ff set no punctuation, as if the Egyptian interrupted him: initially it
seems highly unlikely that anyone would interrupt Cæsar, though if the Egyptian is as nervous and gauche as two
earlier footnotes might indicate, the potential for interruption could be very funny

LS ₄
the words of the text suggest Cæsar is flustered (calling for Dolabella when he has already despatched him on
another errand): Ff's highly irregular verse or prose setting (18/4) clearly highlights the fluster: most modern texts
readjust the passage to slightly long verse lines (11/11 syllables), almost wiping out the original Ff fluster

SD ₅
most modern texts add an exit for Gallus

[Exeunt]
ENTER CLEOPATRA, CHARMIAN, IRAS, AND MARDIAN [1]
[Most modern texts create a new scene here, Act Five Scene 2]

Cleopatra	My desolation does begin to make	
	A better life : Tis paltry to be Cæsar :	
	Not being Fortune, hee's but Fortunes knave,	
	A minister of her will : and it is great	R 364 - b
3445	To do that thing that ends all other deeds,	
	Which shackles accedents, and bolts up change ;	
	Which sleepes, and never pallates more the dung,[2]	
	The beggers Nurse, and Cæsars.	

ENTER PROCULEIUS [3]

Proculeius	Cæsar sends greeting to the Queene of Egypt,	
3450	And bids thee study on what faire demands	
	Thou mean'st to have him grant thee.	
	}	
Cleopatra	What's thy name?	
Proculeius	My name is Proculeius.	
	}	
Cleopatra	Anthony	
3455	Did tell me of you, bad me trust you, but	
	I do not greatly care to be deceiv'd	
	That have no use for trusting.	

If your Master
Would have a Queene[†4] his begger, you must tell him,
3460 That Majesty to keepe decorum, must
No lesse begge then a Kingdome : If he please
To give me conquer'd Egypt for my Sonne,
He gives me so much of mine owne, as I
Will kneele to him with thankes.
}

465	Proculeius	Be of good cheere :
		Y'are falne into a Princely hand, feare nothing,
		Make your full reference freely to my Lord,
		Who is so full of Grace, that it flowes over

R 364 - b / L 365 - b : 5. 2. 1 - 24

SD [1] most modern texts exclude Mardian from the entry, arguing he has neither speech nor action in the scene, and one or other would be expected during the farewells and death of Iras and Cleopatra: however, Cleopatra speaks a very strange phrase 'Sirrah Iras, go', line 3732, page 134 this script, strange in that Iras is a woman: perhaps this is when Mardian leaves, Cleopatra deliberately sparing him witnessing her death

W [2] though most modern texts agree with Ff and set 'dung', one gloss = 'dugge'

SD [3] some modern texts add Gallus and his soldiers to the Proculeius entry, though supposedly unseen by Cleopatra: M. R. Ridley effectively sums up and dismisses the suggested reasons for the addition, pages 247- 255 and footnote to lines 35,36, pages 210-1, *The Arden Shakespeare, Anthony and Cleopatra*, op. cit.

W [4] F2 and most modern texts = 'Queene', F1 = 'Queece'

		On all that neede.
3470		Let me report to him
		Your sweet dependacie,[1] and you shall finde
		A Conqueror that will pray in ayde for kindnesse,
		Where he for grace is kneel'd too.
		}
	Cleopatra	Pray you tell him,
3475		I am his Fortunes Vassall, and I send him
		The Greatnesse he has got.
		I hourely learne
		A Doctrine of Obedience, and would gladly
		Looke him i'th'Face.
3480	Proculeius	This Ile report (deere Lady)
		Have comfort, for I know your plight is pittied
		Of him that caus'd it.[2]

	Proculeius	You see how easily she may be surpriz'd:
		[3] Guard her till Cæsar come.
3485	Iras	Royall Queene.
	Charmian	Oh Cleopatra, thou art taken Queene.
	Cleopatra	Quicke, quicke, good hands.
	Proculeius	Hold worthy Lady, hold:[4]
		Doe not your selfe such wrong, who are in this
3490		Releev'd, but not betraid.
	Cleopatra	What of death too ° that rids our dogs of languish[5]
	Proculeius	Cleopatra,° do not abuse my Masters bounty, by[6]

		Th'undoing of your selfe: Let the World see
		His Noblenesse well acted, which your death
3495		Will never let come forth.
		}
	Cleopatra	Where art thou Death?

W 1
F2 and most modern texts = 'dependancy', F1 = 'dependacie'

SD 2
most modern texts add a stage direction here indicating that Gallus and his troop of Soldiers enter from
behind and seize Cleopatra and reassign Proculeius' next speech to Gallus (line 3483): there are various possible
permutations of the following five short lines, though, as seen earlier, many of them may be spoken one on top of
another

WHO 3
most modern texts indicate this is addressed to Gallus and his Soldiers

SD 4
most modern texts indicate Cleopatra has drawn a dagger, and that Proculeius disarms her during his line

PCT 5
F1 = no punctuation (possibly as if Proculeius interrupts her): F2 and most modern texts print a question mark

LS 6
Ff's irregular setting (6/11/14 syllables) allows Cleopatra a moment of recovery before being firmly interrupted
by Proculeius (see the previous footnote): most modern texts restructure the passage as shown (10/11/10)

	Come hither come; Come, come, and take a Queene Worth many Babes and Beggers.
Proculeius	Oh temperance Lady.

3500 Cleopatra Sir, I will eate no meat,[1] Ile not drinke sir,
If idle talke will once be necessary
Ile not sleepe neither.
                   This mortall house Ile ruine,
Do Cæsar what he can.
3505   Know sir, that I
Will not waite pinnion'd at your Masters Court,
Nor once be chastic'd with the sober eye
Of dull Octavia.
                  Shall they hoyst me up,
3510 And shew me to the showting Varlotarie
Of censuring Rome?
                  Rather a ditch in Egypt.[2]

Be gentle grave unto me, rather on Nylus mudde
Lay me starke-nak'd, and let the water-Flies
3515 Blow me into abhorring; rather make
My Countries high pyramides my Gibbet,
And hang me up in Chaines.

Proculeius You do extend
These thoughts of horror further then you shall
3520 Finde cause in Cæsar.

ENTER DOLABELLA

Dolabella Proculeius,
What thou hast done, thy Master Cæsar knowes,
And he hath sent for thee: for the Queene,
Ile take her to my Guard.

525 Proculeius So Dolabella,
It shall content me best: Be gentle to her,
[3] To Cæsar I will speake, what you shall please,
If you'l imploy me to him.

[Exit Proculeius]

Cleopatra Say, I would dye.

L 365 · b

W [1] the photostatted reproductions of F1 show a somewhat blurred punctuation which could be either a comma or a period: F2/most modern texts set a comma

PCT [2] F3/most modern texts remove the period, and set no punctuation in its place: F2 sets a comma

WHO [3] most modern texts indicate this is addressed to Cleopatra

3530	Dolabella	Most Noble Empresse, you have heard of me. [1]
	Cleopatra	I cannot tell.
	Dolabella	Assuredly you know me. } .
	Cleopatra	No matter sir, what I have heard or knowne:
		You laugh when Boyes or Women tell their Dreames,
3535		Is't not your tricke?
	Dolabella	I understand not, Madam. }
	Cleopatra	I dreampt there was an Emperor Anthony.
		Oh such another sleepe, that I might see
		But such another man.
3540	Dolabella	If it might please ye. }
	Cleopatra	His face was as the Heav'ns, and therein stucke
		A Sunne and Moone, which kept their course, & lighted
		The little o'th'earth. [2]
	Dolabella	Most Soveraigne Creature. }
3545	Cleopatra	His legges bestrid the Ocean, his rear'd arme
		Crested the world: His voyce was propertied
		As all the tuned Spheres, and that to Friends:
		But when he meant to quaile, and shake the Orbe,
		He was as ratling Thunder.
3550		For his Bounty,
		There was no winter in't.
		An Anthony it was,[3]
		That grew the more by reaping: His delights
		Were Dolphin-like, they shew'd his backe above
3555		The Element they liv'd in: In his Livery
		Walk'd Crownes and Crownets: Realms & Islands were
		As plates dropt from his pocket. }
	Dolabella	Cleopatra.
	Cleopatra	Thinke you there was, or might be such a man
3560		As this I dreampt of? }
	Dolabella	Gentle Madam, no.

R 365 - b : 5. 2. 71 - 94

[1] Ff set this line as a statement, ending it with a period: most modern texts end with a question mark

[2] Ff = 'o'th'earth', most modern texts = 'O, the earth', one gloss = 'O o'th'earth'

[3] Ff = 'An Anthony it was', most modern texts = 'an autumn t'was'

Cleopatra	You Lye up to the hearing of the Gods:
	But if there be, nor [1] ever were one such
	It's past the size of dreaming: Nature wants stuffe
3565	To vie strange formes with fancie, yet t'imagine
	An Anthony were Natures peece, 'gainst Fancie,
	Condemning shadowes quite.
	}
Dolabella	Heare me, good Madam:
	Your losse is as your selfe, great; and you beare it
3570	As answering to the waight, would I might never
	Ore-take pursu'de successe: But I do feele
	By the rebound of yours, a greefe that suites [2]
	My very heart at roote.
	}
Cleopatra	I thanke you sir:
3575	Know you what Cæsar meanes to do with me?
Dolabella	I am loath to tell you what, I would you knew,
Cleopatra	Nay pray you sir.
Dolabella	Though he be Honourable.
	}
Cleopatra	Hee'l leade me then in Triumph. [3]
3580	Dolabella	Madam he will I know't.

[Flourish]
ENTER PROCULEIUS, CÆSAR, GALLUS, MECENAS,
AND OTHERS OF HIS TRAINE

All	Make way there Cæsar. [4]	R 365 - b
Cæsar	Which is the Queene of Egypt.	
Dolabella	It is the Emperor Madam.	

[Cleo.{patra} kneeles]

Cæsar	Arise, you shall not kneele:
585	I pray you rise, rise Egypt.

W [1] F3 and most modern texts = 'or', F1-2 = 'nor'

W [2] Ff = 'suites', most modern texts = 'smites', one gloss = 'shoots'

PCT [3] one early editor suggests altering Ff's period (inferring that Cleopatra is making an already understood statement) to a question mark

SD [4] most modern texts delay the entry until after the next line: Ff's placing is probably because the depth of the original stage would set a long entry before Cæsar reached Cleopatra: also it could suggest that while the Roman Soldiers would automatically clear a path for Cæsar, those of Cleopatra's train would (deliberately?) not

Cleopatra	Sir, the gods ° will have it thus,
	My Master and my Lord ° I must obey,[1]
Caesar	Take to you no hard thoughts,° [2]
3590	The Record of what injuries you did us,
	Though written in our flesh, we shall remember
	As things but done by chance.
	}
Cleopatra	Sole Sir o'th'World,
	I cannot project mine owne cause so well
	To make it cleare, but do confesse I have
3595	Bene laden with like frailties, which before
	Have often sham'd our Sex.
	}
Caesar	Cleopatra know,
	We will extenuate rather then inforce :
	If you apply your selfe to our intents,
3600	Which towards you are most gentle, you shall finde
	A benefit in this change : but if you seeke
	To lay on me a Cruelty, by taking
	Anthonies course, you shall bereave your selfe
	Of my good purposes, and put your children
3605	To that destruction which Ile guard them from,
	If thereon you relye. Ile take my leave.
Cleopatra	And may through all the world : tis yours, & wc
	your[3] Scutcheons, and your signes of Conquest shall
3610	Hang in what place you please.
	Here my good Lord.
Caesar	You shall advise me in all for Cleopatra.
Cleopatra	[4] This is the breefe : of Money, Plate, & Jewels
	I am possest of, 'tis exactly valewed,

L 366 - b : 5. 2. 115 - 139

W [1] F1 - 3 set a comma as if Cæsar interrupts her: F4/most modern texts set a period

LS [2] Ff's irregular setting (7/7/10/6 syllables) delicately illustrates the diplomatic, power struggle between the two leaders

    a) Cleopatra's slight pause before and after her first line point up both her refusal to stop kneeling, and her clear statement that to her the gods are more important than Cæsar: the passive-aggressive nature of the remark is emphasised even more with F1-3 setting a comma to end the speech as if her statement was left uncompleted for Cæsar to draw his own conclusions: (most modern texts follow F4 and replace the comma with a period)

    b) Cæsar taking a moment of self-control before replying
most modern texts regularise the passage as shown (10/10/10)

VP [3] F1 -2 set a lower-case 'your', which, if not accidental, would suggest Cleopatra momentarily slips out of verse: F3/most modern texts set the indicator of verse, the upper-case 'Your'

SD [4] most modern texts indicate Cleopatra hands Cæsar a document

3615		Not petty things admitted.
		Where's Seleucus? [1]
	Seleucus	Heere Madam.
	Cleopatra	This is my Treasurer, let him speake (my Lord)
		Upon his perill, that I have reserv'd
3620		To my selfe nothing.
		Speake the truth Seleucus.

Seleucus	[2] Madam,° I had rather seele my lippes,
	Then to my perill ° speake that which is not.
Cleopatra	What have I kept backe.°

3625	Seleucus	Enough to purchase what you have made known [3]
	Cæsar	Nay blush not Cleopatra, I approve
		Your Wisedome in the deede.
	Cleopatra	See Cæsar: Oh behold,
		How pompe is followed: Mine will now be yours,
3630		And should we shift estates, yours would be mine.
		The ingratitude of this Seleucus, does
		Even make me wilde.
		Oh Slave, of no more trust
		Then love that's hyr'd?
3635		What goest thou backe, y̎ [4] shalt
		Go backe I warrant thee: but Ile catch thine eyes
		Though they had wings.
		Slave, Soule-lesse,[5] Villain, Dog.
		O rarely base!
3640	Cæsar	Good Queene, let us intreat you.
	Cleopatra	O Cæsar, what a wounding shame is this,
		That thou vouchsafing heere to visit me,
		Doing the Honour of thy Lordlinesse

SD [1]
since Ff do not set Seleucus a specific point or time of entry, most modern texts have him either come forward or enter once called: for further details see *William Shakespeare: A Textual Companion*, op. cit., page 553, footnote to 5.2.136.1/2792.1

LS [2]
Ff's irregular setting (9/10/5 syllables) provides a tiny pause before Seleucus starts to speak, and a much bigger one after he drops his bombshell before Cleopatra begins her doomed attempt at damage control: not only does the modern texts' restructuring create a new, and strange, irregularity (2/11 or 12/5 + 5 syllables), it also removes the hesitation before Cleopatra replies

PCT [3]
F1 = no punctuation (possibly as if Cleopatra interrupts him), F2 and most modern texts print a period

AB [4]
F1 = y̎, (printed as such because of lack of column width), F2/most modern texts = 'thou'

PCT/W [5]
most modern texts omit Ff's comma and set 'Soule-less Villain'

To one so meeke, that mine owne Servant should
3645   Parcell the summe of my disgraces, by
Addition of his Envy.
                     Say (good Cæsar)
That I some Lady trifles have reserv'd,
Immoment toyes, things of such Dignitie
3650   As we greet moderne Friends withall, and say
Some Nobler token I have kept apart
For Livia and Octavia, to induce
Their mediation, must I be unfolded
With one that I have bred : The Gods! it smites me
3655   Beneath the fall I have.
               [1] Prythee go hence,   L 366 - b
Or I shall shew the Cynders of my spirits
Through th'Ashes of my chance : Wer't thou a man,
Thou would'st have mercy on me.
                    }

3660   **Cæsar**   Forbeare Seleucus. [2]

  Cleopatra   Be it known, that we the greatest are mis-thoght
For things that others do : and when we fall,
We answer others merits,[3] in our name
Are therefore to be pittied.
           }

3665   **Cæsar**   Cleopatra,
Not what you have reserv'd, nor what acknowledg'd
Put we i'th'Roll of Conquest : still bee't yours,
Bestow it at your pleasurc, and beleeve
Cæsars no Merchant, to make prize with you
3670   Of things that Merchants sold.
                    Therefore be cheer'd,
Make not your thoughts your prisons : No deere Queen,
For we intend so to dispose you, as
Your selfe shall give us counsell : Feede, and sleepe :
3675   Our care and pitty is so much upon you,
That we remaine your Friend, and so adieu.

  Cleopatra   My Master, and my Lord.
                  }

  Cæsar   Not so : Adieu.

[Flourish]
EXEUNT CÆSAR, AND HIS TRAINE [4]

L 366 - b / R 366 - b : 5. 2. 161 - 190

[1] most modern texts indicate this is addressed to Seleucus

[2] most modern texts provide Seleucus with an exit, though to leave him on stage till Cæsar's exit could have much theatrical merit

[3] most modern texts move Ff's comma to the end of the line, viz 'others merits in our name,'

[4] this exit should draw extra attention (being printed unusually on a separate line, not alongside the text)

Cleopatra	He words me Gyrles, he words me,

3680

That I should not ° be Noble to my selfe.

¹ But hearke thee Charmian.° ²

Iras	Finish good Lady, the bright day is done,

And we are for the darke.

}

Cleopatra	Hye thee†³ againe,

3685

I have spoken already, and it is provided,

Go put it to the haste.

}

Charmian	Madam, I will.

ENTER DOLABELLA

Dolabella	Where's the Queene?
Charmian	Behold sir. ⁴

}

3690 | Cleopatra | Dolabella. |

}

Dolabella	Madam, as thereto sworne, by your command

(Which my love makes Religion to obey)

I tell you this : Cæsar through Syria

Intends his journey, and within three dayes,

3695

You with your Children will he send before,

Make your best use of this.

I have perform'd

⁵ Your pleasure, and my promise.

Cleopatra	Dolabella,° I shall remaine your debter.

700 | Dolabella | I your Servant :° |

Adieu good Queene, I must attend on Cæsar.

[Exit] ⁶

R 366 - b : 5. 2. 191 - 206

SD ₁ most modern texts suggest Cleopatra whispers to Charmian

LS ₂ Ff's three lines (7/10/5 or 6 syllables) allow time for Cleopatra to come to her understanding of the situation: most modern texts set two slightly longer than normal lines (11/11 or 12 syllables) suggesting an outburst rather than a realisation

W ₃ F2 and most modern texts = 'thee', F1 = 'th e'

SD ₄ most modern texts have Charmian exit here (presumably to arrange for the Clowne to appear with the basket of asps)

LS ₅ the irregular Ff setting (7/11/4) allows tiny moments of unspoken acknowledgement between Cleopatra and Dolabella, illuminating the simple words: most modern texts restructure as shown (11/11)

SD ₆ most modern texts delay the exit until after Cleopatra's next line

Cleopatra	Farewell, and thankes. →[1]
	Now Iras, what think'st thou?
3705	Thou, an Egyptian Puppet shall be shewne In Rome as well[1][2] as I : Mechanicke Slaves With greazie Aprons, Rules, and Hammers shall Uplift us to the view.
	In their thicke breathes,
3710	Ranke of grosse dyet, shall we be enclowded, And forc'd to drinke their vapour.
Iras	The Gods forbid. }
Cleopatra	Nay, 'tis most certaine Iras : sawcie Lictors Will catch at us like Strumpets, and scald Rimers
3715	Ballads[3] us out a Tune.
	The quicke Comedians
	Extemporally will stage us, and present Our Alexandrian Revels : Anthony Shall be brought drunken forth, and I shall see Some squeaking Cleopatra Boy my greatnesse
3720	I'th'posture of a Whore.
Iras	O the good Gods!
Cleopatra	Nay that's certaine.[4]
Iras	Ile never see't? for I am sure mine Nailes Are stronger then mine eyes. R 366 - b
3725	**Cleopatra** Why that's the way ° to foole their preparation, And to conquer ° their most absurd intents.
	ENTER CHARMIAN
	Now Charmian. °[5]
	Shew me my Women like a Queene : Go fetch My best Attyres.
3730	I am againe for Cidrus,[6]

SP[1] Ff's two short lines (4/6 syllables) allow for Cleopatra to come to some form of private decision before turning to Iras: most modern texts join the two lines together

W[2] F1 - 2 = 'aswell', F3/most modern texts = 'as well'

W[3] F2 and most modern texts = 'Ballad', F1 = 'Ballads'

LS[4] the actor has choice as to which two of these three short lines may be joined as one line of split verse

LS[5] Ff's irregularities (6/11/10/3 or 4 syllables) allow Cleopatra a moment before speaking the lines which essentially foreshadow how she will achieve victory over the Romans, and an essential silent moment between her and Charmian (as to whether Charmian has successfully arranged for the basket to be delivered) before issuing the orders to bring her royal robes: most modern texts regularise the lines to 10/11/9 or 10, as shown

N[6] Ff = 'Cidrus', most modern texts = 'Cydnus'

133

To meete Marke Anthony.
                        Sirra Iras, go
(Now Noble Charmian, wee'l dispatch indeede,)
And when thou hast done this chare, Ile give thee leave
3735   To play till Doomesday: bring our Crowne, and all.

[A noise within] [1]

Wherefore's this noise?

ENTER A GUARDSMAN

Guardsman   Heere is a rurall Fellow,
            That will not be deny'de your Highnesse presence,
            He brings you Figges.
                                }
3740 Cleopatra   Let him come in.

[Exit Guardsman]

What poore an Instrument
May do a Noble deede: he brings me liberty:
My Resolution's plac'd, and I have nothing
Of woman in me: Now from head to foote
745   I am Marble constant: now the fleeting Moone
No Planet is of mine.

ENTER GUARDSMAN, AND CLOWNE [2]

Guardsman   This is the man.

Cleopatra   [3] Avoid, and leave him.

[Exit Guardsman]

Hast thou the pretty worme ° of Nylus there,
50   That killes and paines not? °

Clowne   Truly I have him: but I would not be the par-
         tie that should desire you to touch him, for his byting is
         immortall: those that doe dye of it, doe seldome or ne-
         ver recover.

SD [1]   most modern texts suggest Iras exits, some that Charmian goes with her - though one commentator suggests
she stays and readjusts Cleopatra's dress, *The Arden Shakespeare, Anthony and Cleopatra*, op. cit., pages 256-7

SD [2]   most modern texts indicate he brings a basket on with him

LS [3]   Ff's three lines (5/10/5 syllables) allow time for the Guardsman's silent exit, and a moment before the
Clowne replies: most modern texts eradicate both moments by setting two almost normal lines (11/9) as shown

3755	Cleopatra	Remember'st thou any that have dyed on't?

Clowne Very many, men and women too.
　　　　　I heard of
one of them no longer then yesterday, a very honest woman, but something given to lye, as a woman should not
3760 do, but in the way of honesty, how she dyed of the by-
ting of it, what paine she felt: Truely, she makes a verie
good report o'th'worme: but he that wil beleeve all that
they say, shall never be saved by halfe that they do: but
this is most falliable, the Worme's an odde Worme.

765 **Cleopatra** Get thee hence, farewell.

Clowne I wish you all joy of the Worme. [1]

Cleopatra Farewell.

Clowne You must thinke this (looke you,) that the
Worme will do his kinde.

0 **Cleopatra** I, I, farewell.

Clowne Looke you, the Worme is not to bee trusted,
but in the keeping of wise people: for indeede, there is
no goodnesse in the Worme.

Cleopatra Take thou no care, it shall be heeded.

'5 **Clowne** Very good: give it nothing I pray you, for it
is not worth the feeding.

Cleopatra Will it eate me?

Clowne You must not think I am so simple, but I know
the divell himselfe will not eate a woman: I know, that
0 a woman is a dish for the Gods, if the divell dresse her
not.
　　　　But truly, these same whorson divels doe the Gods
great harme in their women: for in every tenne that they
make, the divels marre five.

5 **Cleopatra** Well, get thee gone, farewell.

Clowne Yes forsooth: I wish you joy o'th'worm.

[Exit] [2]

SD [1] some modern texts suggest the Clowne sets down his basket, others wait till he exits

L 367 - b : 5. 2. 249 - 279

SD [2] most modern texts have Iras (and sometimes Charmian) re-enter with Cleopatra's 'royal robe', jewels and crown (see footnote #1, page 134)

Cleopatra	Give me my Robe, put on my Crowne, I have	
	Immortall longings in me.	
	Now no more	
3790	The juyce of Egypts Grape shall moyst this lip.	
	Yare, yare, good Iras; quicke: Me thinkes I heare	L 367 - b
	Anthony call: I see him rowse himselfe	
	To praise my Noble Act.	
	I heare him mock	
3795	The lucke of Cæsar, which the Gods give men	
	To excuse their after wrath.	
	Husband, I come:	
	Now to that name, my Courage prove my Title.	
	I am Fire, and Ayre; my other Elements	
3800	I give to baser life.	
	So, have you done?	
	Come then, and take the last warmth of my Lippes.	
	Farewell kinde Charmian, Iras, long farewell. [1]	
	Have I the Aspicke in my lippes?	
	Dost fall?	
3805	If thou, and Nature can so gently part,	
	The stroke of death is as a Lovers pinch,	
	Which hurts, and is desir'd.	
	Dost thou lye still?	
3810	If thus thou vanishest, thou tell'st the world,	
	It is not worth leave-taking.	
Charmian	Dissolve thicke clowd, & Raine, that I may say	
	The Gods themselves do weepe.	
Cleopatra	This proves me base:	
3815	If she first meete the Curled Anthony,	
	Hee'l make demand of her, and spend that kisse	
	Which is my heaven to have.	
	Come thou mortal wretch,[2]	
	With thy sharpe teeth this knot intrinsicate,	
3820	Of life at one untye: Poore venomous Foole,	
	Be angry, and dispatch.	
	Oh could'st thou speake,	
	That I might heare thee call great Cæsar Asse,° unpolicied.	
Charmian	Oh Easterne Starre.	

SD [1] most modern texts indicate Cleopatra kisses Iras, who falls and dies

SD [2] most modern texts indicate Cleopatra takes an asp from the basket and puts it to her breast

3825	Cleopatra	Peace, peace:° ¹
		Dost thou not see my Baby at my breast,
		That suckes the Nurse asleepe. ⟩
	Charmian	O breake!
		O breake!
3830	Cleopatra	As sweete as Balme, as soft as Ayre, as gentle.
		O Anthony!
		Nay I will take thee too. ²
		What should I stay ——

[Dyes]

	Charmian	In this wilde ³ World?
3835		So fare thee well :
		Now boast thee Death, in thy possession lyes
		A Lasse unparalell'd.
		Downie Windowes cloze,
		And golden Phœbus, never be beheld
3840		Of eyes againe so Royall : your Crownes away, ⁴
		Ile mend it, and then play ——

ENTER THE GUARD RUSTLING IN, AND DOLABELLA ⁵

	1st. Guard	Where's the Queene?
	Charmian	Speake softly, wake her not. ⟩
	1st. Guard	Cæsar hath sent ⁶
3845	Charmian	Too slow a Messenger. ⁷ ⟩
		Oh come apace, dispatch, I partly feele thee.
	1st. Guard	Approach hoa, →
		All's not well : Cæsar's beguild.
	2nd. Guard	There's Dolabella sent from Cæsar : call him.

LS ¹ Ff's irregular setting (14/4 + 2 syllables) allows for the enormous undercurrents of the situation - Cleopatra's onrush, and the women's silences): most modern texts normalise the moment, setting two pentameter lines as shown

SD ² most modern texts indicate Cleopatra takes another asp and places it on her arm

W ³ Ff = 'wilde', some modern texts = 'vile' or 'vild'

W ⁴ Ff = 'away', most modern texts = 'awry'

SD ⁵ since at line 3849 the 2nd. Guard suggests Dolabella be called for, most modern texts delay the entry until Ff's second and solo entry from him, post line 3854: one modern text suggests he enters here, and immediately leaves the stage once he sees the dead Cleopatra and Iras (to clear his head perhaps?), and reenters where Ff suggest

PCT ⁶ F1 sets no punctuation as if Charmian interrupts him: F2/most modern texts set a period

SD ⁷ most modern texts add a stage direction that Charmian now takes an asp and puts it on herself

3850	1st. Guard	What work is heere Charmian? →
		Is this well done? [1]

Charmian It is well done, and fitting for a Princesse
Descended of so many Royall Kings.
Ah Souldier.

[Charmian dyes]
ENTER DOLABELLA

3855 Dolabella How goes it heere?

2nd. Guard All dead.

Dolabella Cæsar, thy thoughts
Touch their effects in this: Thy selfe art comming
To see perform'd the dreaded Act which thou
3860 So sought'st to hinder.

ENTER CÆSAR AND ALL HIS TRAINE, MARCHING

All A way there, a way for Cæsar. [2]   R 367 - b

Dolabella Oh sir, you are too sure an Augurer:
That you did feare, is done.

Cæsar Bravest at the last,
3865 She levell'd at our purposes, and being Royall
Tooke her owne way: the manner of their deaths,
I do not see them bleede.

Dolabella Who was last with them?

1st. Guard A simple Countryman, that broght hir Figs:
3870 This was his Basket.

Cæsar Poyson'd then.

1st. Guard Oh Cæsar:
This Charmian liv'd but now, she stood and spake:
I found her trimming up the Diadem; [3]
3875 On her dead Mistris tremblingly she stood,
And on the sodaine dropt.

Cæsar Oh Noble weakenesse:

R 367 - b / L 368 - b : 5. 2. 325 - 344

LS [1] given the enormity of the situation, the hesitations in Ff's four short lines (3/7 syllables previous page, 6 or 7/4) within this passage are perfectly understandable: most modern texts couple each pair as one longer line

SD [2] most modern texts indicate this is spoken offstage, and before Cæsar and his party enter

PCT [3] to avoid the apparent foolish F1-2 statement, 'trimming up the Diadem;/On her dead Mistris tremblingly she stood', most modern texts follow F3 and remove the punctuation from the end of the first line, and add a comma after 'tremblingly' in the next line, viz. 'trimming up the Diadem/On her dead Mistris, tremblingly she stood': if the F1-2 setting stands it might indicate verbally the shock the sight of the bodies had on the Guard

If they had swallow'd poyson, 'twould appeare
By externall swelling: but she lookes like sleepe,
3880 As she would catch another Anthony
In her strong toyle of Grace.   L 368 - b

}

Dolabella   Heere on her brest,
There is a vent of Bloud, and something blowne,
The like is on her Arme.°

3885 **1st. Guard**   This is an Aspickes traile,
And these Figge-leaves ° have slime upon them, such
As th'Aspicke leaves ° upon the Caves of Nyle.

Cæsar   Most probable ° 1

That so she dyed: for her Physitian tels mee
3890 She hath pursu'de Conclusions infinite
Of easie wayes to dye.
Take up her bed,
And beare her Women from the Monument,
She shall be buried by her Anthony.

3895 No Grave upon the earth shall clip in it
A payre so famous: high events as these
Strike those that make them: and their Story is
No lesse in pitty, then his Glory which
Brought them to be lamented.
3900 Our Army shall
In solemne shew, attend this Funerall,
And then to Rome.
Come Dolabella, see
High Order, in this great Solemnity. †2

[Exeunt omnes]

FINIS

LS 1 the slightly irregular Ff setting (6 + 6/10/10/4) allows the overpassionate split line from Dolabella and the 1st. Guard, and for a pause for Cæsar to come forward (or choose not to) to inspect the body before reply: most modern texts create a different irregularity (6/10/10/6 +4), leaving a great pause before the 1st Guard speaks, and eradicate Cæsar's hesitation

▼ 2 F2 and most modern texts = 'Solemnity', F1 = 'Solmemnity'

APPENDIX A
THE UNEASY RELATIONSHIP OF FOLIO, QUARTOS, AND MODERN TEXTS

Between the years 1590 and 1611, one William Shakespeare, a playwright and actor, delivered to the company of which he was a major shareholder at least thirty-seven plays in handwritten manuscript form. Since the texts belonged to the company upon delivery, he derived no extra income from publishing them. Indeed, as far as scholars can establish, he took no interest in the publication of his plays.

Consequently, without his supervision, yet during his lifetime and shortly after, several different publishers printed eighteen of these plays, each in separate editions. Each of these texts, known as **'Quartos'** because of the page size and method of folding each printed sheet, was about the size of a modern hardback novel. In 1623, seven years after Shakespeare's death, Heminges and Condell, two friends, theatrical colleagues, actors, and fellow shareholders in the company, passed on to the printer, William Jaggard, the handwritten copies of not only these eighteen plays but a further eighteen, of which seventeen had been performed but not yet seen in print.[1] These thirty-six plays were issued in one large volume, each page about the size of a modern legal piece of paper. Anything printed in this larger format was known as 'folio', again because of the page size and the method of sheet folding. Thus the 1623 printing of the collected works is known as **the First Folio**, its 1632 reprint (with more than 1600 unauthorised corrections) the Second Folio, and the next reprint, the 1666 Third Folio, added the one missing play, *Pericles* (which had been set in quarto and performed).

The handwritten manuscript used for the copies of the texts from which both Quartos and the First Folio were printed came from a variety of sources. Closest to Shakespeare were those in his own hand, known as the 'foul papers' because of the natural blottings, crossings out, and corrections. Sometimes he had time to pass the material on to a manuscript copyist who would make a clean copy, known as the 'fair papers'. Whether fair (if there was sufficient time) or foul (if the performance deadline was close), the papers would be passed on to the Playhouse, where a 'Playhouse copy' would be made, from which the 'sides' (individual copies of each part with just a single cue line) would be prepared for each actor. Whether Playhouse copy, fair papers, or foul, the various Elizabethan and Jacobean handwritten manuscripts from which the quartos and Folio came have long since disappeared.

The first printed texts of the Shakespeare plays were products of a speaking-

---

[1]   Though written between 1605–09, *Timon of Athens* was not performed publicly until 1761.

hearing society. They were based on rhetoric, a verbal form of arranging logic and argument in a persuasive, pleasing, and entertaining fashion so as to win personal and public debates, a system which allowed individuals to express at one and the same time the steppingstones in an argument while releasing the underlying emotional feelings that accompanied it.[2] Naturally, when ideas were set on paper they mirrored this same form of progression in argument and the accompanying personal release, allowing both neat and untidy thoughts to be seen at a glance (see the General Introduction, pp. xvi–xxi). Thus what was set on paper was not just a silent debate. It was at the same time a reminder of how the human voice might be heard both logically and passionately in that debate.

Such reminders did not last into the eighteenth century. Three separate but interrelated needs insisted on cleaning up the original printings so that silent and speaking reader alike could more easily appreciate the beauties of one of England's greatest geniuses.

First, by 1700, publishing's main thrust was to provide texts to be read privately by people of taste and learning. Since grammar was now the foundation for all writing, publication, and reading, all the Elizabethan and early Jacobean material still based on rhetoric appeared at best archaic and at worst incomprehensible. All printing followed the new universality of grammatical and syntactical standards, standards which still apply today. Consequently any earlier book printed prior to the establishment of these standards had to be reshaped in order to be understood. And the Folio/Quarto scripts, even the revamped versions which had already begun to appear, presented problems in this regard, especially when dealing in the moments of messy human behaviour. Thus, while the first texts were reshaped according to the grammatical knowledge of the 1700s, much of the shaping of the rhetoric was (inadvertently) removed from the plays.

Secondly, the more Shakespeare came to be recognized as a literary poet rather than as a theatrical genius, the less the plays were likely to be considered as performance texts. Indeed plot lines of several of his plays were altered (or ignored) to satisfy the more refined tastes of the period. And the resultant demands for poetic and literary clarity, as well as those of grammar, altered the first printings even further.

Thirdly, scholars argued a need for revision of both Quarto and Folio texts because of 'interfering hands' (hands other than Shakespeare's) having had undue influence on the texts. No matter whether foul or fair papers or Playhouse copy, so the argument ran, several intermediaries would be involved between Shakespeare's writ-

---

[2] For an extraordinarily full analysis of the art of rhetoric, readers are guided to Sister Miriam Joseph, *Shakespeare's Use of the Arts of Language* (New York: Haffner Publishing Co., 1947). For a more theatrical overview, readers are directed to Bertram Joseph, *Acting Shakespeare* (New York: Theatre Arts Books, 1960). For an overview involving aspects of Ff/Qq, readers are immodestly recommended to Neil Freeman, *Shakespeare's First Texts*, op. cit.

ing of the plays and the printing of them. If the fair papers provided the source text, a copyist might add some peculiarities, as per the well documented Ralph Crane.[3] If the Playhouse copy was the source text, extra information, mainly stage directions, would have been added by someone other than Shakespeare, turning the play from a somewhat literary document into a performance text. Finally, while more than five different compositors were involved in setting the First Folio, five did the bulk of the printing house work: each would have their individual pattern of typesetting—compositor E being singled out as far weaker than the rest. Thus between Shakespeare and the printed text might lie the hand(s) of as few as one and as many as three other people, even more when more than one compositor set an individual play. Therefore critics argue because there is the chance of so much interference between Shakespearean intent and the first printings of the plays, the plays do not offer a stylistic whole, i.e., while the words themselves are less likely to be interfered with, their shapings, the material consistently altered in the early 1700s, are not that of a single hand, and thus cannot be relied upon.

These well-intentioned grammatical and poetic alterations may have introduced Shakespeare to a wider reading audience, but their unforeseen effect was to remove the Elizabethan flavour of argument and of character development (especially in the areas of stress and the resulting textual irregularities), thus watering down and removing literally thousands of rhetorical and theatrical clues that those first performance scripts contained. And it is from this period that the division between ancient and modern texts begins. As a gross generalisation, the first texts, the First Folio and the quartos, could be dubbed 'Shakespeare for the stage'; the second, revamped early 1700 texts 'Shakespeare for the page'.

And virtually all current editions are based on the page texts of the early 1700s. While the words of each play remain basically the same, what shapes them, their sentences, punctuation, spelling, capitalisation, and sometimes even line structure, is often altered, unwittingly destroying much of their practical theatrical value.

It is important to neither condemn the modern editions nor blindly accept the authority of the early stage texts as gospel. This is not a case of 'old texts good, so modern texts bad'. The modern texts are of great help in literary and historical research, especially as to the meanings of obscure words and phrases, and in explaining literary allusions and historical events. They offer guidance to alternative text readings made by reputed editors, plus sound grammatical readings of difficult pas-

---

[3]   Though not of the theatre (his principle work was to copy material for lawyers) Crane was involved in the preparation of at least five plays in the Folio, as well as two plays for Thomas Middleton. Scholars characterise his work as demonstrating regular and careful scene and act division, though he is criticised for his heavy use of punctuation and parentheses, apostrophes and hyphens, and 'massed entry' stage directions, i.e. where all the characters with entrances in the scene are listed in a single direction at the top of the scene irrespective of where they are supposed to enter.

sages and clarification of errors that appear in the first printings.[4] In short, they can give the starting point of the play's journey, an understanding of the story, and the conflict between characters within the story. But they can only go so far.

They cannot give you fully the conflict within each character, the very essence for the fullest understanding of the development and resolution of any Shakespeare play. Thanks to their rhetorical, theatrical base the old texts add this vital extra element. They illustrate with great clarity the 'ever-changing present' (see p. xvi in the General Introduction) in the intellectual and emotional life of each character; their passages of harmony and dysfunction, and transitions between such passages; the moments of their personal costs or rewards; and their sensual verbal dance of debate and release. In short, the old texts clearly demonstrate the essential elements of living, breathing, reacting humanity—especially in times of joyous or painful stress.

By presenting the information contained in the First Folio, together with modern restructurings, both tested against theatrical possibilities, these texts should go far in bridging the gap between the two different points of view.

---

[4] For example, the peculiar phrase 'a Table of greene fields' assigned to Mistress Quickly in describing the death of Falstaffe, *Henry V* (Act Two, Scene 3), has been superbly diagnosed as a case of poor penmanship being badly transcribed: the modern texts wisely set 'a babbled of green fields' instead.

NEIL FREEMAN trained as an actor at the Bristol Old Vic Theatre School. He has acted and directed in England, Canada, and the USA. Currently he is an Head of Graduate Directing and Senior Acting Professor in the Professional Training Programme of the Department of Theatre, Film, and Creative Writing at the University of British Columbia. He also teaches regularly at the National Theatre School of Canada, Concordia University, Brigham Young University in both Provo and Hawaii, and is on the teaching faculty of professional workshops in Montreal, Toronto and Vancouver. He is associated with Shakespeare & Co. in Lenox; the Will Geer Theatre in Los Angeles; Bard on the Beach in Vancouver; Repercussion Theatre in Montreal; and has worked with the Stratford Festival, Canada, and Shakespeare Santa Cruz.

His ground breaking work in using the first printings of the Shakespeare texts in performance, on the rehearsal floor and in the classroom has lead to lectures at the Shakespeare Association of America and workshops at both the ATHE and VASTA, and grants/fellowships from the National Endowment of the Arts (USA), The Social Science and Humanities Research Council (Canada), and York University in Toronto.

His three collations of Shakespeare and music - *A Midsummer Nights Dream* (for three actors, chorus, and Orchestra); *If This Be Love* (for three actors, mezzo-soprano, and Orchestra); *The Four Seasons of Shakespeare and Vivaldi* (for two actors, violin soloist and Chamber Orchestra) - commissioned and performed by Bard On The Beach and The Vancouver Symphony Orchestra have been received with great public acclaim.

SHAKESCENES:
SHAKESPEARE FOR TWO
The Shakespeare Scenebook

EDITED AND WITH AN INTRODUCTION BY JOHN RUSSELL BROWN

Shakespeare's plays are not the preserve of "Shakespearean Actors" who specialize in a remote species of dramatic life. Shakespeare asks to be performed by all good actors. Here in the introduction, "Advice to Actors," and in the notes to each of thirty–five scenes, John Russell Brown offers sensible guidance for those who have little or no experience with the formidable Bard. Thirty-five scenes are presented in newly edited texts, with notes which clarify meanings, topical references, puns, ambiguities, etc. Each scene has been chosen for its independent life requiring only the simplest of stage properties and the barest of spaces. A brief description of characters and situation prefaces each scene and is followed by a commentary which discusses its major acting challenges and opportunities.

paper • ISBN 1–55783–049–5

APPLAUSE

SOLILOQUY!

The Shakespeare Monologues
Edited by Michael Earley and Philippa Keil

At last, over 175 of Shakespeare's finest and most performable monologues taken from all 37 plays are here in two easy-to-use volumes (MEN and WOMEN). Selections travel the entire spectrum of the great dramatist's vision, from comedies and romances to tragedies, pathos and histories.

"Soliloquy is an excellent and comprehensive collection of Shakespeare's speeches. Not only are the monologues wide-ranging and varied, but they are superbly annotated. Each volume is prefaced by an informative and reassuring introduction, which explains the signals and signposts by which Shakespeare helps an actor on his journey through the text. It includes a very good explanation of blank verse, with excellent examples of irregularities which are specifically related to character and acting intentions. These two books are a must for any actor in search of a 'classical' audition piece."

ELIZABETH SMITH
Head of Voice & Speech
The Juilliard School

paper•MEN: ISBN 0-936839-78-3
WOMEN: ISBN 0-936839-79-1

APPLAUSE

THE ACTOR AND THE TEXT
by Cicely Berry

As voice director of the Royal Shakespeare Company, Cicely Berry has worked with actors such as Jeremy Irons, Derek Jacobi, Jonathan Pryce, Sinead Cusack and Antony Sher. *The Actor and The Text* brings Ms. Berry's methods of applying vocal production skills within a text to the general public.

While this book focuses primarily on speaking Shakespeare, Ms. Berry also includes the speaking of some modern playwrights, such as Edward Bond.

As Ms. Berry describes her own volume in the introduction:

" ... this book is not simply about making the voice sound more interesting. It is about getting inside the words we use ...It is about making the language organic, so that the words act as a spur to the sound ..."

paper•ISBN 1–155783–138–6

APPLAUSE

THE REDUCED SHAKESPEARE COMPANY'S
COMPLEAT WORKS OF WLLM SHKSPR
(abridged)

by JESS BORGESON, ADAM LONG, and DANIEL SINGER

"ABSL HLRS." —*The Independent* (London)

"Shakespeare writ small, as you might like it!... Pithier-than-Python parodies...not to be confused with that august English company with the same initials. This iconoclastic American Troupe does more with less."

—*The New York Times*

"Shakespeare as written by *Reader's Digest*, acted by Monty Python, and performed at the speed of the Minute Waltz. So Forsooth! Get thee to the RSC's delightfully fractured *Compleat Works*."

—*Los Angeles Herald*

ISBN 1-55783-157-2 • $9.95 • PAPER

♥APPLAUSE♥

SHAKESPEARE'S
FIRST TEXTS
by Neil Freeman

"THE ACTOR'S BEST CHAMPION OF THE
FOLIO"   —Kristin Linklater
author of *Freeing Shakespeare's Voice*

Neil Freeman provides students, scholars, theatre-
lovers, and, most importantly, actors and direc-

lis-
st

ical
ep-
m-
der
d,
's

writing, but it also did away with some of
Shakespeare himself.

ISBN 1-155783-335-4

APPLAUSE